# Chaos Theory
# & Higher Education

Higher Ed

Questions about the Purpose(s) of Colleges & Universities

Norm Denzin, Josef Progler, Joe L. Kincheloe, Shirley R. Steinberg
*General Editors*

Vol. 9

PETER LANG
New York • Washington, D.C./Baltimore • Bern
Frankfurt am Main • Berlin • Brussels • Vienna • Oxford

# Chaos Theory
# & Higher Education

## Leadership, Planning,
## & Policy

EDITED BY
## Marc Cutright

PETER LANG
New York • Washington, D.C./Baltimore • Bern
Frankfurt am Main • Berlin • Brussels • Vienna • Oxford

**Library of Congress Cataloging-in-Publication Data**

Chaos theory and higher education:
leadership, planning, and policy / edited by Marc Cutright.
p. cm. — (Higher ed; vol. 9)
Includes bibliographical references.
1. Education, Higher. I. Cutright, Marc. II. Series
LB2341 .C485   378—dc21   00-042395
ISBN 0-8204-5110-X
ISSN 1523-9551


**Die Deutsche Bibliothek-CIP-Einheitsaufnahme**

Chaos theory and higher education:
leadership, planning, and policy / ed. by: Marc Cutright.
_New York; Washington, D.C./Baltimore; Boston; Bern;
Frankfurt am Main; Berlin; Brussels; Vienna; Oxford: Lang.
(Higher ed; Vol. 9)
ISBN 0-8204-5110-X

Cover design by Lisa Dillon

The paper in this book meets the guidelines for permanence and durability
of the Committee on Production Guidelines for Book Longevity
of the Council of Library Resources.

© 2001 Peter Lang Publishing, Inc., New York

Printed in the United States of America

# ACKNOWLEDGMENTS

I am indebted, first and foremost, to the authors who have contributed to this volume. The unique qualities of their chapters are noted in my introductory chapter, but what the authors share is that they signed on to this project when it was little more than a concept. I am grateful for their faith, and that of Peter Lang Publishing, and hope that the product justifies it.

In many respects, this volume and my interest in organizing it are direct products of my doctoral studies at the University of Tennessee, Knoxville, and at the University of Calgary as the result of a Fulbright Scholarship. As with any student, those who have contributed substantially to my education and the opportunities to pursue it are too numerous to account in full, but they would surely include Jeff Aper, Ted and Louise Bentley, Alice Boberg, Grady Bogue, Lloyd Davis, Judy Fry, Bryant Griffith, Ruth Liu, Mark Mendenhall, Norma Mertz, Fred Obear, Deborah and Andrew O'Brien, Vince Pellegrino, and Ian Winchester.

Jan Danforth's meticulous and creative preparation of the manuscript made all of the authors look better. She caught many an error, and inched us a little closer to perfection.

And of course, my wife Carol and daughters Kyle and Drew have supported me consistently. For that and so much more, I love them dearly.

# TABLE OF CONTENTS

# CHAPTER ONE

## Introduction:
## Metaphor, Chaos Theory, and This Book

*Marc Cutright*

This anthology is a consideration of some ways that chaos theory might be not only a descriptive metaphor for the conditions of leadership, planning, and policy in higher education, but indeed a prescriptive metaphor, the utilization of which might improve these functions and others. The authors are presidents, vice presidents, deans, other administrators, and faculty members. They represent two-year colleges, liberal arts colleges, and universities. They hail from three nations. Their commonality is that they have all thought carefully about the metaphor of chaos theory as it engages higher education, and how that engagement can improve our practices and outcomes.

Before moving to these specific considerations, however, we need to address more basic questions: Why metaphor? Why chaos theory? And indeed, what is chaos theory?

### Why Metaphor?

A relative of a close friend of mine some months ago suffered a massive and catastrophic stroke. The victim's chances of survival were put at 5 percent. But his resolve to live, the miracles of medical science, and perhaps miracles of source beyond human invention, brought him back from the brink of death. He faced and faces, nonetheless, a slow and difficult recovery.

My friend would tell me about scattered and often nonsensical "conversations" she would have with her relative after he emerged from a coma and became more obviously sensate. In brief and tiring efforts, he would try to tell her what had happened to him. A description recurred: "Hard disk crash. Data lost. Can't reboot. Have to reboot."

Maybe that means nothing. I am neither psychologist nor neurologist, not that they have an uncontestable grasp on how the brain works. But it seems to me that while my friend's relative had lost much of his ability to conceive or express what had happened to his mind and his efforts to heal it, the metaphor of his mind and its processes as a computer, a machine, was alive and explicit.

The importance of metaphor in our conceptions of our selves and our environments should not be underestimated, or considered a mere poetic embellishment of discourse. Since at least Plato's allegory of the cave, we have a record of the significant role played by metaphor in our descriptions of the world around us. Linguist George Lakoff and philosopher Mark Johnson, in their collaborative *Metaphors We Live By* (1980), assert that metaphor is inseparable from conceptualizations of the world and our organization of it:

> [M]etaphor is pervasive in everyday life, not just in language but in thought and action. Our ordinary conceptual system, in terms of which we both think and act, is fundamentally metaphorical in nature. (p. 1)

Further,

> We draw inferences, set goals, make commitments, and execute plans, all on the basis of how we in part structure our experience, consciously and unconsciously, by means of metaphor. (p. 158)

A metaphor for an organization or its processes, then, has utility for shaping our very conceptions of the organization. As Gareth Morgan wrote in the first edition of his book, *Images of Organization*:

> Metaphor is often just regarded as a device for embellishing discourse, but its significance is much greater than this. For the use of a metaphor implies a way of thinking and a way of seeing that pervade how we understand our world generally. . . . [M]etaphor exerts a formative influence on science, on our language and on how we think, as well as on how we express ourselves on a day-to-day basis. (1986, pp. 12–13)

## Metaphor and Organizational Life

Recent decades particularly have seen the emergence of key metaphors for organizational life in higher education. Among the most prominent of these are the "garbage can" and "organized anarchy" models of institutional choice and decision making (Cohen & March, 1974; Cohen, March, & Olsen, 1972). Weick described educational systems, including universities, as "loosely coupled systems" (1976), reminiscent of Cohen, March, and

Olsen's (1972) "uncoupling of problems and choices." Orton and Weick (1990) would return to the idea that loose coupling "baffled and angered" (Weick, 1976, p. 4) administrators in their efforts to plan and otherwise direct colleges and universities. Loose coupling, rather than being perceived as a means by which institutions could be more sensitive to environmental changes, was instead widely perceived as a diametrically oppositional concept to management, and a source of resistance to change (Orton & Weick, 1990). Indeed, George Keller, the most prominent proponent of, and author on, strategic planning, considered both organized anarchy and loose coupling to be crises, not elements of flexibility and adaptability, in confronting a new era of harsh competition for resources (1983).

If metaphor is central to our organization of the world, and if many in higher education would eschew metaphors such as those noted above, then what is, exactly, the operative metaphor, the implicit one, if not the explicit one?

Organizational scholar Gareth Morgan (1986, 1997) is among those who say that the dominant organizational metaphor for our organizations is that of the machine. He notes that this metaphor can be useful, when the environment is stable, when the product is uniform, and when the "human 'machine' parts are compliant and behave as they have been designed to do" (1997, p. 27). The description seems consistent with Frederick Taylor's "scientific management" of the early twentieth century (Taylor, 1911). The model has the characteristics of a machine, in that, consistent with Newtonian mechanics, there's a predictability and replicability to cause and effect; there's a hierarchy of actions and control; and elements of the machine can be isolated and tinkered with.

Margaret Wheatley, writing in her 1992 book *Leadership and the New Science*, holds that we focused our organizational energies on

> structure and organizational design, on gathering extensive numerical data . . . . We believed that we could study the parts . . . to arrive at knowledge of the whole. We have reduced and described and separated things into cause and effect, and drawn the world in lines and boxes. (pp. 27–28)

Oxford physicist and philosopher of science Danah Zohar sees an organizational world of "Newtonian organizations . . . that thrive on certainty and predictability . . . . Power emanates from the top . . . . [Such organizations] are managed as though the part organizes the whole." The emphasis on control and command "isolates these organizations from their environments. They don't interact with or respect those environments, including the people who work with them" (1997, p. 5).

Lincoln and Guba (1985) are among those who argue that such metaphors extend to and dominate our views of educational organizations. Higher education planners and authors Michael G. Dolence and Donald M. Norris describe both the processes and organizations of higher education as being of "classic, late Industrial Age design," a "factory model" characterized by "insufficient flexibility" and a fixation on processes rather than outcomes (1995, p. 11).

### Why Chaos Theory, and What Is It?

The authors of this volume will explore chaos theory as an alternative, and perhaps superior, metaphor for viewing leadership, planning, and policy in higher education. But before moving to those discussions, an explanation of chaos theory itself is in order.

A Virginia commission charged in the late eighties with the development of a master plan or vision for higher education in that state used chaos theory as an analytical framework. That plan and its context are the subject of a chapter here by Jeffery P. Aper. The short definition of chaos theory given in that report serves us well as a beginning point:

> A mathematical concept called, somewhat misleadingly, "chaos," holds that at certain points small changes within systems will produce great and unpredictable results . . . . The mathematics created to conceive . . . 'chaotic' situations is nonlinear: the future does not follow trends established in the past . . . . What [chaos theory] represents to us is the probability that the future will not be simply a linear extrapolation of the past, that small events happening today will cause new patterns to emerge downstream. (Commission on the University of the 21st Century, inside back cover)

Chaos, in the physical sciences, is not the random activity that the term's common use suggests. Chaos theory, instead, holds that many seemingly random activities and systems, in fact, show complex, replicated patterns. The behavior of these systems is nonlinear, that is, behavior feeds back upon itself and modifies the patterns. Further, predictability of the system's behavior is restricted to a relatively short time frame.

Chaos theory's roots in science go back more than a century to Henri Poincare's proof that the gravitational and orbital behavior of bodies in the solar system could not be explained only with simple, Newtonian, linear physics (Hayles, 1990; Ruelle, 1991). But ongoing attention to chaos theory is broadly considered to have begun with the work in more recent decades of MIT meteorologist Edward Lorenz.

Lorenz had been working on computer models of the weather in order to enhance predictability. In one noted episode from the early sixties, he had entered a number of weather conditions into a simple computer and graphed the resulting weather patterns. He sought to replicate the patterns, but this time rounded the mathematical measurements of weather conditions to three decimal places instead of six. He expected only slight deviations in his findings, and for the two graph patterns to reflect similarities. Instead, after only a few iterations of the computations, the patterns began to vary greatly from initial findings, to the point of no correlation at all. Yet within this seeming randomness, boundaries existed on the behavior of the system, and certain weather patterns recurred. These are conditions which characterize actual weather (Gleick, 1987).

Chaotic functions demonstrate *extreme sensitivity to initial conditions* and *extreme sensitivity to influx*. Following from Lorenz's work, this notion is popularly called *the butterfly effect*, where the flapping of a butterfly's wing in Asia may eventually alter the course of a tornado in Texas (Lorenz, 1993).

The explanation of the importance of small factors comes through the circumstance that chaotic systems are dependent upon *feedback*. As opposed to Newtonian concepts that more clearly differentiate between cause and effect and their predictability, feedback is the notion that an effect becomes part of the cause in subsequent *iterations* of the pattern. Depending on the presence, nature, and timing of turbulence and the resulting iterative patterns, small factors can—but not necessarily will—become multiplied over time. Senge (1990) explored this concept as related to organizations in *The Fifth Discipline*.

What, then, allows chaotic systems to develop any sense of pattern, to stay within boundaries? It is the existence of *attractors*. Attractors are those elements in a system that have drawing or organizational power. The presence of multiple attractors, while establishing boundaries on a system, results in unstable, complex patterns, with the attractors acting upon one another, and demonstrating greater sensitivity to influx. It is the presence of attractors that also gives chaotic systems the quality of *self organization*, the ability to recreate order and pattern, at least temporarily, despite continuous compensation for internal and external shocks to the system, or turbulence (Parker & Stacey, 1994).

Chaotic systems demonstrate *self-similarity* at their various levels. The pattern of the whole can be seen in the part. In natural systems, self-similar structuring, called *fractals*, is shown in cloud formation, plant structure, landscapes, circulatory systems, wherever chaotic organization appears. Schwartz and Ogilvy (1979) described this structural principle as holographic, in which the whole is contained in the part.

To summarize, a chaotic system is one in which apparently random activity is, in fact, complexly patterned. Patterns, created by attractors, are disrupted and modified by the presence or influx of smaller or greater levels of turbulence. Attractors work to keep the system within boundaries. Chaotic systems demonstrate self-similarity, or fractal structuring, at various levels of the system. The infinitely varied interactions of attractors and turbulence make pattern predictability difficult in the near term and impossible over the long term. Despite limited predictability, patterns do emerge and are substantially the creation of system conditions and inputs.

A word is in order about the focus on chaos theory as opposed to *complexity* or *complexity theory*. The latter is thought by some to be a more encompassing concept. Others use the term rather interchangeably with chaos. Still others have switched from the use of chaos theory to complexity, perhaps because of the visceral reaction that the word "chaos" engenders when people fail to separate the theory from the conventional description of randomness. Whatever the reasons for those shifts and decisions might be for others, I have found chaos theory as a framework and term to be more than sufficient for the topics of my own work, and I have encouraged the authors of this book to look to chaos first as well. This is metaphoric work, after all, and chaos has a decided advantage over complexity in both basic, accepted definition, and richness of vocabulary. I further find useful the distinction made by Edward Lorenz himself: complexity is irregularity in space, chaos is irregularity in time (1993). Certainly our organizations have literal, spatial dimensions and physical entities, such as committees. But our organizational foci are overwhelmingly concerned with time, and particularly the future, the single element of this dimension over which we have or assert control.

There are dangers in the overextension of metaphors, particularly from science to social systems. Social Darwinism comes to mind, with its rationalization of racism, colonialism, and the abuses of Industrial Age capitalism. A contemporary of Isaac Newton's sought to apply the principles of the theory of gravity to determination of the veracity of courtroom testimony (Cohen, 1994). And within our own, dominant metaphor of machine-like organizations, it's sobering to recall that in the early twentieth century, Frederick Taylor and Henri Fayol were popularizing the concepts of applying physical science to social and business arrangements, just as Albert Einstein was undermining the universality of the Newtonian mechanics upon which "scientific management" was largely based (Fayol, 1984; Taylor, 1911; Einstein, 1961).

But even in light of this caution, it's interesting to note that some of the most impassioned calls for the application of the principles of chaos theory to social systems have come from prominent scientists and mathematicians who have worked in chaos theory at developmental levels. See, for example, Gell-Mann's *The Quark and the Jaguar* (1994); Ruelle's *Chance and Chaos* (1991); and Prigogene and Stenger's *Order Out of Chaos: Man's New Dialogue with Nature* (1984).

Although our intention in this work is to connect life in the academy with metaphors of chaos theory, there are those working in social and organizational sciences who have sought with varying degrees of success to determine literal, mathematical patterns of chaos theory in human relations. These efforts have been particularly notable in such fields as electoral political science and economics, where large quantitative databases have been available for analysis (Gleick, 1987; Priesmeyer, 1992; Brown, 1995; Kiel & Elliott, 1996). In this light, metaphoric application of chaos theory to organizations is not a radical approach, but a conservative one.

A watershed event in the metaphoric application of chaos theory to organizations occurred with the publication in 1992 of Margaret Wheatley's *Leadership and the New Science*. Wheatley took many of the concepts of "new science," particularly chaos theory, and considered them with specific organizational contexts and functions. Gareth Morgan, in his 1997 second edition of *Images of Organization*, broadly considered chaos theory as a metaphor, but did so without much specificity. Other authors, particularly in the business organization realm, have considered the chaos metaphor with detail and prescription. And metaphor has long been an analytical tool for considering our life and functions within higher education. But very little has been done to date in bringing these strands together, to applying the metaphor of chaos theory directly to leadership, planning, and policy in higher education. This volume is an effort in that direction.

## The Chapters That Follow

This introductory chapter has offered a brief explanation of chaos theory and the concept of metaphor, particularly that based in chaos theory, as applied to organizations. The chapters that follow explore those themes in the context of higher education.

The next chapter, by Ronald Barnett, is, in fact, an immediate departure from this general theme. The author, a professor of higher education and dean of professional development at the Institute of Education of the University of London, expresses reservations about chaos theory as a framework for understanding higher education. However, his detailing of the complexity—the supercomplexity—that is common to our higher education environments is compelling, and sets a stage for the challenges of leadership, planning, and policy that are discussed in subsequent chapters.

Jean Swenk, director of institutional effectiveness and planning at National University, California, revisits her model of strategic planning and examines it through the lens of chaos theory. She also expands on the definition of chaos theory offered to this point in the book, as applied to organizations.

I then offer a ten-proposition model of strategic planning, derived from chaos theory and others' work in strategic planning. Some of the model is common to other approaches, but it also accepts limitations about our knowledge of the future and how we might compensate for that and still make our planning relevant.

The chapter by four authors from Blue Ridge Community College, Virginia, considers this model against their own planning experiences. The authors are James R. Perkins, president; Jeffrey B. Lanigan, professor of history; John A. Downey, acting academic vice president; and Bernard H. Levin, professor of psychology.

Jeffery P. Aper considers an early application of chaos theory to planning, that of the state of Virginia as they produced a 1989 report setting goals and directions for colleges and universities in that state. He also considers the aftermath of that plan as new policymakers and public officials came to the scene. He is an associate professor of leadership studies in the College of Education, the University of Tennessee, Knoxville.

Bob Barnetson examines the effects of performance funding and performance indicators on the behaviors of colleges and universities. Specifically, he discusses whether chaos theory might serve as an analytical framework for understanding how these externally imposed criteria might affect the purposes and actions of institutions. He is the research and communications officer for the Alberta Colleges and Institutes Faculties Association.

Two authors from the University College of the Cariboo, British Columbia, take on the fears in the academy that the rapid expansion and utilization of technology in higher education might have the unintended effects of undermining quality and basic philosophies. They suggest that chaos theory might help us to understand and adapt to these changes, even while we maintain core values. Adrian Kershaw is vice president for community and distributed learning services at UCC, and Susan Safford is dean of student development there.

The pace and nature of changes in higher education get the attention of the next two authors. They do this through the double lens of chaos theory and the philosophy of history put forth by R.G. Collingwood. They hold that the latter supports the former. Bryant Griffith is professor of education and former head of that department at Acadia University, Nova Scotia. Lynn Speer Lemisko is a member of the Faculty of Education, Nipissing University, Ontario.

John Dever, in a brief but persuasive chapter, cautions that chaos theory is no substitute for, or excuse to ignore, the critical role of leadership in higher education. He is dean of academic and student affairs at Tidewater Community College, Virginia.

Barbara Mossberg, president of Goddard College, Vermont, draws on her long and personal history with chaos theory, and tells of the many applications she sees in education and leadership. She takes us in dozens of different and provocative directions, perhaps creating as many loose ends as she ties together.

I think that's an appropriate way to end this collection. The merits of any metaphor must be decided by each individual in his or her own circumstances. Every metaphor that illuminates aspects of our reality also blinds us to other aspects, and so there is no absolute answer, no silver bullet. As in so many other aspects of life in the academy, merit lies not foremost with our answers, but with our questions. This is particularly true of chaos theory, which we have just begun to explore and use as a tool to help us fulfill our missions.

# References

Brown, C. (1995). *Chaos and catastrophe theories.* (Sage University Paper series on Quantitative Applications in the Social Sciences, 07-107). Thousand Oaks, CA: Sage.

Cohen, B. I. (1994). *Interactions: Some contacts between the natural sciences and social sciences.* Cambridge, MA: MIT Press.

Cohen, M. D., & March, J. G. (1974, 1986). *Leadership and ambiguity: The American college president.* Boston, MA: Harvard Business School Press.

Cohen, M. D., March, J. G., & Olsen, J. P. (1972). A garbage can model of organizational choice. *Administrative Science Quarterly, 17* (1), 1–25.

Commission of the University of the 21st Century. (1989). *The case for change.* Richmond, VA: Commonwealth of Virginia.

Dolence, M. G., & Norris, D. M. (1995). *Transforming higher education: A vision for learning in the 21st century.* Ann Arbor, MI: Society for College and University Planning.

Einstein, A. (1961). *Relativity: The special and general theory.* New York: Crown Publishers, Inc.

Fayol, H. (1984). *Administration industrielle et générale.* New York: Institute of Electrical and Electronics Engineers.

Gell-Mann, M. (1994). *The quark and the jaguar: Adventures in the simple and the complex.* New York: W.H. Freeman and Company.

Gleick, J. (1987). *Chaos: Making a new science.* New York: Penguin.

Hayles, N. K. (1990). *Chaos bound: Orderly disorder in contemporary literature and science.* Ithaca, NY: Cornell University Press.

Keller, G. (1983). *Academic strategy: The management revolution in American higher education.* Baltimore, MD: Johns Hopkins University Press.

Kiel, L. D., & Elliott, E., eds. (1996). *Chaos theory in the social sciences: Foundations and applications.* Ann Arbor, MI: University of Michigan Press.

Lakoff, G., & Johnson, M. (1980). *Metaphors we live by.* Chicago: University of Chicago Press.

Lincoln, Y. S., & Guba, E. G. (1985). *Naturalistic inquiry.* Newbury Park, CA: Sage Publications.

Lorenz, E. (1993). *The essence of chaos.* Seattle: University of Washington Press.

Morgan, G. (1986). *Images of organization.* Newbury Park, CA: Sage Publications.

Morgan, G. (1997). *Images of organization,* 2nd edition. Thousand Oaks, CA: Sage Publications.

Orton, J. D., & Weick, K. E. (1990). Loosely coupled systems: A reconsideration. *Academy of Management Review, 15*(2), 203–223.

Parker, D., & Stacey, R. (1994). *Chaos, management and economics: The implications of non-linear thinking.* (Hobart Paper 125). London, England: The Institute of Economic Affairs.

Priesmeyer, H. R. (1992). *Organizations and chaos: Defining the methods of nonlinear management.* Westport, CT: Quorum Books.

Prigogene, I., & Stenger, I. (1984). *Order out of chaos: Man's new dialogue with nature.* Toronto: Bantam Books.

Ruelle, D. (1991). *Chance and chaos.* Princeton, NJ: Princeton University Press.

Schwartz, P., & Ogilvy, J. (1979). *The emergent paradigm: Changing patterns of thought and belief.* Monograph from the Analytical Report Values and Lifestyles Program, SRI International.

Senge, P. (1990). *The fifth discipline: The art and practice of the learning organization.* New York: Doubleday.

Taylor, F. W. (1911). *Principles of scientific management.* New York: Harper & Row.

Weick, K. E. (1976). Educational organizations as loosely coupled systems. *Administrative Science Quarterly, 21* (March), 1-19

Wheatley, M. J. (1992). *Leadership and the new science: Learning about organization from an orderly universe.* San Francisco: Berrett-Koehler Publishers, Inc.

Zohar, D. (1997). *ReWiring the corporate brain: Using the new science to rethink how we structure and lead organizations.* San Francisco: Berrett-Koehler Publishers, Inc.

# CHAPTER TWO

## Managing Universities in a Supercomplex Age
### *Ronald Barnett*

### Identifying the Mission: Mission Impossible?

Across the world, universities are faced with a number of competing possible visions of their futures. Different scenarios are unfolded before them, by this government report or that international conference, such that the future of universities appears to take on an unduly challenging character. For one commentator, "colleges and universities will be under severe pressure to perform . . . and many will not survive. The grimness of the 21st Century for higher education . . ." (Skolnik, 1999, p. 48).

The problem, however, is that it is no longer clear what it is for universities to perform. Is it a matter of converting all their courses to on-line provision, making them available to would-be students all around the world to consume in their own time at their own pace? Is it a matter of becoming entrepreneurial, seeking markets for their knowledge services and so generating additional streams of discretionary income to supplement the increasingly inadequate income flowing from state revenues? Is it to become a university of excellence; but then the further problem arises as to excellence by what and by whose criteria? (Readings, 1996). Is it to become an institution fully in tune with and responsive to the local or regional community, offering extended life chances? Is it to become a center for the development of delineated higher order skills for the knowledge economy?

Two answers immediately suggest themselves. One is that universities, in order to survive, should hedge their bets and do all of these things. The difficulty here is that the various strategic options cut across each other, organizationally and conceptually. Organizationally, it is not clear how a single institution can both be an effective world player and be totally immersed in its local community or region. Equally, it is not clear that it can both be a front ranking institution in research and have its faculty who are also investing effort in ensuring that its courses are the most effective in enabling its students to be transformed: the time spent in supporting students, after all, can also be spent in the laboratory or at the word processor, writing a prize-winning book. Can excellence be squared with openness, whether market openness (in going down the on-line route) or civic openness (in admitting would-be students lacking high entry qualifications)? Conceptually, within the multiple missions that stand before the university are ideas that appear to run against each other.

The second and alternative response to the challenge of multiple scenarios opening before every university is to recognize that no one university can or should attempt to do everything. Instead, each institution is to identify and pursue its own mission. In the process, there will be wider diversity across the system as a whole, so ensuring that the total higher education system is maximally responsive to the national and global contexts facing it. Strength and responsiveness through mission diversity: this is the policy agenda that many countries are now trying to pursue in a mass higher education system (cf. HEFCE, 2000).

Behind these questions and dilemmas stand, of course, large socioeconomic and policy contexts. Amid globalization, universities are being positioned or are positioning themselves within an increasingly globalized knowledge economy in which there are rapidly emerging competitors for many of the markets—in relation *both* to teaching and to research—that universities might have thought were theirs. (Between them, corporate universities in the USA *both* conduct research and offer courses on the open market. In 1998, there were some 1,600 plus such companies in the U.S. [CVCP and HEFCE, 2000, pp 30–31].) Amid efforts of governments, universities are being asked to see themselves both as engines of economic regeneration *and* of social integration. Amid the communications revolution, coupled with rising consumerism (fed by more discretionary income and a need for lifelong learning), universities are having to take on board the expectations of those consumers. In the process, course provision and pedagogical relationships may undergo significant change. Individuals paying huge amounts of money for their programs may not take kindly to being denied their diplomas even if their performance is not up to scratch.

Against this background of global economic and social change, it is inevitable that the future of universities becomes uncertain. This uncertainty, as I have indicated, is not just operational. It is, in part, conceptual. What counts *as* a university is now so unclear that it is not even obvious that the matter is worth pursuing any more. The long line of books on the idea of the university, from Cardinal John Newman onwards, is perhaps at an end. The very idea that there could be an idea of the university no longer seems to make sense.

The conceptual uncertainty arises out of an uncertain positioning that universities face. Are they public institutions or are they private institutions? Do they have an allegiance to national or perhaps even local agendas developed through political and representative institutions (in the wake of, say, major government reports) or do they go their own way, becoming entirely entrepreneurial in their own interests as they see it? Again, we might want to play it safe conceptually and suggest that universities are quasi-public institutions. Most, after all, continue to secure a high proportion of their revenues from the state (typically, at least 50 percent). But to say this is to evade the key issue: can a single institution really fulfill a number of agendas that compete against each other?

## Complex Issues

In capturing these preliminary—and by no means exhaustive—reflections about the characteristic condition of universities, we have identified a situation of some complexity: universities are complex institutions having to find their way through a complex environment. Let us identify different forms of complexity that present themselves to universities:

1. *Mission complexity:* In an age of uncertainty, in which perhaps nothing can count as its "core" business, what substance—if any—might attach to a university's "mission"? Is the idea of mission not now simply an attempt to carve out an arena of sureness where none exists?

2. *Priority complexity:* Is it possible for a university to identify definite priorities for itself any longer? Priorities are likely to be undermined by changing national policies and global forces. Increasingly, it appears that there are pressures on every institution to offer and to be "excellent" at a very wide range of activities, if not all possible activities.

3. *Position complexity:* Does the university situate itself regionally, nationally, or globally? Can it do all of them? Who are its principal clients to whom it should be maximally responsive? The state? Today's students? Their potential employers? Society in twenty years' time?

4. *Strategy complexity:* In an age of uncertainty, how can a university form strategy for itself? For strategy implies some stability in prediction as to

the shape of the future; but that might be denied to the university today.

5. *Human resource complexity:* Are academic staff to be considered as autonomous professionals or are they to be considered as employees of an organization to which they owe allegiance? Might academic staff be thought to stand in anything approaching a line-management relationship, being accountable to, and even receiving some direction from, a more senior member of staff?

6. *Communicative complexity:* What forms of communication are conducive to the development of collective understanding of the challenges facing the university? How might the need to make quick decisions be balanced against a desire to be transparent so that the staff feel that they have ownership of decision making?

7. *Operational complexity:* How does the university balance considerations of (a) accountability to state agencies; (b) the academic interests of its faculty; (c) responsiveness toward its (increasingly sophisticated and even litigious) student clientele; (d) its own desires to be "entrepreneurial" and innovative?

8. *Epistemological complexity:* In a world of multiple knowledges, is the university to have epistemological rules or does it allow in all comers? In relation to what knowledge structures—if any—might a university be organized? Do unitary disciplines still have a place? Might the organizational structure deliberately encourage interdisciplinarity, bringing together even noncognate knowledge fields? How far might knowledge-in-use (in the real world) come into play in informing the university's knowledge structures?

9. *Ontological complexity:* How is personal identity to be developed and sustained? Can the university any longer be considered to be a unitary community or is it a set of ephemeral communities such that there are no stable identities available within the university?

10. *Political complexity:* How does a university position itself? What resources can it muster? How does it win friends and influence people? Should it have any scruples as to who its friends might be?

11. *Economic complexity:* How is the university to live within its resources? Can it generate new income streams? What are the possible effects of different forms of internal resource allocation?

12. *Ethical complexity:* By what principles might a university conduct its affairs? How might it balance considerations of civic responsibility with those of its immediate interests? How is it to understand its ethical base? What would an ethical audit reveal?

How might we understand this situation, in which a major social institution—the university—with its 800 years of history, is confronted with such an array of complex challenges? Is this a new situation or have universities always faced these difficulties? Can we say anything more about these forms of complexity? Can we distinguish them at a higher level of generality?

Firstly, on the latter questions, as to their distinguishing characteristics, there are, within these twelve forms of complexity, three distinct species:

1. Complexities concerned with values, ends, purposes, ideas, concepts, objectives and goals: all are open, contestable and challengeable and they *are* contested and *are* challenged. Call these *conceptual complexities.*

2. Complexities concerned with the uncertainty and unpredictability of the total environment within which the university conducts its work. Income streams, stakeholders, and rival institutions offering knowledge services in a knowledge society *and* the university's activities toward and forms of engagement with its wider environment are all open. Even the boundaries of that environment become fuzzy, both in terms of its extension (is it local, national, or global?) and in terms of their distinctiveness (the external world has come into the university and the university acts within the external world such that the internal-external distinction is quickly evaporating). Call these *environmental complexities.*

3. Complexities concerned with relationships and modes of communication *and* associated identities of persons: the idea of a university as a unitary community (one of the meanings of *universitas*, its medieval origin) now seems lost. Again, relationships, communication, and identity come into play both within the university *and* in its interactions with its wider environment. Call these *relational complexities.*

These three varieties of complexity that confront the university—conceptual, environmental, and relational—are not, of course, separate from each other. The conceptual problematics facing universities derive in part from the environmental challenges (such as globalization, a heightened interest in higher education on the part of host states, and rising consumerism). Both the conceptual problematics and the environmental challenges compound the relational complexities in which, for example, their academic identities of university staff evolve. Further, new modes of communication and relationships have impact on the university's wider environment that, in turn, prompt yet more conceptual challenges (over the substance of "the university" as an idea and its proper boundaries).

## Unraveling Is Not an Option

It would be natural, in acknowledging such interrelationships, to form the view that their unraveling is itself a complex matter and that that work of unraveling would be a worthwhile task. Such a sentiment would be understandable but would be somewhat misjudged. The problem lies in the hope implied in the idea of unraveling, the assumption that these matters *could be* worked out and the respective problematics and their interrelationships *could be* laid bare if only one had sufficient resource and time. Such assumptions have to be set aside.

It is not just that, in the twelve, first order set of complexities, and in the three higher order complexities, we have complexity laid on complexity. It is not just that we here—and universities more generally—are confronted with a messy situation. It is, to employ an analogy, not just that we are faced with a tangle of seaweed, with numerous strands of different thicknesses going in all kinds of direction, crisscrossing each other, and entangled in each other such that that complex is itself the seaweed. Unraveling it all would be near-impossible *and*, more importantly, would lose the strength and character of the seaweed. All of this is true; but the main problem of unraveling the complexities of the modern university lie elsewhere.

The difficulty with the idea of unraveling is that, in this situation, unraveling is *impossible*. The impossibility of unraveling lies not in any empirical matter of time, resources, or the near-overwhelming array of elements confronting universities. The impossibility of unraveling in question has a dual character: it is both *conceptual* and *interactional*.

*Conceptually*, the challenges facing the university represent competing and often-incompatible options; and the notions of competition and incompatibility are themselves different. For example, as we have seen, being responsive to the local community may compete with the university's desire to be a global player; the two orientations pull against each other but they are not *logically* incompatible. On the other hand, an orientation toward packaging its courses to sell them to consumers *is* logically incompatible with seeing higher education as a partnership in which students take at least some measure of responsibility for their learning and development. Or, to take another example, a commitment in favor of intellectual openness is logically incompatible with the requirement of some external agencies to have control over any publications that may arise from research that they sponsor, even forbidding any public disclosure in some cases (where, for instance, research may lead to commercially sensitive findings).

Other conflicts are not so easily categorized (through the concepts of competition and (in)compatibility). For instance, a university may espouse a corporate value orientation toward high level teaching but may find itself being pulled more and more to sponsor research and publications. Its internal financing arrangements, its own performance indicators, and its staffing priorities are heavily influenced by an external environment that offers considerable inducements—both symbolic and financial—if the university can be seen to do well according to the externally imposed criteria of performance. Here, operational tensions overlie value tensions: under what conditions is a university prepared to see diminished, if not altogether disappeared, a strong value orientation in its corporate identity?

The university, accordingly, has perforce to swim in conceptually muddy waters, the currents of which may be flowing in opposite directions. In part, this conceptual confusion arises because of the hybrid character of universities being both public and private institutions at once: on the one hand, they are less dependent on the state and are being urged to convert themselves into entrepreneurial businesses; on the other hand, they continue to be reminded by the state that they are public institutions, accountable to external stakeholders according to systemwide criteria and regulatory processes. The conceptual ambiguities to which the university finds itself exposed are, therefore, in part a function of the uncertain structural position that the university occupies in modern society.

However, the conceptual problematic that is the nature of the contemporary university has a further source. It is that our current age is one of multiplying frameworks through which we engage with the world. The causes of this situation would include globalization, the electronic revolution (and the resulting compression of time and space), the global development of research and knowledge capabilities (and not only in universities), the challenge of new and rival epistemologies, the spread of democratic institutions, and the increasing worldwide levels of literacy and educatedness. In such a situation, it is inevitable that our frameworks for comprehending the world will not only proliferate but that they will contend with each other. Certainly, of the multiplication of frameworks, there shall be no end; but, in the process, they will become entangled, will overlay each other, will pull against each other, will sometimes strengthen each other but will also sometimes attempt to suffocate each other. This is a situation less of risk and uncertainty as such (Beck, 1992) but of conceptual confusion. It is also inescapable; it is the character of our age.

Let me turn to the other form of complexity that I mentioned earlier, that of *interactional complexity*. The sense that society constitutes an entity as such, exerting its own influences on human behavior and that there may be unintended consequences of thought and action, is not new; in fact, it is at least two hundred years old (Rosen, 1996). What *is* new is a sense that the interactions between the elements of social life are increasingly complex. Their complexity is evident (a) at different levels: to complexity in relation to society we now have to add complexity both globally and organizationally; (b) in the different "media' in which complexity is manifest: institutions, technology, systems, discourses, language as such, and communication more generally.

Each of these are complexes in themselves: for example, in a sector such as higher education, there are, in any one advanced society, literally hundreds of educational institutions, learned societies, state agencies, interest groups, think tanks, and professional bodies, all interacting in an open-textured policy network. In the "network' society (Castells, 1997), there are horizontal and vertical relationships, made more intensive by electronic media that are themselves a complex of media.

In consequence, to the conceptual complexity outlined earlier, there arises an interactional complexity that characterizes the modern world. This interactional complexity has a dynamism, to be sure; but the dynamism has a number of dimensions to it. Firstly, the components are interacting. Institutions, academic networks, the state, students, and other key stakeholders interact. Further, each of the parties are themselves complexes.

Institutions are comprised of groups competing for attention and resources. Talk of flatter organizational structures has to be qualified in an age in which institutional management and, indeed, leadership, are being accorded increasing attention. And so, too, through each of the stakeholders that influence higher education: each turns out to be sets of networks, looser or tighter, acting reflectively or nonreflectively. These networks are in a state of continual interplay with each other.

In such a setting, the term "system of higher education" is at best a shorthand; at worst, a pernicious fiction. It implies a solidity, a fixity, and a durability that cannot obtain.

## Global Spaces; Local Spaces

This interactional complexity within a society is overlain by global dimensions. It is not just that universities live in global markets, with their client groups increasingly international in character. It is not just that universities proffer their knowledge products on a world stage (both research and teaching). Nor is it just that academics' networks are global in character and increasingly so. And nor is it just, in such an age, that universities compete globally such that their competitors are often in distant parts of the world. More than anything, it is that the very stock-in-trade of universities, their intellectual capital, their knowledges, are global in character (Scott, 1998). Whether they like it or not, universities and their basic units are positioned in global epistemological networks. Some (universities, units, academics) are large players, exerting influence; others are quite marginal.

Markets, networks, and competing interests (reflected in separate stakeholders) combine to form relational uncertainties. These are evident in different league tables: depending on the performance indicator, one university can be on top in one but occupy a lowly place in another.

In these interactions, space and time are compressed (Urry, 1998). And yet new spaces occur. In the process, new challenges occur. Corporate universities arise, causing traditional semi-public universities to rethink their mission. New knowledges arrive in the wider world (relational, emotional, corporate, performative), requiring universities to extend their own knowledge base and so become more epistemologically generous. And new client groups open up for the university's knowledge products, which encourage new knowledge services. Research and teaching find new consumers: the university's epistemologies that allowed it carefully to describe the world still has takers. Now, in addition, the university is being encouraged to develop epistemologies that effect changes in the world. Courses are designed to produce "entrepreneurialism" among students; researchers are called upon to offer consultancy services, not just to recommend changes in organizational life but sometimes to effect those changes. Other researchers set up their own companies to develop and market knowledge products.

There are, here, a mix of levels and orders of interactions overlayered on each other. These interactions take place in several dimensions and with such intensity that time and space become indistinguishable. Local units are in interplay with global forces; apparently single institutions are themselves a complex of actors, each with their different interests; explicit manifestos vie with unstated, and even unrecognized, presuppositions; markets change such that the configuration of actors and their respective market positions change constantly; and the players in the market and, therefore, the character of the goods on offer, also change and yet expand at the same time.

## A Chaotic World?

It would be appropriate to describe this state of affairs as a chaotic situation. Issues, in turn, would naturally arise as to what it is to manage institutions of higher education amid such chaos. There are, however, three difficulties in adopting such a description.

Firstly, there is among many who use the term *chaos* a sense that underlying chaotic patterns of change lie orderly patterns. The assumption appears to be that, if only we are able sufficiently to distance ourselves from events, and displace ourselves as actors, orderly and even aesthetically pleasing patterns can be detected. For chaos as mayhem, read chaos as beauty (Standish, in press). Such an assumption should be rejected. It is an example of hope trying to triumph over reason. There is no reason to assume that fast globalization—as we may term it—offers underlying orderly patterns of change, or of relationships.

Secondly, the belief that patterns of integration are present entirely neglects the conceptual level of change. Here, we can usefully invoke a distinction between complexity and supercomplexity. *Complexity* may be described as an overload of entities, forces, or items of data such that they cannot be assimilated—whether by individuals, institutions, or systems—in the time available. As they are being assimilated, yet others arrive. Time management, data management, systems management, and even knowledge management accordingly become pressing needs. These are real needs. Failures to address them and solve them lead to stress and even breakdown, again at either the individual or system level.

*Supercomplexity*, by contrast, refers to conceptual and framework relationships. It refers, for example, to the ways in which academics, institutional managers, and even institutions understand themselves. Putting it more formally, it refers to the frameworks of meaning that are available by which individuals might understand themselves. In an age of fast globalization, these frameworks multiply and expand. However, the key feature of such a world—of expanding frameworks—is that the frameworks by which we understand ourselves jar and contend with each other.

Amid such conceptual conflict, there will be conceptual incompatibility (to return to an earlier distinction). Some conceptual conflict will turn out to be manageable. Providing students with more autonomy, encouraging them to take more responsibility for their own learning, is not necessarily incompatible with the ideas of academics either as authorities or as having pedagogical responsibilities. Many circles *can* be squared. Conceptual tensions do not in themselves spell conceptual incompatibilities. Their resolution often calls for both conceptual and organizational flexibility. However, conceptual tension may turn out to harbor conceptual incompatibility, which is much less susceptible to resolution. For example:

1. Investing a university's monies without regard to companies' ecological stance is incompatible with that same university's "green" policy.

2. Having no regard to applicants' social situation will be incompatible with that university's declarations in favor of "equal opportunities" (even if to do so will be seen as adversely affecting its standing in certain league tables).

3. In compiling a critical self-assessment for an external evaluation, glossing the facts of the matter so as to present a determinedly positive aspect will be incompatible with that university's declared ethos of being open and honest in its interactions with the wider society.

4. Allowing its academics to establish their own income-generating companies through which they can enhance their own incomes will be

incompatible with developing the university as a single academic community, especially since such opportunities are not uniformly distributed across the disciplines.

5.  Establishing courses entirely "on-line" (because it is felt that certain markets will only follow courses of study in such a mode) is incompatible with the university's assertion that its policy is to pursue a "mixed-mode" approach, a policy adopted since it believes that some face-to-face educational transactions are crucial in assuring the quality of the overall student experience.

6.  Accepting clauses in a research contract that forbid open publication is incompatible with a university's (any university's) upholding of academic freedom.

These incompatibilities are just a few examples culled at random. For the most part, they are *logical* incompatibilities. They also hint at *situational* incompatibilities, of the kind that it is impossible to be in two places at once; but, for the most part, the incompatibilities are logical in character. "P" and "Not-P": wanting to adopt both stances is an increasingly common situation for universities. Continually, universities are finding themselves in a position of wishing to take up mutually incompatible courses of action.

This state of affairs is, by and large, not much admitted on campus. Universities, after all, are supposedly supremely rational institutions, in which it is tacitly assumed that, given enough time, intellectual effort, and openness of debate, fair, just and even true judgments will be reached. This is self-delusion. As we have seen, options present all the time that are logically incompatible, and this is precisely what might be anticipated in an age of supercomplexity. In a networked global world (not a tautology), frameworks of understanding and value multiply. Universities are not immune from such a global characteristic. On the contrary, as we have seen, it has become part of their societal mission to assist in adding to those frameworks; that is partly why we have universities. Second, universities have it as their declared collective mission that they are open to all points of view: mutual incompatibility finds its natural home, therefore, in universities.

Third, universities are semi-public and semi-market institutions: they are, as we noted, a hybrid. Their mission is not theirs alone; it is owned in part by their wider and multiple communities. The idea of mission identification is a nice fiction: it presumes that a university's identity can be identified, cleaned up, and proclaimed. But life isn't like that for universities. They are besieged by multiple and competing networks of consideration, influence, and even force.

## Managing Universities in an Age of Supercomplexity

From this analysis, we can draw a number of considerations and principles for managing universities in the present age.

The first point is a negative one. It follows that setting up management systems and generating large quantities of data on aspects of institutional performance should not be accorded an especially high priority. Information still retains a value but, in an age of supercomplexity, its value can be overstated. Given an overly high profile, a drive for information suggests a management ethos founded on knowledge-based reasoning. But, as we have seen, the assumption that we can manage universities by acquiring more and more information and making decisions on that basis has to be jettisoned. This is *a* model of rational decision making that is past its "sell-by" date. We can still seek for rational decision making, but it cannot take this form.

Universities may be understood, I have implied, as sites in which multiple, proliferating, and competing (and even incompatible) frameworks of understanding jostle together. Of course, that much can be said of any complex organization today, particularly one in the knowledge sector. A key point about universities, however, is that it is their business (a) to generate new frameworks of understanding, (b) to bring into the open and expose to scrutiny existing and often unrecognized frameworks, and (c) to provide a forum in which relationships and, if appropriate, tensions between frameworks, can be negotiated. These dimensions of framework generation, tension, and negotiation clearly apply to academic activities per se. This is what we expect academics to get up to. But the matter of management of our universities can be understood in precisely the same way. That is, management in universities is not about securing knowledge and making "rational' decisions on that basis but is about the generation and the exploration of new frameworks of *institutional understanding* and the negotiation of their mutual differences.

To put it graphically, the task of university management in an age of supercomplexity is that of the generation and exposure of ignorance (cf.

Lukasiewicz, 1994). Ignorance here is to be understood not in a pejorative sense; on the contrary, ignorance—as the gap between our existing or potential frameworks and our capacities fully to comprehend them and their relationships—is inevitable. In some ways, it is the task of management to compound that ignorance by bringing into view more and more frameworks for collective self-understanding. Only by seeing itself under an ever-widening set of frameworks is the contemporary university going to survive in the medium to longer term.

Against these considerations, the following propositions and principles emerge for managing universities in an age of supercomplexity:

1.  *Proposition:*   The frameworks by which a university might understand itself are infinite, even as they are proliferating. Many will contend with each other.

    *Principle:*   The task of management is to identify key frameworks and create a forum in which they can be collectively debated.

2.  *Proposition:*   In an age of supercomplexity, there can be no core business. What counts as core today may be passé tomorrow. (The mission statement that was proclaimed five years ago, as a result of debate over a period of time, is understood to be now hindering the university's self-development.)

    *Principle:*   The university's self-understanding has to be kept more or less permanently under review. No aspect can be taken for granted.

3.  *Proposition:*   That frameworks should be kept perpetually ever open and that the university's mission should be always on the table does not mean that the university has to surrender its values. After all, collectively, through their independence, and through their interrogation of frameworks, universities help to sustain both an open society and a learning society. What does follow is that the university's values should themselves also be kept under review. This is healthy, if only because values tend to become tacit and liable to takeover by hostile forces. In the process, the university is likely to find that it is living—or trying to live—with competing values; and it may feel that it needs to do so.

But this process of value audit will enable the university to be more honest about its value position.

*Principle:* The university should, from time to time, conduct its own ethical and value audit of itself. (External assistance may prove helpful in such a process.) But the university should be prepared to admit to living with competing value systems.

4. *Proposition:* A university can only survive in an age of supercomplexity if its multiple knowledges, multiple goals, and multiple values live in the concrete practices of its staff.

*Principle:* The challenge on management is not just to bring new or different frameworks into view but to encourage staff to embrace new frameworks of academic identity.

5. *Proposition:* Bringing staff to the point where they feel able to embrace new conceptions of academic practice and identity cannot be achieved by managerial fiat. It takes time and effort.

*Principle:* Management in a supercomplex environment requires that process as such be given more effort than goal setting and decision making. Staff have to be enabled to embrace new concepts of self and of university within their own spaces; otherwise, new agendas and new identities will not be taken on with any degree of commitment. Setting up spaces for staff to engage with each other and ensuring that that happens is costly in managerial terms and may appear to be downtime on the finance officer's balance sheet. But the costs of not doing so are going to be even more costly to the university in the medium-long term.

6. *Proposition:* Staff will only come together, especially to explore goal and value matters, if they feel that they know each other. Academic life is brilliant at erecting barriers within itself. If a university is a complex of networks, some of those lines of communication are knotted so that communication is blocked.

*Principle:* Managers have to ease communication among staff by facilitating mutual understanding. Departments, faculties, and the university collectively should conduct their own internal academic and professional audit of every member of staff, and publicize the resulting inventory of staff's expertise and interests. (This exercise needs to be much more nuanced and supple than that typically conducted for the university's press and consultancy offices, to market staff's expertise externally.)

A set of principles such as these is especially appropriate to managing universities in an age of supercomplexity. It will be observed that within the propositions (from which the principles are derived) are the claims that the *task* of management lies in bringing into view within the university environment frameworks by which the university can reenvisage itself and that the *challenge* of management lies in producing an environment such that new frameworks are likely seriously to be countenanced by academic faculty. If these are the key *tasks and challenges*, we might say that the *achievement* of management lies in developing a set of institutional processes such that new frameworks are spontaneously sought and, after due consideration, embraced—even while keeping them under critical scrutiny.[1]

The conception of university management implied by these principles takes seriously the idea of the "network society" (Castells, 1997). University management becomes, in large part, a matter of developing the university as a series of interlocking networks. But, as is apparent, networking is far from being the sum total of the enterprise. The networking is intended to be purposeful, and is aimed at opening spaces, both dialogical and socio-structural, in which new frames of self-envisaging can be, and are likely to be, taken on. This conception of university management, therefore, also takes seriously the idea of the university as a learning organization. But, again, the learning is a steered learning that is oriented toward framework thinking and acting as such.

As we have seen, part of the task of framework thinking is to bring to the surface embedded collective assumptions and values; and part of the collective learning process will lie in recognizing tensions that hold between those assumptions and values. As we have seen, too, those tensions may not be resolvable in any straightforward way; the contending principles and values may continue to be held. But, at least, the university will be more honest and insightful in its self-understanding. It may come to realize, for instance, that it invests two-thirds of its efforts in research and one-third in teaching. That its mission statement contains bland assertions testifying to the "excellence" of both of its main functions just might, then, become something of an embarrassment. The university might then be encouraged to reflect on and make explicit its conception of "excellence" in this context. "Excellence," in any case, is a characteristically empty concept with which the contemporary university tends to cloak itself (Readings, 1996), so it is a particularly appropriate case for self-reflexive scrutiny.

## Leading Values

In an age of fast globalization, frames of understanding are rent asunder. It is an age of fragility characterized by contestability, challengeability, unpredictability, and uncertainty (Barnett, 2000). This fragility has impact on individuals and institutions and invokes both epistemologies (how we know the world) and ontologies (how we live in such a world). Indeed, in such a world, categories collapse upon themselves. Institutions and individuals become fluid networks of associations and ideological currents; knowing the world and living in the word become overlapping rather than discrete issues.

In this maelstrom, the university is not immune. To the contrary, the university is an active player in its production and, as such, must suffer the consequences *and* bear its responsibilities in the matter. But the matter has to be understood. In our present age, notions of complexity and chaos have come to the front. Complexity, however, has a tendency to reduce all phenomena to a single level; and can imply that there is, if only we can understand it, a grand complex into which all the parts fit. Chaos suggests randomness but harbors the hope, too, that there lies within not just a patterning but an orderly and even aesthetically pleasing pattern. On the surface, too, both complexity and chaos appear to underwrite fragmentation and unitization of phenomena; underneath, they hold to a totalizing sense of the world.

The idea of supercomplexity offers a different take on the world. It implies that phenomena are layered and are even hierarchical. Some complexes are more complex than others. Some carry more weight than others. Key to supercomplexity is a sense of the conceptual overload that the contemporary world presents. The dissolution of individuals and institutions is, in part, just this: a realization that they can no longer be characterized under definite conceptual schemes ("academic," "knowledge," "research," "fair-minded," "entrepreneurial") but that any conceptual scheme that might be a candidate for such characterization is itself contested and challenged; and that, especially within a university, *it will be.*

The university, therefore, lives and breathes supercomplexity. Long heralded as a social institution that offers a space for the production and intermingling of ideas, now it has to bear that task whether it likes it or not. Nor can there be any hope that, if only we search deeply enough, a pattern will emerge. The conceptual frames jostling within a university and by which it would understand itself conflict. And nor is one lot easily displaced by another. On the contrary, if the university has a particular place in the contemporary world, it is in large part due to its being open and not arbitrarily excluding potential frames of understanding.

In such a situation, management is charged with creating spaces for ever more new frames of understanding and action to find their way into the university. Nor can there be any hope that the conflicts that there will be between frameworks have any definite resolution to them. The university that generates income by setting up businesses is a different university from one that takes seriously open-ended dialogue for better human understanding for they secrete contending epistemologies (of instrumental and of dialogic reason). The difficulty is that they are typically both part of the same "university."

Is this, then, all that the contemporary university has become, a mélange of proliferating and competing frameworks? And is the task of leadership that of identifying and ushering in new frameworks *and* of managing the resulting tension and discontent? Seen in this way, *the entrepreneurial university* (Clark, 1998) will achieve its success over others by becoming none other than a site capable of tolerating the widest array of frameworks: contemplative knowledge still has a part to play but now alongside practical and even exploitative knowledge.

This is an understandable reading of the university in contemporary times but it is an unduly limited reading. Wiped from it is any sense that the university still retains an enlightenment function and a critical function. Management in an age of supercomplexity is in danger of yielding up just the kind of university that fast globalization seeks, producing universities that are adept at assimilating multiple and contending frameworks without flinching. Fortunately, the university is not quite so pliable. The very production of dialogical spaces for institutional reflection that would encourage the assimilation of new frameworks also turn out to be spaces for critical encounters. The new frameworks cannot just be assimilated by any institution that goes under the name of "university" and this not as a matter of dogmatic assertion but as a reflection on the logic of assimilation in a professional environment.

## Conclusion

The power and the ideologies present in so many of the frameworks that the university is being asked to assimilate do not have to be swallowed wholesale; and won't be, except at the price of the end of the university. The very porousness that opens up universities to new, countervailing, and even oppressive frameworks at the same time opens up new spaces, not just for negotiation or even resistance but also for new presences, new interventions, and new imaginary constructions of the university's own making. In this setting, therefore, university leadership comes to be that of enabling the university to make collective *choices* over the frameworks with which it will be primarily identified, even if other contesting frames are still to be found in the practices and self-understandings of its internal networks.

## Note

1. A better formulation of these points would lie in a distinction between *leadership* and *management*. It would take the general form of the following: the *task* of leadership is that of bringing into view new frameworks; the *challenge* of management is that of producing an environment in which such frameworks can be given a fair hearing; and the *achievement* of leadership/management lies in developing institutional processes such that new frameworks are spontaneously sought. In other words, the concepts of leadership and management *both* do worthwhile work (Middlehurst, 1993) but, in an age of supercomplexity, they overlap each other. Effective leadership requires effective management (we might speak of *leadership-in-action*) and effective management requires effective leadership (having the intellectual generosity to envisage new frameworks of understanding). Clearly, a proper examination of the relationships between leadership and management must await another occasion.

# References

Barnett, R. (2000). *Realizing the university in an age of supercomplexity.* Buckingham: Open University Press.

Beck, U. (1992) *Risk society: Towards a new modernity.* London: Sage.

Castells, M. (1997). *The rise of the network society.* Vol 1. Oxford: Blackwell.

Clark, B. (1998). *Creating entrepreneurial universities: Organizational pathways of transformation.* Oxford: IAU/Pergamon.

CVCP and HEFCE. (2000). *The business of borderless education: UK perspectives.* London: CVCP.

HEFCE. (2000). *Diversity in higher education: HEFCE policy statement.* Bristol: HEFCE.

Lukasiewicz, J. (1994). *The ignorance explosion: Understanding industrial civilization.* Ottawa: Carleton University Press.

Middlehurst, R. (1993). *Leading academics.* Buckingham: Open University Press.

Readings, W. (1996). *The university in ruins.* Boston: Harvard University Press.

Rosen, M. (1996). *On voluntary servitude.* Cambridge: Polity Press.

Scott, P. (Ed.). (1998). *The globalization of higher education.* Buckingham: Open University Press.

Skolnik, M. A. (1999). *Higher education in the 21st century.* HMSO: Office of Science and Technology.

Standish, P. (in press). Higher education and the university. In N. Blake, P. Smeyers, R. Smith & P. Standish (Eds.), *The Blackwell guide to the philosophy of education.* Oxford: Blackwell.

Urry, J. (1998). Contemporary transformations of time and space. In P. Scott (Ed.), *The globalization of higher education.* Buckingham: Open University Press.

# CHAPTER THREE

## Strategic Planning and Chaos Theory: Are They Compatible?

*Jean (Prinvale) Swenk*

Since the early 1980s, this researcher's primary area of scholarship has been organizational behavior and culture in higher education, with particular emphasis on strategic planning. Strategic planning was appealing because of its emphasis on using rational decision making to achieve one's goals. Subsequent studies (Swenk, 1988, 1999) revealed the critical importance of congruence between strategic planning and organizational culture, but the rational underpinnings remained intact. So how does she end up writing an article that, to give away the punch line, argues that chaos theory and strategic planning are in fact compatible?

The author recalls the first time she heard the words "chaos theory" and her amazement that the speaker was not a scientist, but a colleague in her doctoral program. The idea of randomness and unpredictability was intriguing but she doubted its widespread applicability. A decade later, experience as both higher education administrator and faculty, and study results that failed to validate any connection between the use of planning and fiscal condition (Swenk, 1992), convince her that the linear, predictable model of strategic planning is less and less viable.

The chapter begins with a definition and model of strategic planning (based on rational, linear assumptions), followed by a review of the critiques of strategic planning's use in business and education. The second step is a nonmathematical description of chaos theory. The preponderance of the chapter analyzes the congruencies between chaos theory and strategic planning and offers specific suggestions on how strategic planning must change if it is to remain a viable method for change in postsecondary institutions.

## Strategic Planning Defined

Based on an extensive review of the literature (Ackoff, 1970; Ansoff, 1965; Baker & Markin, 1994; Chaffee, 1983; Gilbert, 1991; Hall & Elliott, 1993; Hearn, 1988; Hipps, 1992; Jedamus et al., 1980; Keller, 1983; Migliore, 1991; Mintzberg & Quinn, 1991; Myers, 1996; Townsend & Others, 1992; and Weimer & Jonas, 1995), this researcher defined strategic planning as a formalized and structured procedure during which policy and financial issues are considered, and internal and external factors affecting the institution are assessed, so that the institution can decide how to allocate its resources and implement policies in such a way that the institution's comparative advantage will be improved. It is a conscious process during which an institution assesses its current state and the likely condition of its future environment (Swenk, 1992, 1999). It is a successful and timely adaptation to external events; it is an integrative process; it is a problem-solving device. It is an opportunity to focus attention on the problems confronting the organization and to create a framework within which solutions can be forged. It is the ability to learn from experience, develop methods for improving the learning process, to be self-analytical, and to direct one's own destiny. It is a deliberate process and one that assumes congruity between culture and process. In her earlier research, the researcher did not question that the process included feedback yet was essentially linear in nature; it could be structured. Based on those assumptions, the researcher formulated this nine-step process:

1.  Development of the *planning culture,*
2.  Development of the planning structure and organization,
3.  Development of the institutional mission or vision,
4.  Development of *strategic databases,*
5.  Determination of *objectives,*
6.  Determination of strategies, programs, and plans,
7.  Determination of *goals,*
8.  Determination of constraints and contingency plans, and
9.  *Evaluation* of the planning process and the results of the plans.

Certain assumptions underlie strategic planning. For example, it is assumed that institutions cannot respond effectively to change without formalized procedures for comprehensive planning and decision making. The interdependence between the institution and its environment can be consciously planned for and exploited. Strategic planning means the institution is more confident that the institution's goals are attainable and founded on realistic expectations (Cope, 1987; Hax & Majluf, 1984; Hearn, 1988; Keller, 1983). Strategic planning fosters consistency among the institution's operations (Chaffee, 1983). Strategic planners assume the future does not have to look like the past and recognizes that short-term goals can defeat long-term goals. While strategic planning allows for and encourages risk-taking and takes into account the fact that organizational structures come to have a life of their own, predictability is still assumed to be possible.

Several researchers describe strategic planning in ways that reinforce rationality and predictability. "All organizations, regardless of their specific purpose, need to have a well defined mission, goals, and a *long term plan of action*" (emphasis added) that is "a critical requisite to success . . . . Strategic planners aim to select the best strategy and a *control system* (emphasis added) for monitoring activities and comparing results is needed" (Hall & Elliott, 1993, pp. 295, 306). Ray (1997) echoes the focus on a controlled process during which goals and how to achieve them is determined (which also assumes predictability). Johnson and Jonas (1995) recognize that strategic planning can transform an organization but still the stress is on *organization, time frames*, and *stability* (emphasis added). Finally, while many, including this researcher, acknowledge that contingency plans are essential, steps such as evaluation of the mission statement still reinforce the assumptions of predictability, order, and structure. Promises of unanimity of purpose, predictability, temporal continuity, and resolution of conflicting goals and expectations remain intact (see Swenk, 1988, for in-depth discussion of each planning step).

Noting the persistent emphasis on control and predictability, how can one possibly argue that strategic planning is compatible with chaos theory? In fact, some of the most traditional theorists and practitioners describe planning practices and assumptions that resonate with chaos theory. This will be dealt with in detail later in this chapter, but the flavor is evident in this writer's favorite quote from Keller's 1983 classic: "He who lives by the crystal ball will often eat broken glass" (p. 106). Hines (1991) and Schmidtlein and Milton (1990) note that strategic planning focuses not on prediction but on identifying major directions that will promote institutional health and viability. Finally, King and Cleland write that strategic planning is not routinely projecting the past into the future in a linear manner. It is a method for administrators to "look ahead to seize hold of the future and to guide it, and not just to react to what otherwise will happen" (1978, p. 64).

Another reminder that conceiving of strategic planning as a linear process that assumes the future can be predicted may no longer be accurate (if it ever was, a subject worthy of lively debate) is noted by Schmidtlein and Milton (1990). Institutions spend a lot of time doing planning but evidence from research and literature suggests they are not getting the expected benefits. They argue that the reason may be that planning is so encompassing a concept that it is difficult to distinguish from other organizational functions (p. 1). But this researcher argues that perhaps the lack of evidence is because we have ignored critical components of this new science called "chaos theory."

## Chaos Theory Defined

Chaos theory is one component of what many call the "new science" because it is a departure from the traditional, Newtonian approach and philosophy (Overman, 1996). Since Galileo, humans have been trying to explain complex behavior using linear equations, that is, the belief that "a leads to b." The advent of computers further reinforced this belief with their magnificent power in linear cause and effect. However, it was in fact computer simulation by Lorenz that began the evolution of this new paradigm. In his computer weather simulations in 1961, he discovered that just a tiny error (in this case using numbers out to the third decimal point instead of to the sixth decimal point) became more and more exaggerated, leading to entirely different weather patterns (Gibbons, 1988; Gleick, 1988). The use of the term "chaos" to explain such phenomena was coined by Jim Yorke in the early 1970s but, in fact, was emerging long before then. Key figures in the early development included Lorenz, Mandelbrot, Smale, Yorke, May, and Marcus (Gleick, 1988).[1]

Unlike colloquial usage, chaos theory does not refer to total randomness or pandemonium. Rather, chaos theory is concerned with those instances when doing the obvious thing does not produce the obvious desired outcome (Gleick, 1988; Overman, 1996; Shipengrover, 1996). It is concerned with behavior that varies in such a complicated way that one cannot predict exactly what will happen in the future (Pool, 1989). Chaos theory examines natural systems that are governed by simple laws yet can evolve into extremely complex, volatile behavior. Concepts related to chaos theory include instability, diversity, disequilibrium, and complexity.

Key to understanding chaos theory is the term "nonlinear dynamics." Nonlinear dynamics seeks to understand systems that change in ways not amenable to linear cause/effect models. The change is information from the environment, which acts as "perturbations" or "noise," and iterates (feed back into) the system's own structure (Warren, Franklin, & Streeter, 1998). The results are unpredictable; knowing what happened previously is of minimal, if any, benefit. Furthermore, the effect of the perturbations causes disorganization and constant and, at times, rapid change. Complex systems are composed of interconnections and branching choices that produce unintended consequences and render the universe unpredictable (Tetenbaum, 1998). A major goal of chaos theory is to analyze the disorder described as randomness and dynamic (Shipengrover, 1996; Warren, Franklin, & Streeter, 1998).

Four principles underlie chaos theory: sensitivity to initial conditions, strange attractors, self-similarity, and self-organization. Sensitivity to initial conditions is nonlinearity, i.e., the system itself is influenced by (sometimes to a huge magnitude) its own feedback (iterations). Feedback loops modify the system and, consequently, predictability is possible only in a very short time frame (Cutright, 1999). The expectation is not homeostasis or equilibrium, the characteristics of traditional, Newtonian science. The expectation is constant change, unpredictability, instability, and disequilibrium. As a result of these factors, chaos theorists view systems as those which will become more, not less, complex (Warren, Franklin, & Streeter, 1998). Depending on presence, nature, and timing of turbulence and the resulting iterative patterns, small factors can, but not necessarily will, become multiplied over time (Warren, Franklin, & Streeter, 1998). Lemonick (1993) considers this the essence of chaos theory.

If this principle completely explained chaos theory, then pandemonium and total randomness would be reasonable. However, the second principle of chaos theory explains why this does not happen. The *principle of strange attractors* indicates there are forces (attractors) that keep change within a boundary. Thus, nonlinear growth does not become completely random because patterns of behavior unfold in irregular but similar forms. Tetenbaum (1998) uses the term "chaordic, a combo of chaos plus order" (coined by Dee Hock, founder of Visa) to aptly describe the principle of strange attractors. Warren, Franklin, and Streeter (1998) use the analogy of the "meeting of the proverbial irresistible force and immovable object." A more helpful analogy is that of the snowflake; every snowflake is different but every snowflake (due to "strange attractors") has six arms (Pool, 1989). The point is that within chaos is a hidden pattern of order within disorder. All complex systems break down into chaos at the same points along a transition scale; a short-lived equilibrium develops around the attractor (Brady, 1990). Thus, apparently random activity is, in fact, complexly patterned because of the strange attractors and, as a result, constrained (Cutright, 1999). This is why Tetenbaum (1998) describes chaos in seemingly paradoxical terms: complex, unpredictable, [but] orderly disorder. He notes that chaos can be described as a self-organizing entity. "Stuff" emerges but chaos is still constrained by rules (such as strange attractors) that govern it. He further notes that the essence of chaos theory is that simple agents obeying simple rules can interact to create elaborate and unexplained behaviors.

If strange attractors constrain change, then *the principle of self-similarity* can be viewed as a particular type of "strange attractor." Self-similarity means that although everything else in a system may change, there is always some quality that remains the same (those mystifying pictures of fractals represent the mathematical essence of self-similarity). Shipengrover (1996) notes that the principle of self-similarity means that the parts reflect the whole and each part of the system, she argues, must remain consistent with itself and with all other parts of the system as it changes. Cutright (1999) explains that chaotic systems demonstrate self-similarity at their various levels; therefore, the whole is contained in the part. Many seemingly random activities and systems in fact evidence complex, replicated patterns.

Besides the power of strange attractors and the principle of self-similarity, another factor that prevents chaos from becoming pandemonium is the *principle of self-organization*. This principle is understood within the context of dissipative systems. Dissipative systems tend to lose energy over time and the energy cannot be regained. Death results unless the energy is replaced. Complex dissipative systems replace lost energy by importing new energy from the environment (Warren, Franklin, & Streeter, 1998). Nevertheless, they also are governed by the principle of self-organization so that pandemonium does not result (Lemonick, 1993). There is "order through fluctuation" (Mathews, White, & Long, 1999).

The principle of self-organization explains why, given the potential for radical discontinuities in system behaviors, some systems seem to evolve away from the extremes of complete order, inertia, and statis on the one hand and complete randomness and chaos on the other. Self-organization suggests that many systems naturally evolve to a critical state poised between order and disorder (Mathews, White, & Long, 1999).

In summary, chaos theory can be viewed as the capacity of systems to generate new forms from inner guidelines rather than only from the external imposition of form (Mathews, White, & Long, 1999). Unlike Newtonian science, which imposes structure on an organization from above, chaos theory represents the biological model. This model views organizations (or systems) as living, self-organizing, complex, and self-adaptive (Tetenbaum, 1998). The principle of self-organization also shows us, according to Shipengrover (1996), why systems have their own agenda, why growth is found in chaos, not order, and why the new system that results is consistent with the system's prior history.

Some dispute that chaos theory represents a dramatically new way of looking at scientific issues; after all, turbulence always has been part of the natural order (Brady, 1990). This researcher disagrees. While disorder and turbulence are nothing new, this viewpoint overlooks the fact that chaos theorists do not assume linearity and they accept, if not embrace, ambiguity and disorder. That is why chaos theory can be a valuable component of strategic planning. More forcefully, that is why successful strategic planning must incorporate the "chaordic" philosophy.

### What Chaos Theory Contributes to Strategic Planning

Scientific thought and experiment always have had a strong influence on administrative theory and practice (Overman, 1996). Strategic planning is no exception. The belief in the possibility of rational decision making, for example, reflects the Newtonian belief in linear cause and effect. Yet, the increasing influence of chaos theory reveals what Schmidtlein and Milton (1990) noted a decade ago. Some worldviews are incompatible with the scientific perspective, such as a belief in a world of random or unpredictable events, a world viewed as being more than sum of its parts, and the belief that unpredictable human beings cannot be analyzed. Unfortunately, many ". . . planners still think they are agents of efficiency instead of inventors of the future, their calculus of rationality reflects theories of behavior that are necessarily simplified . . ." (Benveniste, 1982, quoted in Schmidtlein & Milton, 1990, p. 4).

Fortunately, alternatives to rational, linear decision making are not new. That gives hope that administrators who implement strategic planning will not ignore the power of chaos theory. For example, the literature on higher education demonstrates the powerful influence of nonlinear theories such as Cohen and March's "garbage can theory" and Baldridge's concept of political decision making (Schmidtlein & Milton, 1990).

What elements of chaos theory are relevant to the implementation of strategic planning in higher education? One crucial contribution is that chaos is not necessarily pandemonium. Chaos theory's principles of self-similarity, strange attractors, and self-organization testify that it is from these very circumstances that new structures and relationships can emerge. Furthermore, these experiences are the rule, not the exception (Overman, 1996).

However, arguably the most important and revolutionary concept of chaos theory when applied to planning is the principle of sensitivity to initial conditions. An excellent example in higher education is the results of retention studies which reveal that one initially negative experience can lead to loss of an enrollment (Mossberg, 1998).

Strategic planning has always recognized the criticality of external environmental influences. The sensitivity principle reveals that another reason institutions of higher education (systems) are chaotic and unpredictable is because feedback iterates back into the system (the institution) itself. Furthermore, that is beneficial because "genuinely complex structures can take advantage of the possibility of the sudden changes inherent in online dynamics while maintaining the order necessary for continuity" (Warren, Franklin, & Streeter, 1998). This is consistent with one primary goal of strategic planning: to provide the flexibility for taking advantage of sudden changes so they can be manipulated to the institution's advantage.

Chaos theory also offers an explanation for a common organizational puzzle: how one seemingly simple error can lead to lasting change. Because cause and effect are not "close in time and space" (Shipengrover, 1996), "[I]n a complex system, errors and uncertainties multiply, cascading upward through a chain of turbulent features" (Gleick, 1988). Chaos theory reminds planners that a more accurate perspective is to view institutions (systems) as complex structures which, because they respond to feedback, grow, adapt, and are self-organizing, and can break norms, experiment, and reorganize. Chaotic systems are characterized by a flexibility lacking in more orderly systems. In fact, Warren, Franklin, and Streeter (1998) state "extremely ordered systems will not give birth to anything new." Specifically, it is these very nonlinearities (sensitivities to initial conditions) in a process that builds on itself that enable changes in the organization to happen with surprising speed.

Scholars of planning are familiar with the skepticism and cynicism often surrounding planning. Tetenbaum (1998) observes that planning has been successful but maybe that is more serendipitous than purposeful, a function of relatively quiescent times.[2] "There is a lack of empirical research that measures whether strategic planning enables an institution of higher education to change more efficiently or more effectively than through the use of other planning or decision making processes. Numerous and interesting case studies and anecdotes are available but the lack of a rigorous research design severely limits comparability or generalizability beyond the specific institution described" (Swenk, 1992, p. 2).

Chaos theory offers a new, more realistic perspective that recognizes that planning to predict and control is probably both illusory and dangerous and allows a false and debilitating sense of security (Tetenbaum, 1998). Successful systems are those at the transition between order and chaos (Matthews, White, & Long, 1999). The management of organizations ultimately requires the management of contradiction. The rules governing success are changing. Today's environment requires an approach that accepts instability and unpredictability (Tetenbaum, 1998).

While sensitivity to initial conditions may be the most revolutionary element of chaos theory, the remaining three principles—strange attractors, self-similarity, and self-organization—also are essential. These three principles explain how and why, in the midst of chaos, planning has any usefulness in a world characterized by discontinuous change occurring at geometric rates, ever increasing competition, complexity, globalization, and paradox (Tetenbaum, 1998). The point is that these principles provide the hope that the manner in which planning occurs and its underlying assumptions constrain chaos so it does not become totally random.

Cutright (1999) endows strange attractors with particular importance in planning by defining strategic planning as the process of discovering a system's attractors. Strange attractors organize the system despite turbulence, establish its boundaries, and give it a general direction for the future. Attractors allow actors within the system to make decisions consistent with the organization's collective identity, purposes, and goals. If the attractors are ignored when imposing new goals and purposes, there will be an early separation of plans from reality.

The need for consistency between decisions and the organization's identity highlight how one strange attractor can be the organizational culture. Swenk's 1988 and 1999 studies reveal how planning can fail when such congruence is not sought. The alternative is to recognize how conscious attention to culture—the system of informal rules that spells out how people are to behave most of the time (Deal & Kennedy, 1982; also see Porras & Collins, 1994)—is one attractor that can nudge change in the desired direction. One reason is that culture provides clarity about the purpose and direction of the organization. This reminds us too of the value of vision and mission.[3] Other likely strange attractors (constraints on the direction of change) are structure and resource limitations (Warren, Franklin, & Streeter, 1998).

As noted above, chaos theory postulates that, while everything else in a system may change, some quality always remains the same. Each part of a system must remain consistent with itself and with all other parts of the system as it changes. Identifying the strange attractors, such as culture, can aid in understanding what will and will not change. Chaos theory's principles of strange attractors, self-similarity, and self-organization also signify that there is leverage in finding patterns in the midst of the disorder and chaos. Revealing the underlying patterns helps the organization shift away from a focus on the random events and forces to which the organization reacts.

Warren, Franklin, and Streeter (1998) state that systems tend to adjust to the environment in a harmonious manner; the environment that systems respond to will make complementary responses. They refer to this as "structural coupling." This is further evidence that structure can act as a factor propelling toward self-similarity and self-organization. Shipengrover explains this is because each part of the system is free to express itself within the context of the history, values, and traditions of the whole. Therefore, the new system can maintain its overall character and identity while better managing the complexity of its environment (1996). Even revolutionary changes must have logical connection to the organization's existing structure and have significant buy-in in order to be institutionalized (Levin, Lanigan, & Perkins, 1995). "Life seeks order in a disorderly way . . . mess upon mess until something workable emerges" (Wheatley, 1992). However, this researcher reminds the reader that the principles of iterative feedback and nonlinearity suggest it is unwise to assume that harmony implies that any specific change is always positive and desirable.

## How Strategic Planning Should Change Because of Chaos Theory

Models of strategic planning are numerous and in her previous research (1988, 1992), this writer developed a nine-step strategic planning process. While each step is still essential, chaos theory illustrates that sensitivity to initial conditions and iterative feedback requires administrators who allow flexibility as the strategic planning process unfolds. The linearity of the planning steps must be abandoned. For example, while administrators begin by creating a planning culture, diligent attention must be paid to this task throughout the planning process. It is not unusual for the novelty of planning to wear off after a few weeks or months; it is at that point that cultural changes, such as recognizing heroes of the planning process, may be warranted. Likewise, step two of the process is creating a planning structure, such as a committee chaired by an outside consultant. Even if this tactic is supported widely, chaos theory teaches us that the influence of the consultant may be radically different from what was expected. Therefore, the attentive administrator will possess the flexibility needed to change the structure, even if it means firing the consultant, based on the feedback received. In a similar vein, feedback may reveal new internal leaders who should assume roles in the process. When strategic planning is implemented at departmental levels, chaos theory may explain why different departments need to have different types of process.

According to Shipengrover (1996), there is leverage in accepting that change cannot be fully predicted or guided with precision. Chaos theory provides a rationale for structuring the planning process in a way that keeps options open. Then the institution can take advantage of big results from small changes (sensitive dependence on initial conditions). Once again, flexibility assumes primary importance as a characteristic of the institution's strategic planning process.

As stated, step one of the planning process is to create a planning culture. The challenge is to cultivate "planful attitudes" and proper time perspectives (Swenk, 1988). Step 2 is developing a planning structure. The development of a strategic planning structure is more than just deciding what kind of committee will perform strategic planning. This is just one of four issues that must be addressed. The scope and span of strategic planning must be determined, deadlines and priorities must be set, the roles and responsibilities of the participants must be clarified, and the specific structure within which planning will occur must be established.

While both steps are necessary and important, chaos theory suggests both the structure and culture of strategic planning also must embody features that allow for high levels of cooperative behavior, promote risk taking and experimentation, and embrace disorder. A key feature is flexibility of both structure and culture so the organization is free to choose actions and reward behavior that deviate from accepted norms. Flexibility of structure and culture recognize change happens rapidly and unexpectedly and encourages participants in the institution to embrace disorder and experimentation since that is the type of organization that successfully transforms itself. Finally, such flexibility is consistent with the recognition that successful strategic planning occurs when people can avoid formal structure in order to relate or communicate with each other despite a rigid hierarchy.

Noted above was the idea that change and chaos can be leveraged to an institution's advantage. Shipengrover (1996) discusses trust as a strange attractor that is one of the most important factors needed to make high leverage change more likely. The variables she delineates that can foster trust highlight the need for flexibility of both the planning culture and structure: sharing power by decentralization, empowering informal leaders, providing structures and support to help everyone hone skills, encouraging collaborative relationships, risk taking, experimentation, protecting the freedom to fail, and trusting people to find their own level of involvement.[4]

Another concept of chaos theory related to planning structure (and, indirectly, planning culture) is interconnectedness. Planning structures generally are orderly and conform to the internal organization of the college or university. An organizational chart can be drawn. What this linear structure often ignores is the informal yet powerful lateral connections that transcend established boundaries. If, as Tetenbaum (1998) states, "knowledge is a primary precondition for emergent change," then the planning structure must enable the institution to discover and utilize the collective intelligence of the institution's constituents at all levels (also see Cutright, 1999; Mossberg, 1998). The planning structure must be sufficiently flexible that it is open to the sharing of information and to answers coming from anywhere in the organization. In fact, ". . . full participation and communication by members of the community serve as a uniting force[5] within the process" (Weimer & Jonas, 1995). Such an institution engages in planning that consciously takes advantage of the randomness and iterative feedback that characterize chaos theory. Structure is needed for routine tasks but probably has to be abandoned so change can occur (Schmidtlein, 1990).

A further implication of the attentiveness to sharing information and seeking it from all possible sources is an emphasis on teamwork. However, homogenous teams, just like hierarchies, inherently seek order and tranquility (Janis, 1971; Whyte, 1989). They wish to sustain their power and position. The randomness and unpredictability of change posited by chaos theory underscore the long-term futility of such top-down, closed approaches. The alternative is to create teams that are fluid; membership can change as well as their specific purposes. Teams must be heterogeneous both in fact and in spirit; dissenters must not just be tolerated but encouraged (Tetenbaum, 1998).[6]

Higher education institutions often are stereotyped, even among their own members, as extraordinarily slow to change. No doubt numerous institutions display remarkable traditionalism and conservatism. Some institutions are able to withstand enormous pressures for change and sustain success. However, one suspects that in today's world of instability and phenomenal rates of change, most institutions cannot enjoy this invulnerability if they wish to survive, much less prosper. Planners who understand chaos theory realize that sudden and unpredictable changes are typical. Furthermore, sudden changes can affect goal outcomes, such as loss of expected fiscal resources. But sudden, unpredictable change, due to iterative feedback and sensitivity to initial conditions, also explains why collective decision making and group processes unfold in startling ways. According to Warren, Franklin, and Streeter (1998), groups go through an initial phase in which members learn to react to one another, i.e., a process of building feedback loops occurs. At some point, the feedback loops become tight and dense enough so the system begins to show sensitivity to initial conditions. It is now in a chaotic state and rapid change is possible. As uncomfortable as this can be, remembering that chaos and disequilibrium are not abnormal can help participants resist abandonment of their goals and purposes. If the planning structure has incorporated flexibility of membership, interconnectedness, freedom to take risks and voice dissent, then collapse of the group is not inevitable. Rather, the group can have the power to adapt itself, and the institution, to the turbulence.

The turbulence can be viewed as a "reservoir of possibilities and paths towards change" (Warren, Franklin, & Streeter, 1998). Turbulence is perceived as a position of strength since the alternative, homeostasis, means eventual death. Chaos theory underscores why strategic planners should pay as much attention to the processes of change as to the interventions needed to promote change (Warren, Franklin, & Streeter, 1998).

Step three of the strategic planning process is the development of the institutional mission or vision. How does an understanding of chaos theory guide this activity? First, the principle of strange attractors reveals that mission and vision can serve as constraints on change. But the inevitability of unpredictability and rapid change counter any complacency that even mission or vision statements that have successfully guided the college or university in the past are immune from evolutionary or even radical revisions. Chaos theory signals that the institution's planners need to rely on the collective knowledge of the institution's internal constituencies to ensure that appropriate responses to the feedback occur. Just as important, the institution must actively seek to interpret the feedback from its external constituencies and whether it indicates changes to the institution's basic purpose are needed. This does not mean that fundamental changes to the institution's purpose occur casually. As Porras and Collins (1994) explain, companies that are "built to last" are characterized by unwavering commitment to their basic purposes. At the same time, these authors provide numerous examples of companies that failed to reconsider their basic purposes and are, therefore, no longer leaders. Chaos theory is one more admonition that college administrators and planners cannot afford to ignore the influence of iterative feedback and unpredictable change that are part and parcel of today's complex environment.

The remaining five steps of planning are the development of strategic databases; the determination of objectives, strategies, programs, and plans; goals; the creation of contingency plans; and the evaluation of the plan's outcomes and the process itself. As has been discussed, chaos theory highlights how essential it is to monitor actively all sources of feedback for the institution. Obviously, assessment is integral. This is not unique; however, strategic planners have traditionally focused on the use of environmental forecasting and assessment of the external environment. What distinguishes the contribution of chaos theory is its emphasis on the criticality of flexibility.[7] How familiar we are with institutions that spend hundreds of hours and large sums of money to create an elegant set of objectives, goals, and strategies that collect dust on a shelf. In contrast, colleges and universities must view their goals and plans as constantly changing within the context of an institution that asks, and keeps on asking, fundamental questions (Ray, 1997). Chaos theory exemplifies that the institution that uses strategic planning as an excuse to stop learning may fail. All levels of the college and university must be involved in continuous learning (Tetenbaum, 1998; Schmidtlein, 1990).

When objectives, goals, and plans are developed during strategic planning, creativity and flexibility are often difficult to embrace. Humans naturally seek certainty and order. The principle of sensitivity to initial conditions, however, exemplifies how little complexity in a system is needed to produce complicated phenomena (Pool, 1989). As a holistic process, chaos theory can help participants tolerate the chaos with its focus on continual analysis. Chaos theorists address local variables while simultaneously considering existing turbulence and that generated when introducing an agent of change (Wertheimer & Zinga, 1997). This consideration of the multitude of factors that influence the institution, especially many that are unpredictable, can nudge people away from the tendency to focus on static, inflexible goals and plans. So can a constant reminder by planners that systemic change in chaotic systems can be gradual, incremental, evolutionary or sudden, discontinuous and revolutionary (Mathews, White, & Long, 1999). For those desiring scientific support, chaos theory's principles of iterative feedback and sensitivity to initial conditions provide a scientific rationale for investing time in the examination of the individual and peculiar properties of a system (Peca, 1992).

Shipengrover (1996) illustrates another valuable contribution of chaos theory to the need for ongoing analysis. She notes that chaos theory helps us see deeper patterns underlying behavior and events in our organizational lives that are surprising and seemingly out of control. Understanding those patterns can lead to a restructuring of how we think and, therefore, the nature of the objectives and goals that are developed. Therefore, those involved in planning have the rationale for seeking far and wide for input and not accepting the obvious or the status quo (also see Kershaw & Safford, 1998).

The "small change-big result phenomenon" (Shipengrover, 1996; Warren, Franklin, & Streeter, 1998) yields an appreciation for the power that examining actions and changes in structures may have in fostering significant, lasting improvement. Sensitive dependence suggests there is often little leverage in acting on the most obvious symptoms of problems. Rather, chaos theory indicates that maximum leverage can be gained if effort is focused on identifying a change that, with a minimum of effort, would lead to lasting improvement. Chaos theorists remind planners to look in places that might have been previously ignored (for example, the effects of feedback internally). The results are objectives, goals, and plans radically different from what was expected. Change breaks down existing relationships and habits and forces systems to relinquish the status quo and trust in a destination not fully known (Shipengrover, 1996). Chaos theory underscores the need to counteract the tendency to label erratic and sudden behavior a crisis and explains why conflict and disorder are an essential part of a dynamic system (Mossberg, 1998). The dynamic system is one that can sustain conflicting agendas and that can adapt to and manipulate early resistance so that the institution has time to self-organize (Mossberg, 1998).

The next-to-last strategic planning step, development of contingency plans, is obviously congruent with chaos theory. When administrators develop contingency plans, the administrators describe how the institution will modify its plans and strategies to deal with anticipated constraints. While it is impossible to anticipate every possible change, exploring constraints and developing contingency plans generally will enable the institution to respond more quickly and more effectively when changes do occur.

However, much of the planning literature implies, directly or indirectly, that these constraints can be discovered and controlled. Chaos theory reveals the impracticality of that assumption. Strategic planners who integrate chaos theory into their processes recognize that institutions must budget fiscally and psychically for failure (Cutright, 1996). Strategic planners who accept the inherent instability implied by chaos theory recognize that the development of stable objectives, goals, and plans is unrealistic. They avoid the temptation to commit to specific actions more than six months in advance of implementation (with some obvious exceptions, such as facilities planning). Instead a planning process is created that is flexible, in part because information as input is sought continuously (Levin, Lanigan, & Perkins, 1995). Feedback must be constant (Mossberg, 1998). Strategic planning, including the development of contingency plans, becomes a process that allows the institution's members to attempt to prove one's self wrong, on an ongoing basis, to challenge thinking, find flaws, and experiment and test every possible alternative (Tetenbaum, 1998). The underlying assumption is that administrators predict the unpredictable and ensure that the process and the budget reflect this attitude (Mossberg, 1998). Measures and criteria for success are long-term (Mossberg, 1998). One is not defined by others' sense of crises and their agendas. The leaders, planners, and participants in a chaos-theory-based strategic planning institution remain centered and able to respond subtly and strategically. Messiness does not mean failure or no progress. Rather, conflict and turbulence are signs of progress as energy is processed according to systemic law, i.e., energy causes turbulence (Mossberg, 1998). "Strategic planning embraces the fact that the past has a conflict with the future and this creates the present. Nothing creative happens until energy is forced into it. These two ideas are united when strategic planning is used to leverage an org" (Weimer & Jonas, 1995, p. 1).

## Conclusion

This writer's analysis of the principles governing chaos theory and the implementation of strategic planning in institutions of higher education reveals that the two phenomena are not incompatible. The consideration of the external environment, the focus on process and not just product, and the vital role played by information, are traditional components of strategic planning consistent with the "new science" of chaos theory (Cutright, 1999; Swenk, 1999; Tan, 1994). Furthermore, she argues that if strategic planning is going to be useful and effective in today's environment, strategic planners need to consciously adopt elements of chaos theory.

Kershaw and Safford (1998) write about the "sea change" occurring in Canada and the United States regarding our perceptions of the relationships between institutions and students (see Gilbert, 1991, for a similar perspective). These factors are familiar to members of higher education institutions. Driven by imperatives of telecommunications, the hard, strong boundaries of the past led logically to a "notion of a range of good or service geographically, politically, socially." Today, however, boundaries between institutions are fuzzy. The relationship between student and institution has reversed. Students have more power because they have much more freedom of choice. They express a common theme of why chaos theory must be integrated into strategic planning: to remain viable and vibrant, institutions must develop new social technologies that allow for much more flexible responses. Chaos means vitality; higher education institutions must change significantly so the focus is on promoting acceptance of the need for change.

Chaos theory, like strategic planning, is an interpretive tool that can enable a more realistic assessment of reality. Chaos means vitality. Chaos theory provides the principles by which we can implement a strategic planning process that helps us deal with the "turbulence of permanent white water" (Shipengrover, 1996) and allows order to emerge from the messiness of disorder through experimentation and trial and error, not rigidity and rationality. Chaos theory is the foundation by which genuinely complex structures can take advantage of the sudden change inherent in online dynamics while maintaining the order necessary for continuity (Warren, Franklin, & Streeter, 1998).

The literature on strategic planning provides numerous examples of the mixed results associated with the use of strategic planning in higher education (Cutright, 1999; Swenk, 1992; Schmidtlein & Milton, 1990). Several dilemmas are not explained or are overlooked by strategic planning. For example, strategic planning is not always equal to the challenge of explaining how we cope with uncertainty and rapid change. Much of what happens was not planned in the first place. Organizational cultures, policies, and structures are not likely to be changed merely through careful planning. And planning only works in the short-term because specifying objectives may induce a temporary vision to bolster confidence. Then, when new changes begin to encroach on the task at hand, leaders rush to restore order and return to the main agenda. Models of strategic planning look for order in a disorderly world and rely heavily on rational assumptions of cause and effect (Shipengrover, 1996).

Dever (1997) presents a thoughtful rationale why chaos theory may be more easily accepted in higher education. Chaos theory is a radical departure from traditional business practices and, therefore, the discipline most likely to be resisted in the corporate world. But the strength of academic freedom can allow for risk taking and experimentation. The academic discipline of history is consistent with systems thinking and its stress on the need to identify the long-term and complex effects that follow from causes often far removed in time. Critical thinking, convergent discourse (Cutright, 1999), continuous learning, and discovery of new knowledge also are educational values that interconnect nicely with the requirements of chaos theory. The dual hierarchies that characterize higher education and the emphasis on consensual decision making (Swenk, 1992, 1999) also are characteristics that can counteract the rigidity associated with clearly defined hierarchical structures. The integration of chaos theory and strategic planning may be the best way of alleviating the views of faculty and administrators who view planning as futile since the future cannot be predicted because the emphasis shifts to a flexible process of identifying and managing change. The shift is to a way of looking at the world, not a linear process for creating plans and guiding activities. Namely, the ideal outcome of planning is planning (Cutright, 1996). Institutions can be hierarchically organized for the purpose of maintaining tight control over routine recurring tasks. Yet chaos can still reign internally. At these institutions, planning is continuous, evolving, and chaotic. Planning is driven by values and by the institutional vision and is fed by a continual flow of an ever-expanding information base (Levin, Lanigan, & Perkins, 1995). "The better futures will be reserved, as always, for those able to act more often than simply to react" (Gilbert, 1991, p. 118).

It is natural to choose order rather than disorder as a means of coping with conflict, paradox, and ambiguity (Tetenbaum, 1998) by choosing order rather than disorder. Siegfried, Getz, and Anderson wrote that there was surprisingly little correlation between the characteristics of institutions and the speed at which innovations were adopted or accepted (1995, quoted in Levin, Lanigan, & Perkins, 1995). How long will this remain true? How will institutions of higher education survive when events in today's environment overwhelm the system's capacity to cope? If these institutions engage in ongoing strategic planning characterized by "fluid organizational dynamics that promote continuous learning, rigorous analysis, and creative responses" (Dever, 1997), then there is optimism that the future will not be just the result of chaos and external influences. The future can be an invention that contains "creative elements of the dreams, values, and ambitions" (Cutright, 1999) of those who care deeply about the institution. Effective planning involves ambiguity and chaos (Hines, 1991). Effective strategic planning requires the integration of chaos theory.

## Notes

1. For a readable and most enjoyable history of the emergence of chaos theory, see Gleick (1988).

2. See Swenk, 1988, 1992, for detailed critiques of the use of strategic planning in business and higher education.

3. The literature on the value of mission, vision, and the role of culture is voluminous but will not be discussed here.

4. Levin, Lanigan, & Perkins, 1995, also emphasize the important role played by informal leaders.

5. Expressed in the language of chaos theory: "acting as a strange attractor . . . ."

6. The concept of *groupthink* exemplifies the importance of dissent (Janis, 1971; Whyte, 1989)

7. Schmidtlein noted this in his 1990 analysis of strategic planning.

# References

Ackoff, R. (1970). *A concept of corporate planning.* New York: Wiley and Sons.

Ansoff, H. I. (1965). *Corporate strategy: an analytic approach to business policy for growth and expansion.* San Francisco, CA: McGraw-Hill.

Baker, D., & Markin, R. J. (1994). *A framework for strategic planning and change in higher education: The case of a business school.* Paper presented at Association of Institutional Research. Washington, DC: ERIC Clearinghouse. (ED 360918).

Barnett, R. (2000). *Realizing the university in an age of supercomplexity (Introduction, Chapter 8).* Philadelphia: Society for Research into Higher Education and Open University Press.

Brady, D. (1990, November 19). The roots of chaos: An exciting theory stirs the scientific world. *Maclean's, 103*(47), 46–47.

Brown, T. (1997, April). The essence of strategy. *American Management Association, 86*(4), 8–14.

Chaffee, E. E. (1983). *Rational decision making in higher education.* Boulder, CO: National Center for Higher Education Management Systems.

Cohen, M. D., & March, J. G. (1986). *Leadership and ambiguity* (2nd ed.). Cambridge, MA: Harvard Business School Press.

Cope, R. G. (1987). *Opportunity from strength: Strategic planning clarified with case examples* (8). Washington, DC: ASHE-ERIC.

Cope, R. G., & Delaney, G. (1991). Academic program review: A market strategy perspective. *New Strategies in Higher Education Marketing*, 63–86.

Crittenden, W. F., & Crittenden, V. L. (1997, Spring). Strategic planning in third-sector organizations. *Journal of Management Issues, 9*(1), 86–103.

Cutright, M. (1996). The implications of chaos theory for strategic planning in higher education. Abstract. Washington, DC: ERIC Clearinghouse. (ED 393376).

Cutright, M. (1999, April). *Planning in higher education: A model from chaos theory.* Montreal: Paper presented at the Annual Conference of the American Educational Research Association.

Deal, T. E., & Kennedy, A. A. (1982). *Corporate cultures: The rites and rituals of corporate life.* Reading, MA: Addison-Wesley.

Dever, J. T. (1997, Fall). Reconciling educational leadership and the learning organization. *Community College Review, 25*(2), 57–63.

Drohan, W. (1997, January). Principles of strategic planning: A step by step approach. *Association Management, 49*(1), 85–87.

Gibbons, A. (1988, July). Chaos and the real world. *Technology Review, 91,* 5.

Gilbert, A. (1991, October). Current issues and future developments in higher education. *Journal of Tertiary Education Administration, 13*(2), 117–130.

Gleick, J. (1988). *Chaos: Making a new science.* New York: Penguin Books.

Hall, M. C., & Elliott, K. M. (1993). Strategic planning for academic departments: A model and methodology. *Journal of Marketing for Higher Education, 4*(1/2), 295–308.

Hax, A. C., & Majluf, N. S. (1984). *Strategic management: An integrative perspective.* Englewood Cliffs, NJ: Prentice-Hall.

Hax, A. C., & Wilde, D. L., II. (1999, Winter). The Delta model: Adaptive management for a changing world. *Sloan Management Review, 40*(2), 11.

Hearn, J. (1988). Strategy and resources: Economic issues in strategic planning and management in higher education. In J. Smart (Ed.), *Higher education: Handbook of theory and research* (Vol. 4), (pp. 212–281). New York: Agathon Press.

Hines, G. (1991, April). Strategic planning made easy. *Training and Development Journal,* 39–43.

Hipps, G. Melvin (Ed.). (1982). *Effective Planned Change Strategies.* San Francisco: Jossey-Bass Inc.

Hurst, P. J. (1994). Enhancing strategic planning through campus surveys. Paper presented at AIR, Louisiana, 5/29-6/1/94. Washington, DC: ERIC Clearinghouse. (ED 373651).

Janis, I. L. (1971). *Groupthink.* Boston: Houghton Mifflin

Jedamus, P., Peterson, M., & Associates. (1980). *Improving academic management: A handbook of planning and institutional research.* San Francisco: Jossey-Bass.

Johnson, T., & Jonas, P. (1995, May). *Participative strategic planning with an eye toward economic analysis.* Washington, DC: ERIC Clearinghouse. (ED 387015).

Keller, G. (1983). *Academic strategy: The management revolution in American higher education.* Baltimore: Johns Hopkins University Press.

Kemerer, F., Baldridge, J. V., & Green, K. C. (1982). *Strategies for effective enrollment management.* Washington, DC: American Association of State Colleges and Universities.

Kershaw, A., & Safford, S. (1998). From order to chaos: The impact of educational telecommunications on post-secondary education. *Higher Education, 35,* 285–298.

King, W., & Cleland, D. (1978). *Strategic planning and policy.* New York: Van Nostrand Reinhold Co.

Lemonick, M. D. (1993, February 22). Life, the universe and everything. (complexity). *Time, 141*(8), 62–63.

Levin, B. H., Lanigan, J. B., & Perkins, J. R. (1995, August). *Strategic planning in a decentralized environment: The death of linearity.* Asheville, NC: Paper presented at the 24th Annual Conference of the Southeastern Association for Community College Research.

Liff, A. (1997, January). Avoiding eight pitfalls of strategic planning, *Association Management, 49*(1), 49, 120–123.

Mathews, K. M., White, M. C., & Long, R. G. (1999, April). Why study the complexity sciences in the social sciences. *Human Relations, 52*(14), 439–440.

Migliore, R. H. (1991, Winter). Strategic planning/MBO with a human resources emphasis in educational administration. *CUPA,* 15–19.

Montuori, A. (1992, December). Creativity, chaos, and self-renewal in human systems. *World Futures, 35*(4), 193–208.

Mintzberg, H., & Quinn, J. B. (1991). *The strategy process: concepts, contexts, cases* (Second ed.). Engelwood Cliffs, New Jersey: Prentice Hall.

Mossberg, B. (1998, October/November). Why I wouldn't leave home without chaos theory. *The Inner Edge*, 5–8.

Myers, R. S. (1996, Summer). Restructuring to sustain excellence. *New Directions for Higher Education, 94*, 69–82.

Overman, E. S. (1996, September-October). The new sciences of administration: Chaos and quantum theory. *Public Administration Review, 56*(5), 487–491.

Peca, K. (1992). Chaos theory: A scientific basis for alternative research methods in educational administration. Abstract. Washington, DC: ERIC Clearinghouse. (ED 361843).

Pfeffer, J., & Salancik, G. R. (1978). *The external control of organizations: A resource dependence perspective.* New York: Harper & Row.

Pool, R. (1989, July 7). Chaos theory: How big an advance (part 6). *Science, 245*(4913), 26–28.

Porras, J. L., & Collins, J. C. (1994). *Built to last: Successful habits of visionary companies.* New York: Harper Business.

Ray, D. E. (1997, August). Strategic planning for non-profit organizations. *Fund Raising Management, 28*(6), 22–23.

Robson, K. (1996, February). A funny thing happened on the way to the future: Regenerating our academic institutions. Paper presented at Fifth Annual International Conference for Community and Technical College Chairs, Deans and Other Organizational Leaders, Arizona. Washington, DC: ERIC Clearinghouse. (ED 394568).

Schmidtlein, F. (1990). Planning for quality: Perils and possibilities. Paper presented at the European Association for Institutional Research, Lyons, France.

Schmidtlein, F., & Milton, T. (1990). *A review of literature on higher education institutional planning.* 45 pages, Washington, DC: ERIC Clearinghouse. (ED328189).

Scott, W. R. (1992). *Organizations: Rational, natural, and open systems. Third Edition.* New Jersey: Prentice-Hall Inc.

Shipengrover, J. (1996, Spring). If it doesn't embrace chaos, can it be called a strategic plan. *CUPA Journal, 47*(1), 1–6.

Swenk (Prinvale), J. (1988). Achieving distinction in an uncertain future. *Proceedings of fifth annual conference: Academic chairpersons: In search of academic quality.* Orlando, FL: Kansas State University, National Issues in Higher Education.

Swenk (Prinvale), J. (1992). *What happens when colleges plan? The use of strategic planning in four-year colleges and universities.* Unpublished dissertation. Stanford University School of Education, Stanford, CA.

Swenk (Prinvale), J. (1999). Planning failures: Decision cultural clashes. *The Review of Higher Education, 23*(1), 1–21.

Tan, D. (1994, Summer). The state of strategic planning: A survey of selected research universities. *CUPA Journal, 71*(1), 24–32.

Tetenbaum, T. J. (1998, Spring). Shifting paradigms: From Newton to chaos. *Organizational Dynamics, 26*(4), 21–31.

Townsend, B., & Others. (1992). *Creating distinctiveness: Lessons from uncommon colleges and universities.* Washington, DC: ERIC Clearinghouse. (ERIC Digest: ED 356753).

Trygestad, J. (1997). Chaos in the classroom: An application of chaos theory. Abstract. Washington, DC: ERIC Clearinghouse. (ED 413289).

Warren, K., Franklin, C., & Streeter, C. L. (1998, July). New directions in systems theory: Chaos and complexity. *Social Work, 43*(4), 357–373.

Weimer, D., & Jonas, P. M. (1995). Strategic planning: A participative model, Cardinal Stritch College, pp. 1–6. Washington, DC: ERIC Clearinghouse. (ED 390324).

Wertheimer, R., & Zinga, M. (1997). Attending to the noise: Applying chaos theory to school reform. Abstract. Washington, DC: ERIC Clearinghouse. (ED 408707).

Wheatley, M. (1992). *Leadership and the new science.* San Francisco: Berrett-Koehler Publishers.

Whyte, G. (1989). Groupthink reconsidered. In Kolb, D., Osland, J., & Rubin, I. (1995), *The Organizational Behavior Reader* (16th ed.). Englewood Cliffs, NJ: Prentice-Hall. pp. 251–267.

# CHAPTER FOUR

## A Chaos Theory Metaphor for Strategic Planning

*Marc Cutright*

### Circumstances and Roots

Robert Birnbaum is among the scholars and practitioners in higher education to revisit strategic planning in that venue, and to cast substantial doubt on its effectiveness. Indeed, he counts it prominently among the management "innovations" in the academy that he discusses in *Management Fads in Higher Education: Where They Come From, What They Do, and Why They Fail* (2000). In a history of about twenty years, we've seen an early zenith of enthusiasm about the concept, and its subsequent, perhaps inevitable, fall. Does it have utility, or is strategic planning just another suit from the world of business, fit poorly to the college and university?

Strategic planning in higher education received an early definition and a strong boost from George Keller with the publication in 1983 of *Academic Strategy: The Management Revolution in American Higher Education.* The author estimated that while no more than a dozen of 3,400 colleges and universities nationwide were engaged in strategic planning at the time of the book's publication, a decade later perhaps a quarter of those institutions were engaged in strategic thinking and acting. Yet Keller also acknowledged that a considerable number of the efforts in that decade had failed (Keller, 1993). Other expert opinion was more pointed; by one accounting, for every three institutions that had initiated a planning process in the 1980s, two had fallen away from it and had gone back to "business as usual" (Jones, 1990, p. 52). A study published in 1994 by the American Council on Education (Schuster et al.), inspired by Keller's work and seeking to examine the state of strategic planning as shown on eight campuses Keller had originally studied, found mixed results from strategic planning efforts, and some outright failures. This revisionism is certainly not contained to the United States. Australian higher education authors Peter Coaldrake and Lawrence Stedman, for example, note that strategic planning is commonly asserted by institutions in that country. But they also say that such planning is often rote and unthinking, intended merely to meet government mandates, and unable in its product to differentiate one institution from another. "The net result is that much administrative time is wasted in tick-a-box activity and little strategic light is shed" (1998, p. 153).

Strategic planning enjoys a longer and more storied history in the corporate setting than in higher education, and so Henry Mintzberg's publication in 1994 of *The Rise and Fall of Strategic Planning* is of interest. Among other assertions coming from his broad study of many strategic planning processes, Mintzberg suggested that the mid-nineties were an appropriate time for the publication of the book and his prescriptions for strategic planning's revival. Had he published earlier, he felt, his points might well have been lost in the 1980s' backlash against strategic planning.

Of course, considerations of the limitations, failures, and cultural conflicts of planning and related issues within higher education predate Keller and the economic conditions of the 1980s which pressed consideration of institutions' market placements. Cohen and March, in their 1974 classic *Leadership and Ambiguity*, noted that the many presidents they interviewed voiced virtually unanimous support for the importance of planning and the idea that central responsibility for such planning resided within the office of the president. Yet Cohen and March determined four categories of answers when these same presidents were pressed for their plans (p. 113):

1. Yes, we have a plan. It is used in capital projects and physical location decisions.

2. Yes, we have a plan. Here it is. It was made during the administration of our last president. We are working on a new one.

3. No, we do not have a plan. We should. We are working on one.

4. I think there's a plan around here someplace. Miss Jones, do we have a copy of our comprehensive 10-year plan?

Cohen, March, and Olsen tied such patterns of institutional action and culture into their "garbage can" and "organized anarchy" models of institutional choice and decision making. Problems, solutions, participants, and choice opportunities were conceived and described as a rather random mix given to uneven results and low predictability (Cohen & March, 1974; Cohen, March, & Olsen, 1972).

Karl Weick described educational systems, including universities, as "loosely coupled systems" (1976), reminiscent of Cohen, March and Olsen's "uncoupling of problems and choices" (1972, p. 16) in garbage-can decision making, rather than as tightly controlled, centrally managed organizations. Weick identified advantages to such systems. Loose coupling can allow an organization to be more sensitive to environmental changes and able to adapt to them, as well as having lower administrative costs. Although Weick noted in 1976 that loose coupling "baffled and angered" (p. 4) administrators in their central planning activities and resulting expectations that an organization could be changed by such planning, he later expressed further and more detailed concern that loose coupling had frequently been conceptualized as a diametric opposite to management of organizations and was often cited as a cause of perceived resistance to change (Orton & Weick, 1990). Keller (1983), indeed, considered the conditions of garbage-can decision making and loose coupling to be crises, not elements of flexibility and adaptability, for the then-emerging era of harsh competition for resources.

## Can We Do Better?

Anyone who has lived awhile in the world of the college or university likely has a personal history with strategic planning, as a participant or "victim." I have seen it touted and occasionally practiced in small colleges, large universities, professional schools, and state systems. The result is that I have substantial sympathy for Birnbaum's perspective. Following is a worst-practices composite description of strategic planning in my experience. See if it's familiar:

- Planning is mandated by, and executed only to meet at a minimal level, the policies of external agencies such as governing boards, state legislatures, or accrediting agencies.

- Planning is periodic, episodic, and discontinuous.

- Plans are crafted from sketchy and limited information, almost all of it statistical. Only persons of a certain status are allowed to input this information, which is gathered along conventional chains of command.

- The planning process avoids conflict, particularly as it might question the institution's core purposes and reasons to exist.

- Planning is directed and controlled to a very high degree by the institution's chief executive officer.

- Planning assumes that a sufficient amount of information on current circumstances will yield an accurate prediction of the future.

- Plans are highly detailed, project far into the future, and depend on a deliberate sequence of events.

- Budgets and plans are linked in one of two ways: not in the least, or in rigid lock, with no room for contingencies.

What if one was to define an alternative, potentially a best-practices model, merely by turning these elements on their head? We'd then have:

- Planning driven by an institution's desire to identify and develop its potential.

- Planning that's continuous.

- Planning open to a broad range of opinion, information, aspiration, and argument from throughout the broadly defined constituency of the institution.

- Planning that is focused on the priority of articulating the institution's core purposes and priorities.

- Planning that is energized, but only generally directed, by the chief executive officer.

- Planning that points a direction, but that is not overly detailed and hard to remember.

- Planning that allows for the pursuit of opportunities that arise in the future but are not currently foreseen.

That would be a framework largely reflective of both the most enduring—and most recent, sound thinking—about strategic planning in higher education. It would also be a framework highly reflective of perspectives about the future, and our relationships to it, that can be derived from a consideration of the metaphoric or literal principles of chaos theory.

I now put forward ten propositions about strategic planning, propositions derived from a coincident consideration of both chaos theory and best practices in strategic planning. The propositions form an extended metaphor, a model, which provides a conceptual coherence for successful practices in strategic planning, and therefore a general, prescriptive approach for institutions embarking on planning efforts. Some of these propositions are stated in blunt and provocative terms. If we accept that mechanical metaphors are largely default conceptions of how our organizations work, they have to be pushed aside, summarily if temporarily, to allow for adequate consideration of this alternative.

While these propositions have roots in relatively abstract thought, and the planning research and practice of others, they were examined and refined by case-study consideration of the planning experiences of a number of institutions. Foremost among these cases were Carson-Newman College, a denominational college in Tennessee; the University of Calgary, an institution that would be considered a Carnegie Research I university in the American context; Blue Ridge Community College, a public institution in Virginia; and Red Deer College, a public two-year college in Alberta, Canada. Only Blue Ridge Community College among these four operated from an explicit metaphor of chaos theory, and so their experience is recounted in detail later in this book. While examples of practice and experience from these cases would beneficially illustrate these propositions, length considerations dictate otherwise.

## Propositions of a Chaos Theory Metaphor for Planning

**Proposition 1: The ideal outcome of planning is planning, not a plan.**
Dwight Eisenhower was more direct: "Plans are nothing. Planning is everything" (Keller, 1983, p. 99). Keller (1983) noted that strategic planning is not the production of a blueprint, or a fat, detailed document. Rather, it is a strategic direction and central strategy, which adjusts to changing conditions.

Cohen and March (1974) alluded to the prime role of planning *vis-à-vis* plans in higher education. As they noted, many students of planning, to that point, had asserted that the interaction brought about by planning was more important than the plan itself. "Occasionally that interaction yields results of positive value," Cohen and March wrote, "But only rarely does it yield anything that would accurately describe the activities of a school or department beyond one or two years into the future" (p. 115), given the importance of environmental turbulence such as changes in personnel, political climates, foundation policy, and student demand.

This is not to suggest that plans should not produce goals and targets for an organization. Mintzberg (1994) was critical of post hoc rationalizations of failed planning efforts in the planning-itself-is-the-goal vein. Yet it is important to note that the failures of which he speaks are products of overly detailed efforts, constructed by management fiat and heavily dependent upon narrowly considered and shaky data. As to simplicity, Mintzberg wrote: "The more elaborate the planning procedures become—in response to the failure of the simpler ones—the greater seemed to be their failures" (p. 295). Mintzberg ultimately argued for planning that emphasizes process ahead of product.

Large, detailed plans, issued on a long time horizon of five, ten, or more years, are common in higher education. Further, they are sequentially structured, with each step dependent upon the completion, within a specified time frame, or precedent steps. This is, suggests one author, somewhat like playing a game of pool by specifying, before the commencement of play, each and every shot through the sinking of the eight ball (Priesmeyer, 1992).

Academic planners James Morrison (editor emeritus of the planning journal *On the Horizon*), George Wilkinson, and Linda Forbes note in their Web-published book *Common Sense Management for Educational Leaders* (1999) that many others have said that "it is the process, and not the plan that counts." They appear to endorse this general viewpoint with their instruction: "Keep this in mind: *The product you are seeking at each step is not a written report. It is a strategic mind-set of the senior leadership, indeed the whole organization*" (emphasis in original).

Rebecca Stafford, president of Monmouth University and an established author and consultant in strategic planning, has noted where she believes many strategic planning processes go wrong (1993). Among her key cautions: most plans are far too detailed, or worse, burdened with fairly meaningless language disguised as details. She advises that the strategic initiatives in a plan should be few and specific.

**Proposition 2: Planning begins with a distillation of the institution's key values and purposes.** These elements are not dictated from above, but discovered from within. In the paradoxical context of chaos theory, they provide a constant source of reference but are always open to challenge and modification. This process, within the context of chaos theory, is the discovery of a system's attractors, those principles that organize the system despite turbulence, establish its boundaries, and give it a general direction for the future. The attractors allow the actors within the system to make decisions consistent with the organization's collective identity, purposes, and goals, and to make decisions about the deployment of finite resources.

If colleges and universities are considered as chaotic systems, then the attempt to import principles, or their imposition by executive fiat, are alien to reality. Attractors already exist in the system, chaos theory states, and attention must be paid to them. Imposing new goals and purposes, without discovering and reconciling those already operational for the system actors, will result in an early separation of plans from reality. Failure to recognize the existence of attractors operant at various locations within an organization also ignores the centrality of fractal structure. A college may profess dedication to the quality of teaching as a central principle, but unless this principle is a goal and motivator at all levels of the organization, it is unlikely that this central dedication will be reflected in the experience of students.

This discovery of attractors would rarely be accomplished by reference to a college's mission statement. As many have noted and many more have experienced, these documents are often "kitchen sinks" of collected ideas and goals, good and bad, littered with platitudes, and with little sense of priorities. These elements may be attractors, but they have limited organizational power because of their multitude and lack of priority. Mintzberg (1994, p. 297) similarly decried the presence of "empty platitudes" at the heart of most planning processes. Newson and Hayes (1990), in an analysis of nearly 100 different college and university mission statements, found those mission statements to be largely indistinguishable, of little focusing power, and exercises in institutional compromise. They include nearly all objectives suggested within the particular institution and reject very little in potential identity and mission. "Not surprisingly, few colleges find much use for their mission statements. They are usually not guidelines for serious planning" (p. 277). David Dill, commenting particularly on the Newson and Hayes study, asserted that there is intention in this situation: such mission statements are externally oriented, rather than internally, and are meant to keep an institution's options wide open. Dill has also observed the power of mission statements more simply and narrowly stated. When a mission statement is more focused, and "grounded in the culture and traditions" of the particular institution, then that mission statement is "central to the implementation of a successful planning and resource allocation process" (1997, p. 188).

Neumann and Larson considered the circumstance of a president, particularly a new one, who develops an institutional "vision" without consideration of operative imperatives within the college or university. Not only is this lack of recognition a neglect of opportunities and momentum already in operation, but institutional culture presents many opportunities to thwart an alien vision through resistance and sabotage (1997).

Chaffee and Jacobson were even more pointed. Their scan of planning history yields the lesson that "the planning process that is inconsistent with organizational culture is doomed to fail" (1997, p. 231). Chaffee and Jacobson noted that operative cultures are based on underlying and deep values and assumptions. When vision and the institution's resident values go head to head, the result is almost always the same: "Culture 1, Planning 0" (p. 230). Morrison et al. (1999) stress the importance of seeking the broad involvement of institutional stakeholders and reaching agreement, as much as is possible, about mission and vision as preliminary to focus on the issues key to institutional success and the development of a strategy for their accomplishment.

**Proposition 3: The widest possible universe of information should be made available to all members of the institution. This universe of information includes ongoing, rich, and current feedback.** Keller's (1983) advancement of the concept of environmental scanning and information gathering as critical to good planning has become widely accepted. Where chaos theory perhaps advances the concept of information gathering and sharing is an emphasis on the importance of feedback. The discussion and creation of plans themselves are elements of the informational landscape. They create feedback loops, whether planners recognize them or not. Schuster et al. (1994) exaggerate the importance that Keller (1983) places on the need for secrecy and confidentiality in the deliberations of the Joint Big Decision Committee, Keller's generic name for a campus's central planning body. But chaos theory does support Schuster's argument for open planning, and Keller subsequently to his 1983 book would revise his view on the Joint Big Decision Committee; more open communication engenders trust, he concluded (1988). Chaos theory suggests that planning executed in secret or with an air of exclusion will deny itself the creativity, vitality, and connection with reality that open— that is to say, feedback-rich—planning processes enjoy.

Chaffee and Jacobson (1997) held that information should not only be widely shared, but shared in a variety of ways, including reports, speeches, newsletters, and other ways. This sharing should include sensitive information. Likewise, they write, the planning process should be open to information offered from any source; the openness of the administration with information sets the tone for receptiveness and allows the process to capture information that otherwise would escape. This is consistent with Peterson's contextual planning model (1997), which emphasizes widespread participation in the information-gathering and planning processes.

## Proposition 4: Dissent and conflict are creative, healthy, and real. The absence of conflict is reductionist, illusory, and suspect.

Chaos recognizes and respects the power of turbulence. It is the essence of creativity in chaotic systems. Ideas uncontested are suspect in their power and frequently unable to withstand the inevitable influx of turbulence. Yet how much of our planning is characterized by a desire to minimize conflict, to subtly suppress dissent, and to reach early consensus? Keller (1983) noted this desire for tranquility as a root of the smothering of organizational creativity when he quoted the president of Indiana University: "Many presidents spend much of their time trying to anger the fewest people rather than trying to produce something really good . . ." (p. 173). Keller further noted that many presidents see planners as creators of problems, not solvers of them.

Mary Parker Follett, an organizational theorist and consultant writing seven decades ago, distinguished our various ways of dealing with conflict as domination, compromise, and integration (1925, in Fox and Urwick, 1973). Chaos theory would suggest that domination, the simple victory of one side over another, merely delays the turbulent effect of the losing side's resistance to, or outright sabotage of, compliance with the "winning" position. Compromise, more ostensibly cordial, likewise delays or ignores turbulence, in that agreement is typically reached at a fairly low and superficial level, and leaves the turbulence as an unrecognized, background element. Integration, solutions in which the desires of all sides have been met and skillfully combined, is the creative resolution of conflict, and the resolution most consistent with chaos theory. Neither did Follett suggest nor would any other observer hold that all conflict is resolvable by integration. But without recognition, even encouragement, of conflict, without all sides putting their cards on the table, integration is impossible.

Consonant with Follett, Zohar (1997) holds that "debate, the contesting of preset positions to victory or defeat," has become the dominant Western form of solving disagreements and arriving at decisions. But before debate, in ancient Greece, was *dialogue*. *Dia* means "through," and *logos* is translated as "words." But an older translation of *logos* would be "relationship." Ancient Greeks, before the assignment of debates to representatives in republican government, would meet in the agora, or marketplace, and hold dialogue on issues. "This allowed for the emergence of collective insight, collective wisdom, and a nonconfrontational way of solving problems . . . . Dialogue is about finding out, about discussing something openly until I break through to some new knowledge or insight . . . . Dialogue involves my emotions and my deeper sensitivities, as well as my best intellectual thinking facilities" (pp. 137–138).

Neumann and Larson (1997) found relevance in these general perspectives for contemporary strategic planning. Academic culture itself is built largely upon "communities of divergent discourse" (p. 194). What is to be avoided is the emergence in planning of an administrative, "single-minded view that stifles the disciplined growth of certain lines of thought in favor of others" (p. 194). Openness to various points of view can, Neumann and Larson cited as an example, lead to the blending and mutual consideration of viewpoints that might be pigeonholed early on as self-interested or irrelevant. Tierney (1992) echoes this perspective. Rather than suppress difference, he writes, we should honor it, and "build across our differences a commonality that encompasses them" (p. 18). Holton (1995) suggested that conflict is not the problem, but the solution; conflict "can be cathartic, providing opportunities for revitalization, energizing, and creativity by all involved in the academy" (p. 94).

**Proposition 5: Linearity doesn't work in strategic planning. It doesn't work in dictation—planning and plans imposed from above—or in collation—planning and plans created solely by the collection of unit information.** By this point in the argument, the reader may see the obvious incompatibility of top-down, executive-committee-dictated planning with chaos theory. Attractors are not identified, feedback is denied, faint recognition of the environment is inevitable, and the implementation of plans is made virtually impossible by the lack of fractal structure. But it may be less obvious that the planning structure opposite to dictation—collation—is equally unsuitable.

Collation is the collection of individual "plans" by the department, the collection of these departmental collations by the college or school, and so on up the structure, until they are united at the top level of the organization. As Keller wrote (1983), strategic planning "is not a collection of departmental plans, compiled and edited . . . . A university is more than the aggregate of its parts" (p. 141). It is possible to mistake this sort of collation for a sort of empowerment, or a democratic process, but collation can at best only identify individual desires and directions.

Chaos theory would inform us that this process lacks the connectivity between elements of an organization that is inherent in systems. Collation without feedback creates only linear and upwardly directed information paths. Collation without feedback and the identification of organization attractors does not contribute to self-organization and sustained direction.

The type of bottom-up strategic planning element suggested by chaos theory is more akin to the "grassroots" model of strategy formation championed by Mintzberg (1994): "Strategies grow like weeds in a garden, they are not cultivated like tomatoes in a hothouse" (p. 287). Such strategies spring up unbidden throughout the organization, but they do not become organizational until they "become collective, that is when the patterns proliferate to pervade the behavior of the organization at large" (p. 288). Management's role, according to Mintzberg, is to recognize these emergent patterns and to nurture their growth throughout the organization. Chaos theory would suggest that such a role is an acknowledgment of the centrality and power of fractal structure.

Neumann and Larson (1997), in their consideration of processes which flaw planning processes, noted that even when planners use feedback mechanisms, they may fail to seek out negative feedback (such as disagreement or initiative failure). Such planners give attention instead to feedback that supports leaders' preconceptions. It is a "good news" approach to planning that robs the process of vitality and relevance. It is a partial, truncated, and flawed approach.

**Proposition 6: The institution should budget—fiscally and psychically—for failure. Pilots are alternate futures. Not all can be realized or succeed.** Several of these propositions are stated with attention-getting provocation, and none more so than this one. Experimentation and striking out in new directions are often viewed heroically on the front end, but disparaged on the back side after less than favorable results. We should recognize that in planning, as in financial investment, higher returns are made possible by higher risk. The challenge is to improve—not assure—the chances of success.

Universities are historically averse to change, even those changes which are ultimately and broadly adopted in higher education (Seigfried et al., 1995). This might be characterized as an overly developed aversion to Type I statistical error, that is, an aversion to making a change even when strong evidence exists that change is beneficial.

However, strategic planning by its nature attempts to make some tentative decisions about and preparations for an uncertain future. As Keller wrote (1983), ". . . strategic planning increases risk taking. It fosters an entrepreneurial spirit, a readiness to start new ventures" (p. 142). Dolence and Norris caution that if we wait until "the vision is perfectly clear and risks have vanished, the opportunities will have passed, as well" (1995, p. 4); the costs of lost opportunity are collected more quickly in a more rapidly changing environment. Morrison et al. (1999) encourage that "you and your [planning] colleagues must be imaginative, innovative, and willing to take risks," and "that means you are flexible, and not wedded to a set of strategies or action plans that you cannot change."

Chaos theory suggests that the predictive timeline is shorter than likely is the start-up and testing times of complex projects. Chaos theory suggests that strategic planning can at best identify likely or possible futures, but cannot, through the compilation of adequate data, foretell the future through longitudinal projections. Therefore, tests and pilots should be launched, with the knowledge that not all possible or likely futures will come to pass. Even though strong data collection and ongoing feedback can result in what might be called "wise piloting," some pilots will fail.

Keller (1983) recognized this in an element of his prescription that is perhaps less closely observed than other elements: "To foster change, have a venture capital fund ready to support those on campus who are the most creative and entrepreneurial" (p. 169). Later work by Keller (1997) supports this idea even more emphatically: "Unless money follows new ideas, the strategic priorities will not get adequate support and the planning exercise will be perceived as a sham" (p. 168).

It is more difficult to document, but it follows that institutions are as psychically averse to piloting as they are fiscally averse to it. If we subtly punish or isolate those whose pilots seemed reasonable and which were blessed, but fail, and we quickly distance ourselves from failure rather than examine it for lessons, we discourage the experimentation necessary to discover the future.

Weick, who confessed a "mild affection" (1976, pp. 6–7) for loose coupling, saw as one of its benefits the ability to test "mutations and novel solutions" it develops in response to its "many independent sensing mechanisms." Weick cautioned that this same structure that permits these mutations to flourish may prevent their diffusion. This would support Mintzberg's (1994) suggestion that a role of management is to identify and promote promising strategies throughout an organization.

**Proposition 7: The considerable expense of time on the front end is an investment. It is recouped, with interest, in the future.** There can be little doubt that top-down, stripped-down, feedback-free planning is faster. This is a false economy. Fast plans may be convenient, even poetic, but without a rich understanding of the environment, the discovery of attractors, and the creation of iterative structure, they will, more often than not, fail. Time and resources will be inefficiently spent as institutional leaders attempt to impose a plan alien to the system's actual dynamics. Alternately, a plan developed from these dynamics, and not against them, will be more fully implemented, more reflected at fractal dimensions of the organization, more in concert with the organization's attractors, and more successful.

Keller (1983) noted that genuine strategic planning is broadly participatory. But Newton (1992) suggested that conflict carrying out this involvement may arise from the clash between the corporate culture of administration, on the one hand, and the academic culture on the other. The managerial bent of the former values quick decisions in response to rapidly changing environmental conditions, top-down decision making, and an expectation of organizational compliance. The latter culture values extended conversations, deliberation, and the testing of ideas over time and circumstances. Efforts to impose a corporate culture in domination of the academic culture, within the planning arena, often brings the planning process to a bad end.

Neumann and Larson (1997), who emphasize the importance of detecting organizational patterns and values that may be subtle but are nonetheless deep, note the many models of leadership and strategic planning emphasize broad involvement, but they note as well that in practice these principles are often ignored. Invitations to participate, or the creation of open forums, are not enough of an effort to gather broad input and diverse participation. Conversation, wrote Neumann and Larson, "must also permeate space and time." This expanded conversation involves not only formal meetings, but hallway talk, and entails an active effort on the part of planning coordinators to bring the thinking of groups and individuals to the attention of other groups and individuals. This is a process heavily dependent upon feedback, and feedback, in turn, is heavily dependent upon the investment of time.

Chaffee and Jacobson (1997) tie planning to institutional culture, and changing or redirecting culture, they note, can take substantial time. But they maintain that the "payoff can be immeasurably large." The payoff includes enhanced environmental sensing aided by many eyes and ears, the greater creativity made possible by many minds, and broad buy-in to the results of institutional planning, "in ways that the central administration could never have imagined or planned for" (p. 244). Conversely and "often, in the final analysis, [a] plan cannot be implemented, because key players have not agreed to it" (Innes, 1996, p. 470).

**Proposition 8: The executive is not demoted or minimized. The executive is the most critical shaper and champion of the process. Ultimately, the executive is empowered by the process.** All of this may suggest, without intention, that the executive becomes figurehead in a planning process informed by chaos theory. Descriptions of chaos-related metaphors and management viewpoints have perhaps reinforced this perception. Gareth Morgan writes, "In complex systems, no one is ever in a position to control or design system operations in a comprehensive way . . . . At best, would-be managers have to be content with an ability to nudge and push a system in a desired direction by shaping critical parameters that can influence the course of system evolution" (1997, pp. 272–273).

James Fisher, himself a former president and a longtime commentator on the institution of the presidency, gave voice to the suspicion that constituent-involving processes are in fact an abdication of presidential power and responsibility (1994). "In a misguided sense of democracy" (p. 60), board members, faculty, students, and others are engaged in an "unending and totally unproductive morass of committee meetings, faculty meetings, formal and informal dialogues" (p. 62), leading to paralysis and undistinguished, lowest-common denominator compromise.

John T. Dever, vice president for academic affairs at Blue Ridge Community College in Virginia, has written (1997) critically of Senge's (1990) and others' ignoring or downplaying the role of formal leadership in organizational processes. Dever writes of the academic arena:

> A president can produce results for weal or woe because he or she occupies an office from which force can be leveraged throughout the organization . . . . The leader must design, teach, husband, and deploy resources; but at times, he or she must energize the organization. (p. 60)

Further:

> Presidents and senior administrative staff leading these educational enterprises will need to be comfortable with fluid organizational dynamics . . . . However, they also will need to be prepared to intensify their leadership efforts when they must advocate forcefully, maneuver deftly, and, as required, do battle on both internal and external fronts. (p. 62)

I would suggest that the president active in the promotion and advancement of strategic planning may be seen, in the language of chaos theory, as a strange attractor, a basic element in the formation of a system's patterns. He or she can speed or slow the process, give or deny it legitimacy, and provide energy to the process when necessary.

Ultimately, the president can be empowered by the process. He or she should have a more clearly defined mandate, and should be able to make decisions, hire and fire personnel, allocate resources, and commence and terminate programs. The president should draw power, a greater level of consensus, and support for great operational leaps if he or she can tie decisions to the institution's goals and visions emerging from the chaos-informed planning process.

Keller (1997) noted specific, critical points for presidential intervention in and direction of the planning process, regardless of the openness of that process. The president needs to make a compelling case for the need for a strategic plan. The president needs to lay out a plan for the plan: a timetable and outline or nature of what is expected in the final product. The president or other respected campus leader needs to be prepared to step in and reenergize or direct planning processes that are stalled or sidetracked. The president should be prepared to produce timely implementations from the planning process, even while it is in progress, in order to contribute to the sense of urgency and empowerment. Finally, the president, once basic strategic directions are agreed upon institutionally, should be prepared to compel compliance and cooperation, to turn from the carrot to the stick.

Peter Fairweather (1997) advocates that the president and other leaders can sustain and energize institutional transformation through "small wins" in numerous areas. This makes change conceivable, palatable, and realistic for those whom massive change is too huge and abstract to comprehend. Further small, successful change enables people to support larger-scale change going in a similar direction.

However, the "strong" president, one who acts in virtual sole proprietorship of power, one who enforces his or her will with scant regard for opposition, feedback, or organizational attractors, has the potential to become an attractor of a different sort—a point attractor. Like a pendulum swirling toward a point of rest, the patterns of the institution become tighter and tighter, tending toward inertia. Feedback is of a different sort: lowered morale and commitment, leading to more rules and regulation, in a cycle that quickly overcomes all other dynamic inputs to the system. The actors on the scene become resigned to treading water instead of making waves (Platje & Seidel, 1993). Bensimon and Neumann (1993) describe the circumstance of the president prone to action without consultation as contributory to an executive staff, which is given to only going through the motions of deliberation among themselves, and with the president. Tierney (1992) encouraged us to view leadership, in planning and in broader contexts, more in terms of "facilitation" than "direction . . . . Leaders create the conditions for dialogue rather than acting as if they are the ones who define the reality of the organization" (p. 19).

It would seem rather critical that any model of any significant aspect of organizational function would devote substantial attention to the role of the executive. As Harvey (1998) writes, "effective leadership . . . is indispensable in guiding a campus through the treacherous waters of strategic planning . . . . [L]eadership is the capstone" (p. 7).

**Proposition 9: That which can be quantified is not to be overvalued, and that which cannot be quantified is not to be discounted.** Much of the circumstance of unpredictability comes from our inability to discern which factors in our environment, which "butterfly wings," will be absorbed by the most powerful dynamics of the system, and which will gain great power, from iterative dynamics, far out of proportion with the seeming insignificance of their genesis. The American G.I. Bill was such a butterfly wing. The bill's most ardent supporters in the closing days of World War II believed its promise of unemployment benefits for veterans to be the bill's most significant feature. Few thought that many returning veterans would take advantage of the bill's educational benefits. Yet more than two million veterans jumped at the chance to attend college. More significantly, access to higher education in America was transformed, in the public's mind, from a privilege for the few to an entitlement for virtually all people (Kiester, 1994).

None of the contributing factors to the effects of the G.I. Bill were identified, except in retrospect, by quantification. On the other hand, over-dependence upon quantification has yielded incorrect conclusions. The dominant "fact" of the planning future going into the eighties was a declining pool of potential students, which would result in the closing of at least 10 percent, and perhaps as many 25 percent, of America's colleges and universities in the decade then ahead (Keller, 1983). The realized future was an increase in college enrollments through the eighties, and the survival of the great majority of the institutions placed on death watch. Linear planners perhaps took too few factors into account, including the power of institutional creativity and adaptability. Such planners are heavily dependent for their projections upon that which can be more easily quantified (Wheatley, 1992; Frances, 1991).

Overreliance upon quantifiable data, and the concurrent under-consideration of such elements as opinion, desires, and ambitions was put into perspective by Albert Einstein: "Not everything that counts, can be counted; and not everything that can be counted, counts" (Marino, 1995, p. 218).

**Proposition 10: The future is a creation, not a prediction. This power of agency is the distinguishing context of human chaotic systems.** Despite the difficulty of prediction, the certainty of uncertainty, it would be a grave error to take from chaos theory the idea that planning is futile, because the future is unpredictable. Rather, the primary lesson is that the future can be created. Conventional, linear planning is based largely on the assumption of high predictability. Linear planning puts an emphasis on trend lines, projecting them into the future, and tends to make insufficient accounting for the influx of turbulence, foreseen or not. Linear planning postulates a future far over the horizon, but it is rarely realized in any recognizable form. Directors of linear planning attempt to execute the future less than they attempt to create it, and they are often wrong. Priesmeyer, a proponent of nonlinear management, described "forecasting," a linear approach, as (p. 176) "the process of using historical data exclusively to make estimates of the future." Such approaches, he added, fail to recognize the presence of free will, and are, therefore, "naive for any system in which humans participate." Mintzberg touches upon this in his description of the "grand fallacy" of strategic planning: "Because analysis is not synthesis, strategic planning is not strategic formulation" (1994, p. 321). Analysis is decompositional, according to Mintzberg, and is, therefore, incapable of the creation of novel strategies.

Peterson encourages us to regard the future and the environment as "complex but malleable" (1997, p. 134). But the ability to make long-term changes in the future is dependent upon our willingness, as actors within the university or social system, to make "long-term commitments" and to apply "consistent effort" toward desired ends (p. 153). Peterson specifically distinguishes this from a strategic planning perspective, which places a higher premium over environmental evaluations and scanning, as opposed to desired outcomes.

Participants in nonlinear planning, by contrast to linear planners, come to realize that the future is an invention; the external and internal environments are strong creative elements of the future, but so are dreams, values, and ambitions. Metaphorically, the flutter of a wing can move not only the breeze but the system, particularly if applied with consistency and in partnership. These "small" elements gain power over time, and can overcome substantial resistance.

# References

Bensimon, E. M., & Neumann, A. (1993). *Redesigning collegiate leadership: Teams and teamwork in higher education*. Baltimore: Johns Hopkins University Press.

Birnbaum, R. (2000*). Management fads in higher education: Where they come from, what they do, why they fail*. San Francisco: Jossey-Bass Publishers.

Chaffee, E. E., & Jacobson, S. W. (1997). Creating and changing institutional cultures. In Peterson, M. W., Dill, D. D., & Mets, L. A. (Eds.), *Planning and management for a changing environment: A handbook on redesigning postsecondary institutions* (pp. 230–245). San Francisco: Jossey-Bass Publishers.

Coaldrake, P., & Stedman, L. (1998). *On the brink: Australia's universities confronting their future*. Queensland, Australia: University of Queensland Press.

Cohen, M. D., & March, J. G. (1974, 1986). *Leadership and ambiguity: The American college president*. Boston, MA: Harvard Business School Press.

Cohen, M. D., March, J. G., & Olsen, J. P. (1972). A garbage can model of organizational choice. *Administrative Science Quarterly, 17*(1), 1–25.

Dever, J. T. (1997). Reconciling educational leadership and the learning organization. *Community College Review, 25*(2), 57–63

Dill, D. D. (1997). Focusing institutional mission to provide coherence and integration. In Peterson, M. W., Dill, D. D., & Mets, L. A. (Eds.), *Planning and management for a changing environment: A handbook on redesigning postsecondary institutions* (pp. 171–190). San Francisco: Jossey-Bass Publishers.

Dolence, M. G., & Norris, D. M. (1995). *Transforming higher education: A vision for learning in the 21st century*. Ann Arbor, MI: Society for College and University Planning.

Fairweather, P. (1997). Using small problems to make big changes. *Planning for Higher Education, 25*(3), Spring, 39–43.

Fisher, J. L. (1994). Reflections on transformational leadership. *Educational Record, 54*, Summer, 60–65.

Follett, M. P. (1925). Constructive conflict. Paper presented before a Bureau of Personnel Administration conference group. In Fox and Urwick, eds.

Fox, E. M., & Urwick, L. (Eds.). (1973). *Dynamic administration: The collected papers of Mary Parker Follett*. London: Pitman.

Frances, C. (1991). Uses and misuses of demographic projections: Lessons for the 1990s. In Bess, J. L. (Ed.), *Foundations of American higher education*. Needham Heights, MA: Simon & Schuster/ASHE.

Harvey, B. C. (1998, Summer). The perils of planning before you are ready. *Planning for Higher Education, 26*(4), 1–9.

Holton, S. A. (1995). Where do we go from here? *New Directions for Higher Education, 92*, 91–95.

Innes, J. (1996). Planning through consensus building: A new view of the comprehensive planning ideal. *Journal of the American Planning Association, 62*(4), 460–472.

Jones, L. W. (1990). Strategic planning: The unrealized potential of the 1980s and the promise of the 1990s. *New Directions for Higher Education, 70*, 51–57.

Keller, G. (1983). *Academic strategy: The management revolution in American higher education.* Baltimore: Johns Hopkins University Press.

Keller, G. (1988, February). Academic strategy: Five years later. *AAHE Bulletin*, 3–6.

Keller, G. (1993). Strategic planning and management in a competitive environment. *New Directions for Institutional Research, 77*, 9–16.

Keller, G. (1997). Examining what works in strategic planning. In Peterson, M. W., Dill, D. D., & Mets, L. A. (Eds.), *Planning and management for a changing environment: A handbook on redesigning postsecondary institutions* (pp. 158–170). San Francisco: Jossey-Bass Publishers.

Kiester, Jr., E. (1994, November). The G.I. Bill may be the best deal ever made by Uncle Sam. *Smithsonian, 25*(8), 129–139.

Marino, J. (1995). Clearcutting the groves of academe. In Laxer, G., & Harrison, T. (Eds.), *The Trojan Horse: Alberta and the future of Canada* (pp. 209–222). Montreal: Black Rose Books.

Mintzberg, H. (1994). *The rise and fall of strategic planning: Reconceiving roles for planning, plans, planners.* New York: The Free Press.

Morgan, G. (1997). *Images of organization*, 2nd edition. Thousand Oaks, CA: Sage Publications.

Morrison, J., Wilkinson, G., & Forbes, L. (1999). *Common sense management for educational leaders.* Retrieved February 1, 1999, from the World Wide Web: http://horizon.unc.edu/projects/monograph/csm.

Neumann, A., & Larson, R. S. (1997). Enhancing the leadership factor in planning. In Peterson, M. W., Dill, D. D., & Mets, L. A. (Eds.), *Planning and management for a changing environment: A handbook on redesigning postsecondary institutions* (pp. 191–203). San Francisco: Jossey-Bass Publishers.

Newson, W., & Hayes, C. R. (1990, Winter). Are mission statements worthwhile? *Planning for Higher Education, 19*(2), 28–30.

Newton, R. (1992, Fall). The two cultures of academe: An overlooked planning hurdle. *Planning for Higher Education, 21*(1), 8–14

Orton, J. D., & Weick, K. E. (1990). Loosely coupled systems: A reconsideration. *Academy of Management Review, 15*(2), 203–223.

Peterson, M. W. (1997). Using contextual planning to transform institutions. In Peterson, M. W., Dill, D. D., & Mets, L. A. (Eds.), *Planning and management for a changing environment: A handbook on redesigning postsecondary institutions* (pp. 127–157). San Francisco: Jossey-Bass Publishers.

Peterson, M. W., Dill, D. D., & Mets, L. A. (Eds.) (1997). *Planning and management for a changing environment: A handbook on redesigning postsecondary institutions*. San Francisco: Jossey-Bass Publishers.

Platje, A., & Seidel, H. (1993). Breakthrough in multiproject management: How to escape the vicious circle of planning and control. *International Journal of Project Management, 11*(4), November, 209–213.

Priesmeyer, H. R. (1992). *Organizations and chaos: Defining the methods of monlinear management*. Westport, CT: Quorum Books.

Schuster, J. H, Smith, D. G., Corak, K. A., & Yamada, M. M. (1994). *Strategic governance: How to make big decisions better*. Phoenix, AZ: American Council on Education/Oryx Press.

Seigfried, J. J., Getz, M., & Anderson, K. H. (1995, May 19). The snail's pace of innovation in higher education. *Chronicle of Higher Education*, p. A56.

Senge, P. (1990). *The fifth discipline: The art and practice of the learning organization*. New York: Doubleday.

Stafford, R. (1993). Sheep in wolves clothing. *Planning for Higher Education, 22*(1), 55–59.

Tierney, W. G. (1992). Cultural leadership and the search for community. *Liberal Education, 78*(5), 16–21.

Weick, K. E. (1976). Educational organizations as loosely coupled systems. *Administrative Science Quarterly, 21* (March), 1–19

Wheatley, M. J. (1992). *Leadership and the new science: Learning about organization from an orderly universe*. San Francisco: Berrett-Koehler Publishers, Inc.

Zohar, D. (1997). *ReWiring the corporate brain: Using the new science to rethink how we structure and lead organizations*. San Francisco: Berrett-Koehler Publishers, Inc.

# CHAPTER FIVE

## Chaos Theory Applied to College Planning: A Case Study in Defense of Ten Propositions

*James R. Perkins, Jeffrey B. Lanigan,
John A. Downey, and Bernard H. Levin*

Blue Ridge Community College, a small rural college in the Shenandoah Valley of Virginia, is in many ways a typical two-year institution of higher education in America. Our curricula are designed to meet the needs of our local community, our organizational structure is largely traditional, and our primary focus is on providing a good learning environment for our students. We are recognized in Virginia for a strong technology environment and for a willingness to take leadership roles at the local and state levels. The college has a reputation of being a good place to work and a place where things get done properly. To an outside observer, nothing particularly unusual marks the institution.

To those on the inside, however, Blue Ridge Community College is a very different college. It is different because of the leadership framework that helps guide institutional planning and decision making. Inspired by the writings of Wheatley (1999), Mintzberg (1993), and Greenleaf (1983), Blue Ridge Community College has moved away from traditional management and planning models based on theories adapted from the classical Newtonian sciences. Instead, we view our institution as one that operates more as a living organism and less as a nonliving mechanism following the principles of classical mechanics. We do not, for example, aspire to keep our organization running like a well-oiled machine. Instead, we describe our organization as a family. Occasionally, we experience behaviors in "our family" that we wish were not present. More often, the initiative and creative thinking exhibited by the most unlikely among us surprise and enlighten us all.

For Blue Ridge Community College, chaos theory has provided an excellent institutional and management framework to guide our organizational thinking. Key elements of the chaos theory model that have influenced our thinking include the concepts of nonlinearity, strange attractors, and the butterfly effect. To operate effectively within this model, traditional notions of hierarchical decision making have been modified and greater emphasis placed upon cooperation and collaboration. Robert Greenleaf's (1983) principles of servant leadership have provided us with excellent guidance as we have learned to adapt to a more collaborative organizational model.

Chaos theory-driven organizations understand that institutional values and organizational vision become the "strange attractors" that nurture creativity, individuality, and initiative. At the same time, values and vision serve to help us redirect behavior that violates the culture. The president helps serve as a moral compass, as do peers within the institution. Chaos theory-driven institutions are not "chaotic organizations" as most understand the meaning of chaos. They are highly flexible organizations operating within parameters that are widely known and accepted. Individuals and groups are given latitude and responsibility, information is shared broadly, and outcomes are continuously evaluated to ensure improvement with each succeeding effort.

Institutional leaders of chaos theory-driven institutions know that the smallest event, if properly nourished, can have a profoundly positive effect on an organization. Such events can emanate from within or from outside the organization and often emerge as threats to the college. At other times, these events are so small they initially escape institutional notice. Left unattended they grow like weeds in a garden. Nurtured and cultivated, an amazing and unexpectedly beautiful garden can emerge. This "butterfly effect" (Lorenz, 1993; Cutright, 1999) can make a significant difference in the life of an institution. The trick is to know what to support and what to "weed." Institutional vision and values help shape organizational response. Organizations consciously aware of the "butterfly effect" provide incentives for creativity, reward success, and view failures as learning opportunities.

Planning within a chaos theory-driven organization recognizes failures inherent within traditional models that embrace linearity and predictability. Mintzberg's (1993) classic, *The Rise and Fall of Strategic Planning*, provides ample evidence of the failure of traditional planning models. At Blue Ridge Community College, we have created a planning process that places heavy emphasis upon directional thinking developed through intense environmental scanning, grassroots input, widely shared information flow, and continuous evaluation. Our planning documents are short and carefully worded, then multiple drafts are distributed throughout the college community for comment.

We focus on principle and direction, eschewing details of implementation. We have found that, like many other institutions, we are tempted to seek refuge in detail but when we yield to that temptation, the documents are obsolete before they are published. Instead, we ask organizational units annually to establish work plans that support the strategic directions, and campus governance committees to review and approve agreed upon "charges" that guide their work. A campus-wide planning committee evaluates progress and advises the president and the campus community on issues needing attention. Our strategic directions document would not be viewed by most outside observers as revolutionary, except perhaps for its brevity. In fact, to some it would be considered rather ordinary. To us, it is very important, not necessarily because of what it says, but because of how it was developed. As chaos theory-driven organizations know, it is not the plan, but the planning process that is important. An institutional family that understands the organization's values and visions, and works together to find strategic directions to advance those visions and values in a context that rewards initiative, celebrates successes, and uses failure as an opportunity to learn, is using principles supported by chaos theory.

The role of the college president in an organization that embraces the principles of chaos theory is both challenging and invigorating. The effective president articulates institutional values, helps frame an institutional vision, clarifies mission, serves as an internal and external ambassador, and empowers others. By sharing insights, suggesting professional resources, and ensuring that everyone participates, the president leads the process and achieves results that would be impossible in more traditional structures. However, because the planning process involves everyone employed at the college, the plan and the decisions derived from the plan are seen as the work of the entire college, not of the administration. Thus, buy-in is almost never an issue.

The president's job is to help facilitate the direction and the priorities that flow from the process. Everyone at the college understands that, if desired results are to be achieved, the president must sometimes take direct action. Effective presidents know when to let the process run its course and when the process has become stagnant and action at the top level is necessary. Clearly, the successful president operating in a "chaotic" environment must possess both sensitivity and a sense of timing, and must daily resist the temptation to "fix" things. The president, employees at all levels, and others concerned with the success of the organization need to have developed a trust in the planning process.

Marc Cutright (1999) has offered ten propositions concerning planning and decision making in chaos theory-driven organizations. Each of these propositions was derived from assumptions inherent in chaos theory, and can be better illustrated by specific examples that have emerged from our experiences at Blue Ridge Community College. What follows is a case study of a campus engaged in organizational chaos theory; a case study that demonstrates the profound effect that emerges from a college that relies upon the unique strengths of each and every member of its community.

**Proposition I**
**The Ideal Outcome of Planning Is Planning, Not a Plan**

At Blue Ridge Community College we view Cutright's (1999) first proposition as metaphorically representing three distinct aspects of the planning process. First, we consider the proposition to reflect the importance of strategically engaging the entire organization in the planning process. Secondly, the proposition implies an inherent flexibility required of the process itself. Finally, we consider the proposition to reflect the idea that the final product of planning must not be a rigid prescription for what must be done organizationally, but rather a broad-based outline of the direction toward which the organization aspires. Each of these distinct facets is evident in the manner we approach planning at Blue Ridge Community College.

**1. Planning requires planning, such that the entire organization contributes to and embraces both the process and the outcome.** In organizations that value participatory governance, the planning process does not occur without preparation. In order to engender the individual and organizational buy-in that is *the* critical payoff of chaos-oriented planning, planners must carefully and continuously consider who is participating, what ideas are being embraced or rejected by the college community, and how meaningful contributions can be elicited from those normally on the margins of the planning process. It takes planning to build consensus and to promote the value that everyone's ideas are viewed as important contributions to the final plan. Without the belief of all individuals in the organization that they possess the opportunity to shape the final draft of the strategic document, the principal desired outcome of strategic planning cannot be realized. The final desired outcome is not the plan itself, but a collective vision, shared, embraced, and widely believed, that the college is capable of advancing toward a specific, collectively valued outcome.

The role of the president, discussed later in this chapter, is critical in this process of consensus building. However, leadership for institutional buy-in emerges from all corners of the institution. Indeed, the president alone cannot sustain the notion of involvement. It exists only in relation to the organizational culture that believes in broad-based participation, and which organizational members at all levels must promote.

At Blue Ridge Community College, we began each of our last two processes for developing strategic directions documents with college-wide retreats. The fact that we had retreats was not particularly remarkable, but the manner in which the retreats were structured was vital to our belief that the process of planning demands planning, particularly in regard to building consensus. At the suggestion of a staff association member who had several years of experience in the banking industry, several members of the planning committee became trained in nominal group process facilitation. The suggestion was made after members of the planning committee were bemoaning the fact that, despite ample opportunity, relatively few organizational members were contributing to the development of the original strategic directions document. The nominal group process helped counter that problem during the college retreat because it required involvement from virtually every college employee.

**2. Planning requires planning, such that the organization embraces flexibility as an expected and integral part of the process.** Cutright's (1999) proposition, that the ideal outcome of planning is planning, implies that institutions must be willing to abandon previous planning efforts in light of recent and relevant information. In 1995, Blue Ridge Community College did just that.

The college's first real attempt to engage in strategic planning began in 1990. Although the process was collective, the result looked like the first-time effort it was: long, prescriptive, and bogged down with details and deadlines. Goals that were too specific and narrow, such as hiring a reading professor or purchasing a specific number and type of computers over a given number of years, were clear indications that our first attempt at a planning document was mired in linearity and minutiae. The plan revealed, in retrospect, our overconfidence in predicting the future. The document was based on our assessment of where we were in 1990 as opposed to where we should be going. We soon learned that predicting anything but the broad landscape of the future was futile and that relying on ideas generated by the conditions of the present was counterproductive.

The rapid pace of emerging technology was the most salient factor in Blue Ridge Community College's realization between 1990 and 1995 that we needed to radically rethink our approach to planning and embrace chaos theory. As the future emerged, our first plan rapidly declined into irrelevance. During that time we were first introduced to the concept of chaos theory, and we developed a position paper (Levin, Lanigan, & Perkins, 1995) that highlighted the problems of linearity in the planning process. That paper embraced the notion of chaotic systems and, as a result of our research, we dedicated ourselves to a shorter and broader strategic planning document. In the true spirit of chaos theory, we embraced a staff employee's suggestion that we call the document "strategic directions," rather than a strategic plan. That simple suggestion changed the whole document for us, from a detailed, prescriptive plan to a more general discourse on where we wanted to be heading as an institution during the next few years.

We also began our second attempt at strategic planning with the knowledge that Blue Ridge Community College was on the cutting edge for technological leadership among the colleges of the Virginia Community College System. We knew we wanted to remain in that position. We also admitted, however, that we did not know specifically how technology would shape our quest for educational excellence, how technology itself would change, or how small contributions from a wide variety of institutional players would forever change our future.

We created our strategic directions document around a collective vision of where we wanted to go technologically, not how we would get there. Implementation subsequently occurred on a day-to-day basis, to coincide with an environment that changes on a day-to-day basis. Our willingness to view the process as flexible, not operating in a specified manner, or by a specified time, increased the salience of the resulting document.

We view our strategic directions in much the same manner as the United States Constitution might be viewed. The Constitution has survived as a living, breathing document because it has a flexibility that allows for constant reinterpretation. Our country's founders were interested in creating a framework that would remind the American people of what our core values were, and what principles we ought to embrace as we planned our way through time. Clearly, the founders' intention was not to prescribe what specific steps needed to be taken day-by-day, month-by-month, and year-by-year over the next several centuries. We view our strategic planning documents as guiding our institutional decisions in much the same manner.

**3. Planning requires planning, such that its final product is not a rigid prescription for what must be done, but rather a broad-based outline directing the organization toward its collective vision.** At Blue Ridge Community College, we consider planning as encompassing two essential elements, collective process and outcome. Many institutions err by expending tremendous amounts of energy in the creation of a specific and detailed plan. Soon afterward, these colleges are forced to consume even more energy, either desperately clinging to an obsolete plan or abandoning it altogether. Planning should be an ongoing activity designed to advance long-term strategic directions agreed upon by the college community.

Our contention is that the planning process, in order to be successful, must be anchored in long-term, idealized, visionary directions toward which institutions strive to achieve. Otherwise colleges may easily lose the forest for the trees. The ideal outcome of planning is the establishment of direction, not a listing of how departments must implement that direction. Detailed and rigid plans do not take into account the chaos that is endemic as an institution moves through time. Rigidity renders such plans irrelevant at some future point, and usually sooner rather than later. In many cases, these long-term plans can even become detrimental to the institution, forcing decisions that no longer make sense. Inertia rarely is a friend. The amount of time and work that goes into the development of a five-year plan makes it difficult for an institution to abandon, but the costs of hanging on to such plans come in the form of wasted fiscal and human resources, as outdated elements of the original plan are implemented despite irrelevance.

Strictly interpreted plans are particularly dangerous in today's economy, as colleges aim at the expensive and rapidly moving target of the technological age. The effects of these changes in technology are not limited to the simple notion that "Now we can do the same things faster than we did them in the past." Technology has affected the very core of colleges and has created philosophical debates on basic notions of mission, academic freedom, and general education. Higher education now struggles not only with traditional curricular issues but also with the basic notion of what constitutes a liberal education. When institutions can now employ distance education to meet the employment training needs of the next generation, legitimate questions concerning the intangible benefits of education that cannot be easily addressed through distance means are debated in faculty forums. No college in 1995 could have created a prescriptive plan with a reasonable expectation of understanding the technological opportunities and the resulting philosophical challenges facing institutions in the year 2000.

## Proposition II
### Planning Begins with a Distillation of the Institution's Key Values and Purposes

The establishment of collective values is crucial for the creation of successful strategic directions. The values serve as the "attractor" or foundation of the institution. Like strategic directions, they should be short and to the point so that everyone, no matter how employed at the college, can comfortably understand and internalize them. Collective development of these values is essential. It is a difficult process that requires numerous drafts and discussions. Each word is carefully, even painstakingly, analyzed until all are aware of, understand, and agree with the document's meaning. The priceless product of these efforts is shared values, along with a collective understanding of what is important for the institution. The result is a shared understanding of the principles behind the day-to-day tasks that need to be accomplished.

Although a values statement serves as an institution's foundation, it must not be viewed as carved in stone, never to be altered again. Values must be reexamined from time to time, as fixed values do not permanently suit a changing world. In both 1995 and 2000, as Blue Ridge Community College began the process of developing new strategic directions, we revisited our values statements and indeed, some needed adjustment. We discovered that while our core values largely remained the same, new language that emphasized enduring values emerged in response to a changing environment. Our Values Statement now consists of a one-page summary of our collective vision concerning four general principles:

- *Learning*
- *Excellence*
- *Relationship to community*
- *Campus and culture*

Our ability to agree to institutional values made the development of strategic directions infinitely easier. As the institution set directions, it was easy to determine if those directions coincided with the College's Values Statement. However, our collective determination of institutional values served another critical purpose as well. We learned that once strategic directions were set, the day-to-day life of the college continued at a rapid pace. In chaotic systems, the idea that unpredictable challenges arise continuously is embraced. We found that as the college formulated action, there often existed in our community varied interpretations of the strategic directions we all agreed to. We learned that strategic documents are rarely clear when they are confronted with an unexpected future. Various people and groups within the community interpret or emphasize portions of the document differently. The dynamic energy resulting from discussions led to more creativity on campus. In fact, we discovered that a strategic document best serves as a game plan rather than a playbook. We learned to look to our institutional values as the grounding force for actions that needed to be taken.

One example at Blue Ridge of the struggle that can occur as a result of varied interpretations of strategic directions statements involved a contentious and divisive battle over whether the college should close for Labor Day. Since Labor Day occurs so early in our fall academic calendar, faculty unanimously argued that it was educationally more important for students to have an October fall break and that classes should be held on Labor Day. College staff, tired after working to enroll thousands of new students over the course of a long summer, voted unanimously that the college should close. Administrators debated the true motivation of each of these constituency groups, surveyed the students, argued the educational merits of each side, and could not agree on a suitable course of action. Finally, the president reaffirmed the shared institutional value of learning and stated firmly that this value would be the final arbiter of whatever decision would be rendered. He then asked his administrative staff to seek a solution that would uphold this institutional value and meet the interests of each constituency group to the extent possible. The result, although unusual, would not likely have been possible to achieve in a linearly motivated institution. After consultation with faculty, staff, and student groups, classes were held on Labor Day with an understanding that traditional support services would be limited. Staff did have the day off, and faculty held classes. Student attendance was strong, and the educational process did not suffer. Some may argue that disputes like this one, over whether and how to administer a holiday, reveal weakness and indecisiveness within the administration. We believe the resolve to maintain the institutional value of participatory governance requires leadership beyond the norm, sometimes in the face of intense lobbying for a firm decision to be made at the highest level.

## Proposition III
## The Widest Possible Universe of Information Should Be Made Available to All Members of the Institution. This Universe of Information Includes Ongoing, Rich, and Current Feedback.

Even in the most chaos theory-oriented institutions, linearity tends to assert itself at times. At Blue Ridge, this became evident as our various constituency groups and subcultures debated the extent to which their "own business" should be communicated to the other constituency groups within the college community. The faculty senate fretted that the college administration would be privy to discussions critical of administrative decisions. Administrators struggled with the idea of instituting a 360-degree evaluation process in which supervisees could provide feedback on each supervisor's work style. Deans debated whether minutes from their staff meetings should be shared with the college community, and whether any member of the college could choose to attend such meetings.

In the end, each of these struggles was resolved, more or less, in favor of a cultural standard at the college whereby information about decisions are distributed to the widest possible membership of our community. These struggles were not easily resolved, however. The deans remained uncomfortable with open meetings, and the faculty senate resisted suggestions to change bylaws that precluded the widespread distribution of their minutes. Yet, when the president set the tone by inviting the chairperson of the faculty senate to his weekly staff meetings, the deans also compromised by agreeing to distribute their staff meeting minutes via the internet, and to e-mail those minutes to the chairperson of the faculty senate. Ultimately, when these decisions were acted upon by the administration, the faculty followed suit by amending their bylaws and distributing their minutes each month by e-mail.

There is little doubt in our community that the widespread dissemination of information reduces suspicion. Whenever widespread communication was not well cared for at the college, initiatives associated with that lack of communication have been halted, at least until such communication could occur. Often, it has been the perceived lack of information about a particular initiative, rather than an actual intent to withhold information, that has caused discontent on campus. Such discontent subsided in direct proportion to the amount of communication that subsequently took place regarding the initiative.

## Proposition IV
### Dissent and Conflict Are Creative, Healthy, and Real.
### The Absence of Conflict Is Reductionist, Illusory, and Suspect.

At Blue Ridge Community College, conflict and dissent are not strangers. Similar to other institutions, we don't relish conflict, we don't look for it, and we don't engage in it when it can be averted. However, we also view conflict as an unavoidable, and even necessary element of organizational growth. In fact, when there is no conflict, we begin to worry. The absence of visible conflict and dissent is our signal that the organization might be stagnant. Passivity usually means that the institution is not engaged, employees or students feel threatened, or there is a feeling that opinions don't matter.

In general, we work to establish a campus climate that encourages personal engagement in organizational initiatives, and the free and open exchange of ideas. This climate works at the college largely because of a trust that has been built within our community, a trust that emanates from a fundamental belief that we share the organizational values we espouse. Trust in each other helps keep conversations frank but civil. Conflict emerges from these discussions because of differences in the beliefs that participants hold concerning organizational priorities or the manner of implementing such priorities. However, conflict rarely derives from questioning the fundamental mission, values, or vision of the goals we are collectively aspiring to achieve.

An excellent example of the type of conflict that is typical on our campus involves a current debate regarding distance learning, known commonly on campus as "The Cyber-College." In keeping with our strategic directions, the college has provided substantial support to faculty who teach web-based, television-based, and compressed video courses. However, the rapid growth of the cyber-college, particularly the unforeseen popularity of web-based courses, has not enabled the institution to participate in the careful discussion and planning in which we usually engage. In fact, without any institutional plan, the cyber-college has grown within a couple of years such that over 14 percent of the college's students are now enrolled in cyber-courses. In the early stages, some faculty questioned the college's purpose in promoting the development of web-based courses. These faculty members argued that a college-wide discussion of the cyber-college was necessary prior to the expansion of such offerings. They believed that distance education initiatives needed a mission statement, a greater degree of regulation, and strategic planning.

Other faculty argued that regulations and detailed planning are the best way to stifle faculty initiative. These faculty asserted that whether Blue Ridge Community College participated or not, distance education initiatives were taking place all around us. To delay our own implementation of these initiatives amounted to a restriction of academic freedom and faculty creativity. Distance education, they argued, was merely another course delivery method.

Despite passionate arguments on both sides of this issue, the cyber-college growth has occurred unabated. Even so, the conflict itself, a conflict that has not yet ended on campus, has fostered among the faculty creativity about the entire curriculum that was not evident prior to this debate.

On one side of the continuum, the most unlikely of professors emerged as cyber experts, having developed course methodology that critics have not been able to denounce. On the other end, those most vocal of professors, who argued that cyber instruction lacks the intangible benefits present in direct faculty-student interaction, have been able to harness that criticism to develop a proposal for an enhanced general education program for selected students in our transfer program.

Conflict in an environment where peer relationships prevent its personalization has fostered on our campus a creative energy that prevents stagnation. Conflict-based interactions are difficult to witness, and even more difficult to participate in. Without the safe expression of conflict however, great ideas would be suppressed at all levels of the organization and the college would be less dynamic as a result.

## Proposition V
## Linearity Doesn't Work in Strategic Planning.
## It Doesn't Work in Dictation:
## Planning and Plans Imposed from Above;
## Or in Collation: Planning and Plans Created
## Solely by the Collection of Unit Information

Linear thinking is counterproductive to organizational planning (Levin, Lanigan, & Perkins, 1995). Linear thinking is incompatible with chaotic organizations—such thinking inevitably forces organizations into conflict with emerging realities. Blue Ridge Community College is no different from other organizations in this way. Some form of linearity has been connected to each of our most contentious campus issues over the past decade.

One aspect of linearity we found interesting to examine critically is the idea that timelines are essential to the planning process. Timelines may indeed be a virtue in some places, but in a chaotic institution they have limited utility. We have repeatedly tried establishing timelines, attempting to stick to deadlines in each planning process we have engaged in. Every time we tried to value the timeline over the process, the product failed. "All things in good time" works well, but time-bound plans generate little. Perhaps the best example of the failure of the timeline-driven approach was our experience with the development of a college marketing plan.

The college had never had an effective marketing plan. In fact, over the years, even the term "marketing" developed such offensive connotations that its mere mention fired tempers. The president, having identified the need to develop a reasonable plan to streamline marketing functions, worked with a small committee, hired a consultant, and then assigned four competent administrators to create a plan together. The president communicated to the college community at each step of this initial process. Therefore, there was generally widespread acceptance of his idea that four key administrators, already directly responsible for key aspects of marketing, should develop a workable plan. These administrators then agreed to set strict deadlines to develop detailed responses across four general categories: Product, Promotion, Student Tracking, and Initial Campus Impressions. However, after nearly a year of quiet work during which little college-wide communication on marketing took place, they presented their draft of a marketing plan to the college planning committee. Almost immediately, the controversy began. The plan was so prescriptive that few people could support its content. Several members of the college community argued that the plan took us in an entirely wrong direction and included tasks that had not been discussed with the very people charged to carry them out.

Of course in retrospect, the reason for the plan's failure was, despite a very linear adherence to the logical steps required to develop a marketing plan, too few people had been involved in the process. As a result, the plan was developed right on schedule, but the product was not palatable to the institution.

As a result of the conflict at the planning committee meeting, a group of volunteers emerged to assume a coordinating role. They began by affirming many of the merits of the recently presented plan, and employed only minor wording modifications of the same basic structure developed by the administrators: product, planning, student connections, and initial impressions. This group began drafting and redrafting based on feedback elicited from widely distributed drafts via e-mail to college administrators, faculty, and staff. Endless drafts were produced, critiqued, rejected, and redrafted. In the end, our patience paid off and the marketing plan was accepted unanimously by both the planning committee and the entire College Assembly. The approved plan had generally the same structure as the rejected plan, but it was far less prescriptive and allowed wide latitude for those carrying out the initiatives under each of the four categories to do so in a manner that takes into account the constant change in environmental conditions.

### Proposition VI
### The Institution Should Budget—Fiscally and Psychically—for Failure.
### Pilots Are Alternative Futures. Not All Can Be Realized or Succeed.

Embracing chaos theory means institutions create flexible structures for the future even as they admit the future is unpredictable. Alternative ideas for the future are also unpredictable. Gambling on people and their ideas is an integral part of creating a future as opposed to predicting or reacting to it. Successful chaotic institutions are willing to budget risk capital (fiscal and human) and prepare for the unknown. The establishment of this mentality must become a part of the institutional culture. Colleges that value change and exude a sense of competence to prepare for the future are more likely to take the leaps required to take advantage of the future. However, this eagerness to engage the future is not without peril. Chaotic colleges must also be prepared for the inevitable failures. Two examples from our experiences at Blue Ridge Community College illustrate significant budgetary and human resource investments in the future without accompanying guarantees of success. The first example can now be labeled a great success, but the initial risks associated with the project's development were considerable. The second example is an instance of a recently launched project whose success or failure is still unknown. Yet both projects represent a college culture in which funding for risk-laden ideas is carefully and routinely considered as a part of our budget development process.

The first example involves the opening of our Harrisonburg Center, a location north of the college's central campus in Weyers Cave, Virginia. Our Weyers Cave location is geographically situated between three cities, all roughly the same size. For many years we have operated a center in Waynesboro, southeast of the main campus. However, with the exception of a few classes at a local high school, Blue Ridge Community College never had a physical presence north of the main campus.

The north is the fastest growing geographical area served by the college. In 1995, an opportunity in the city of Harrisonburg arose through which the college could take over part of a downtown building at minimal cost. There were considerable risks for doing so. The building needed extensive renovation, computer infrastructure support, security, and parking facilities. Deciding to support this initiative meant we would be required to restructure our off campus administration and hire additional people. Furthermore, the building is located near James Madison University, an aggressively growing public four-year institution, and we were unsure whether that fact would help or hurt the initiative.

As a college, we decided to pursue the opportunity, largely because of the expressed and perceived needs of our constituents. We believed that the future was right for our physical presence in the northern part of our service area. Enrollment at the center was strong initially, and remains so. We are currently in the process of expanding our space at the facility. The investment we made in the computing infrastructure allows us to offer noncredit courses to the downtown population looking to upgrade their skills, and we have been able to provide a lower cost alternative for a wide range of courses for James Madison University students.

Despite an overall perception of success, some problems remain. The parking issue was never fully resolved, personnel challenges associated with coverage of the center are still being evaluated, and class-scheduling conflicts between the centers north and south of the campus have emerged as an issue in productivity discussions. Although failure of this initiative is now entirely unlikely, budgetary risks remain as we attempt to take advantage of the full potential of the center. We emphasize once again, however, that the decision to open the Harrisonburg Center was never based primarily on an assessment of risk. The risk factors were assumed because of our collective decision that we needed to respond proactively to an emergent community need associated with the rapid growth of a particular area of our service region. It is important to note that if the decision had been based on risk, we might never have acted. Institutions of higher education are notoriously conservative and risk-averse. Chaotic institutions, on the other hand, see change as a friend, and must tolerate a certain degree of fiscal and emotional risk within the decision processes that are compatible with change.

A second example of the process we use to fund new initiatives, despite the associated risks, involves the rapid expansion of our Veterinary Technology program through distance education. Blue Ridge Community College has a highly successful and innovative Veterinary Technology program that is one of only two in the Virginia Community College System. Students from all over the state come to Weyers Cave to attend this popular on-campus program, for which there is an enrollment waiting list. There was no pressing reason to tamper with the highly successful program. Still, based on our desire to provide technological leadership and the statewide demand for the degree, we made the decision to invest sizable resources in an experiment to deliver the program via distance education methodology to other Virginia community colleges.

Costs for the innovative program, including additional personnel and equipment, are significant for maintaining an accredited program through compressed video. The risks for such a venture are high. Many questions remained unanswered as we began the project, and the need for the initial investment of resources was quite high. Did we accurately assess demand for the enrollment? Would the Veterinary Technology accrediting agency be satisfied with a clinical program delivered by nontraditional means? Would we have the capacity to grow if demand for the program grows? Would the significant investments associated with program development ever end?

Despite these unanswered questions that describe the risks, we clearly realized from the start that the payoff for creating such a program could be enormous. If done properly, the initial investment would be offset by the manner in which the program would meet a significant need in the Commonwealth. Blue Ridge Community College has the potential to become a national model for the high-quality delivery of Veterinary Technology instruction. More fundamentally, we would become an institution that had identified a specific need, proposed a high-quality solution for that need, and created a fiscally responsive method of instituting that solution.

This past year, we graduated our first cohort class of this initiative, and we recently learned that every enrolled student who took the national exam for licensing veterinary technicians has passed it. The students we served received the highest quality instruction in a manner convenient to their busy lifestyles. Behind the scenes, we engaged in great struggles as we argued among ourselves about the philosophical and fiscal needs associated with building the program. Today, as we begin the process of enrolling the second cohort to the same distance location, we also decided to begin expanding our service to a second location. Even though many controversial issues remain about resource deployment and instructional methodology, we embrace these risks because we know that if we did not, we would irresponsibly remain an institution meeting its own needs rather than those of the public we serve.

Throughout the process of building and establishing new initiatives, it has been clear to us that in chaos theory-driven institutions, the risks associated with new ideas are never fully diminished. Still, those ever-present risks are associated, at least more so than in linear-driven institutions, with a creativity and inventiveness that keeps the college dynamic and responsive to the needs of the community we serve. Risk culture feeds upon itself. Institutions that budget for risk, and accept the potential for failure, often benefit by learning from the successes but also from the organizational education caused by the failures. If risk-taking becomes part of the values of a college, such that people engage less in blame behavior and more in innovative reactions to failure when it comes, people become more willing to attempt innovative ideas.

We caution, however, that institutions must retain a healthy prudence regarding risk behavior. Colleges must realize, accept, and prepare for the fact that a certain proportion of innovative ventures will not pan out. The entire college community must understand this fact from the outset. Otherwise, people will look to point fingers at one another when failure does occur. This behavior is common in linear organizations when the organizational leader demands to know the reasons why a planned initiative failed. Such a culture discourages risk, and, therefore, innovation. Here, the ways in which the president, administrative leadership, and a risk-taker's colleagues respond to failure is critical to the maintenance of the risk-tolerant culture.

## Proposition VII
## The Considerable Expense of Time
## on the Front End Is an Investment.
## It Is Recouped, with Interest in the Future.

At Blue Ridge Community College our experiences reveal how closely proposition seven is related to proposition three. In fact, we view them as virtually indistinguishable. The considerable expense of time on the front end at our college is almost entirely devoted to creating and nurturing the widest possible universe of information. This also relates to proposition one in that it takes the investment of time to ensure buy-in and participation to the process of chaos-oriented planning.

The collective development of both an institution's values and strategic directions is an essential element of institutions embracing chaos theory. Otherwise, these values and stated directions mean nothing to anyone outside of the persons who developed them. Therefore, all members of the college community must not only be informed, but also educated on college issues.

Participatory governance does not mean that everyone should debate every decision made at the college. Obviously, this would grind the institution to a halt. However, inclusiveness on the surface seems so logical and obvious that even many linear-driven institutions begin their processes with the intention or perception of a collective process. The greatest challenge is sustaining this value over time.

Blue Ridge Community College has committed itself to collective decision making on all matters that have a significant effect on the institution. (It is reflected in our Values Statement.) *This is hard to do!* It sometimes even demands a fundamental debate on what constitutes a "significant effect." The process often takes long periods of time, involving people having to read a seemingly endless series of draft proposals, and often resulting in cries of "Just make a decision" or "Just tell me what to do." Sometimes it even means that after a decision has been made, individuals have the right to question that decision and to plead the case that it has a significant impact, such that it should be discussed within the governance structure.

The perception that the administration is unable to decide upon important issues is the most common criticism expressed by community members who disagree about participatory governance. However, the vast majority of college employees clearly see the reward for resisting the urge to decide at the highest level of organizational structure: that everyone ends up working in close proximity to the same vision. Perhaps a more tangible reward is a decrease in the passive-aggressive criticism that is prevalent at so many colleges.

Colleges are full of highly educated, analytical people who, if allowed to be marginal, can create divisiveness by spending time focusing on what is wrong. Collective decision making greatly reduces the potential for such divisiveness. Colleagues who are informed by their own experiences in the decision-making process are highly resistant to the negative arguments that would otherwise find friendly ears. This value is not automatically evident, however, and some great challenges exist in bringing new employees into a culture that is not easily understood initially. Participatory governance is so foreign a notion to most new employees that many resist or ignore the personal challenge that it demands: an engagement in the process of deciding what is important for an organization to value. No organizational task is more demanding. It is no wonder that many demand for decisions to be made for them. When properly nurtured, however, no task is more rewarding because it increases the commitment that individuals have to the institution and to the people who are affected by every decision the institution makes.

The development of our strategic plan in 1995 is an excellent illustration of how shared information and collective decision making can work. It was a long, ten-month process. We began with a college-wide retreat that lasted for two days and which took place in a hotel away from the campus. As stated earlier, we used a nominal group facilitation process at the retreat that allowed for all employees at the college to express their own ideas about what the institution could strive for in the future. As a result, from the first day, there was ownership of the process, and the outcome, by everyone who attended that retreat.

After the retreat, the planning committee took all the information acquired from the brainstorming process, analyzed it, categorized it, and began to work on the draft strategic plan. Thirty-six drafts (each of which were distributed by e-mail to the entire college community) and ten months later, the final draft of the strategic directions document passed unanimously in the College Assembly.

This process has also worked for us in different venues. We employed it in the development of our Technology Plan, Mission Statement, Vision Statement, and Values Statement, as well as during the restructuring of our Governance Model. Still, even with the obvious success of each of these developmental processes, the temptation to ignore the participatory process for reasons of expediency, or lack of appreciation for its merits, remains real.

Our experience with the development of the college marketing plan, described earlier in this chapter, demonstrates the danger of that temptation. We mentioned that, as the process of developing a marketing plan began, many in the college community, including many faculty members, paid little attention. Frankly, the misguided notion shared by many was that this project simply involved the development of an external plan to publicize the college in the community. Thus, it was viewed as not having a significant impact on the institution from the perspective of those not directly involved.

When the plan was finally released after a year of development, it was then viewed as having an impact because of the significant details regarding instructional delivery methodology that it contained. There was a strong temptation on both sides of the argument, first to throw out the entire year's worth of work that had gone into the development of the plan and also to keep the plan merely because it took so long to develop. Only because the college was committed to the value of collective input on significant decisions was there a strong feeling to do neither. Acknowledging the portions of the process that were not inclusive, the president made a firm commitment to the four administrators that their work would not be summarily discarded. At the same time, he expanded representation on the committee, asked a new committee chair to develop a participatory process, and to release drafts of the revised plan via e-mail to ensure that all interested members of the college community could contribute to the final version.

Collective decision making on college-wide issues, and the free flow of information, are an integral part of our college culture. It would have been easy to treat that first marketing plan as "water under the bridge" and to say we wouldn't make such a mistake again. It would have been easy to mandate the implementation of the unpopular plan, or even easier to discard it altogether. However, chaos theory suggests that we not only acknowledge mistakes, but also that we learn from them. The chaos theory-driven process is infectious. Once empowered, members of the college community were unwilling to abandon our commitment to inclusiveness. This commitment meant, in the case of the marketing plan, a year's delay in its development, but the resulting payoff has been threefold. First, faculty members who saw a specific threat to curricular control became participants in curricular improvement. Secondly, college employees who were frightened about being told how to do their jobs in carrying out marketing now can decide how they best can support the general goals of the plan. Finally, college administrators who were in danger of having to implement an unpopular plan are now enjoying widespread support for implementation.

### Proposition VIII
### The Executive Is Not Demoted or Minimized.
### The Executive Is the Most Critical
### Shaper and Champion of the Process.
### Ultimately, the Executive Is Empowered by the Process.

The concept of leadership has many meanings. Some argue that leadership involves the ability to make a tough decision, even when unpopular. Others believe it involves an ability to persuade others of the direction an organization should take. A substantial amount of literature exists regarding the efficacy of various leadership styles in higher education (e.g., Fisher & Koch, 1996). We indicated earlier that our organization has been heavily influenced by Greenleaf's (1983) concept of servant leadership. Cutright's (1999) eighth proposition is closely related to our understanding of servant leadership.

Leadership in a chaos theory-oriented institution is far more complex than in a traditionally linear institution. The president in a chaotic institution plays a far more important role than in more traditional colleges. In traditional institutions, a firm hand at the helm, a modicum of intelligence, a pleasing smile, and a firm handshake at cocktail parties might be enough to get by. In a chaotic institution, such a president would be lost. Life in chaos is far too complex. The president must be a social maven, academically credible, principled, an effective communicator with even the crankiest college denizens, and a far-seeing self-restrained polymath.

Because chaotic institutions are inherently nonlinear, control from the top is simply not possible. Therefore, presidents of chaos-driven institutions must employ a wider range of skills and abilities than a simple reliance on the power inherent in their position. The power of the position is still relevant, but what is even more important is the president's ability to remain comfortable in an environment that demands patience, persuasion, and a leap of faith in the abilities of the most unlikely of college personnel. Power is carefully and subtly utilized to ensure the opportunity for participation and input from all members of the organization.

Chaotic institutions are inherently flat, so the top is not very far from the bottom. As a result, leaders of such environments are comfortable relying upon an open door policy, accessible to all. The president must view himself or herself as one of the many contributory players to the collectively determined institutional vision. The presidency is not a command position but rather an influential one, where he or she acts as a sort of shepherd guiding the entire organization toward a vision of what the organization could become. The president works to develop a culture of participation; to ensure that the college's most quiet voices can still be heard. Frankly, the most difficult decision for the president of a chaotic institution is when to, and more importantly when not to, become involved in an issue. Once the decision is made to become more involved, the president's manner of acting is as important as the action taken. How to ensure inclusion, the timing for yielding a greater degree of influence, and the manner in which viewpoints are shared by a president all demand a keen awareness of the power that chaos theory principles produce through the process itself.

At Blue Ridge Community College, faculty, staff, and even administrators, at all levels of the organizational structure, routinely storm into the president's office, ranting about one problem or another. Ironically, many at the institution complain in those meetings with the president, that he should render an immediate decision in their favor, or that actions are not implemented quickly enough, or that the faculty is allowed to make too many institutional decisions. Just as commonly, however, the opposite event occurs, with individuals demanding more input on specific decisions, or decrying the lack of information presented prior to a rendered decision, or arguing that a decision should be reopened within the governance structure. The president's role and typical action in these situations has been to listen. That listening role is an *active* process whereby the person leaves the office not with a resolution but with a distinct sense that their criticism has been heard and analyzed, not judged, counter-argued, or ignored. The president makes a point in these situations not to decide, even in the face of tremendous pressure from those people who argue quite vigorously for a decree to be issued forth, instantaneously. In effect, this process is the president's prime means of intelligence collection, of cultural assessment. It is his ultimate weapon of empowerment because he alone can understand the entire culture of the institution. In a chaotic institution, it is when people stop knocking on that open door that the president knows the institution is in trouble. When no one enters that open door, the president can suspect that the atmosphere has not properly been developed for achieving the vision of participation in decisions at all levels of the organization.

The president's primary role in a chaotic institution is to serve as an intellectual, ethical, and even emotional guide. That role is not one to which he or she is appointed, but one that must be earned. A president earns that role through trust, built over time, as a result of interacting with the members of the community as a peer. The president cannot wage battles, must not take sides, and ought not wield power to obtain some predetermined outcome. If battles occur, the president cannot seek to win them. Instead, the president can, and must, assist his peers (the other employees of the college) understand and strive for what they really want, and then create a shared value, spoken or unspoken, that articulates that desire. A president lacking in intellect, ethical leadership, and principled social skills is simply incompetent to run a chaotic institution.

Two particular situations describe for the reader the manner of leadership style that works well for our president as he functions in the chaos of decision making that is Blue Ridge Community College. The first situation involves the manner in which he dealt with an administrative retrenchment at the college, and the second involves how his vision helped guide individual participants to create and implement a successful Title III grant at the college.

In 1995, the Commonwealth of Virginia offered a onetime, unique, early retirement offer to a limited group of state employees. Individuals weren't automatically eligible for the offer, but could request the permission of the president to accept the buyout. The offer was aimed at the specific task of downsizing state government, and as such, had some very unusual strings attached for any agency that agreed to allow their employees to take advantage of it. The college was allowed to retain the saved salary funds, but they were not allowed to refill the position vacated by the departing employee. The result, of course, was that the work typically done by that employee would have to be spread across the remaining employees in the department, or across the college.

Normally, the news that employees would be required to do more with less would not be positively received on most campuses. In fact, in addition to Blue Ridge Community College, only one of the twenty-three other eligible institutions in the Virginia Community College System agreed to the buyout because of such concerns. However, our president saw the challenge of downsizing as an opportunity to reengineer existing processes, and thus to better align the organization to respond to the changing needs of our students.

The president employed his position of power, not to determine the method or manner of reorganization, but rather to communicate his vision of the opportunities he saw that the downsizing could create. The administrative structure at the college was used as a brainstorming forum to discuss how technology could be employed to broaden the service options for our students. A total of six employees sought the buyout and the president successfully pursued an exemption to the policy that would allow two of the six to be replaced. The other four positions were permanently eliminated.

One of the positions not replaced was that of a mid-level student services administrator. In her stead, two student services professionals, one in admissions and another in the counseling center, were asked to assume joint responsibility for both direct service to students and administrative decisions. Their enthusiasm for this new structure, which they helped to establish with the president's encouragement, was employed to help both service areas reengineer processes that had not been very responsive to the work schedules of students. After reengineering, students were able to register by telephone or e-mail, and the window of opportunity for doing so was greatly expanded. Employees within student services were allowed to function with a wider range of responsibility than they had held previously, and students were able to access services from a wider range of trained employees than in the past.

Would it be possible that such responsiveness to student needs could have happened through an administrative directive in a linear-oriented institution? Perhaps, although we argue that even if it were to occur, the manner in which it would be carried out would not be implemented as enthusiastically or with such dynamism as it was on our campus.

A second example of our president's ability to champion and shape a process concerns the procedure we used to develop a successful application for a federal Title III grant. Anyone familiar with the application process for this type of federal grants knows what a daunting process it is to produce an effective application. Although an institution may receive significant financial assistance, the money is designated to very specific tasks that must be envisioned as far as five years into the future.

Blue Ridge Community College began the application process for our Title III grant by first applying for and receiving a planning grant. The planning grant provided the college with the opportunity to brainstorm a variety of needs that we could use federal assistance to address. An example of a specific need identified through this brainstorming process was our hope to develop a technological infrastructure that would elevate the college to a state-of-the-art facility assisting students in accessing information for their studies.

The brainstorming process was effective at identifying a rich variety of very specific and diverse institutional needs. Yet the process also resulted in stagnation for the grant development process, as specific special interests arose across different departments. Individuals began to advocate for their own departmental technological advancement, without a clear vision of how the college as a whole would be improved.

At this point, the role of the president proved invaluable. It was the president, in this chaotic and inharmonious atmosphere, that patiently listened while a wide variety of constituency groups, individual faculty members, and department administrators advocated for their own computers, technical equipment, and personnel positions. It was the president who didn't panic when entire sections of the grant failed to materialize and when those that were written were not coherent or competitive. Ultimately, it was the president who chose exactly the right moment, in the presence of the right people, to clearly articulate a coherent vision for the entire application. The president outlined his idea that the first activity section of the grant could concentrate on employing technology to achieve student success by accurately assessing incoming students in career and academic development. He suggested that the second activity might focus on employing technology for the professional development of faculty, so that they might provide students with the tools for academic success. Finally, the president recommended that the third activity could focus on employing technology to design long-term funding strategies that would keep the first two activities solvent at the end of the life of the grant.

When the president presented his vision, hewed from the chaos that developed from the advocacy of special interest groups, the grant practically wrote itself. Three authors went to work and put his interpretation of the college's vision to paper. The result was a successful application that yielded a successfully implemented grant. The specific implementation strategies of the grant changed drastically from the original application, but the overarching vision never changed. The result was an entirely different college than we had, a college which fostered the vision he expressed not because it was mandated, but because it was believed in and taken to heart.

## Proposition IX
### That Which Can Be Quantified Is Not to Be Overvalued, and That Which Cannot Be Quantified Is Not to Be Discounted

In the age of accountability and assessment, the blind worship of data is an inherent danger in most institutions of higher education. While state and federal governmental officials are right to pressure colleges to document the utility of the services they provide, they often fail to acknowledge the immeasurable outcomes that education provides to the students we serve. Few members of the higher education community would argue against the proposition that part of the role of education is to broaden students' perspectives and increase their ability to critically assess the world around them. Values such as citizenship, an internal work ethic, a love for learning, a commitment to excellence, and a sense of service to one's community are all outcomes that many general education programs profess to instill in college graduates. Attempts to quantify these values are almost always problematic. Still, few would argue that abandonment of the effort to teach these qualities is appropriate for lack of an adequate measure.

We have repeatedly asserted that institutions of any sort must be motivated by vision. With chaotic institutions that contention assumes even a more critical importance. Too much reliance on data inherently centralizes power in those who possess, generate, and interpret the data. Hierarchy and chaos are fundamentally incompatible. While at Blue Ridge Community College there are few secrets, and data are given to anyone who wants them, there remains a tendency to follow the trend lines instead of thinking outside the box.

In order to achieve a vision for the future, we must abandon quantitative projections and rely instead on less rigid environmental scans. Data that helps provide a vision for where the world is going is more important than data that helps people look back to where the world has been. Bean counting is antithetical to chaos theory. Managers count beans; chaotic leaders embrace and welcome and anticipate more nebulous trends. Leading chaotically is risk-laden but the courage to gamble is an essential part of successful chaotic systems.

The important things in institutional futures, such as reputation in the community and credibility in business and industry, are best measured qualitatively. Structured surveys won't get at it adequately. Quantitative numbers cannot adequately tell an institution whether its values are a proper fit, which interviewee to hire, or which opportunities to pursue. Although it may be handy to know whether an institution is staying near its budget, whether it has sufficient students, and whether its staff members are getting paid, that information merely provides either reassurance or threat, not guidance for the future.

Even the planning for apparently simple things, like a replacement for our archaic telephone system, can defy the logic of quantitative data analysis. First, we did exhaustive comparative analysis of various phone systems, and finally decided a more modern PBX system was the only way to go. Suddenly, a new technology emerged, called "voice over ip." We began to lean toward this new technology until further analysis suggested that voice over ip would not be reliable for several years. After that decision was agreed to and announced, new information emerged which suggested that the second-generation voice over ip was more reliable than the first release. A week later we reversed ourselves and announced we would implement the voice over ip telephone system.

If we merely relied on quantitative data alone to make decisions, we would be an institution with a smooth decision-making process and technology that was state of the art in the 1980s. Instead, we muddle through, sense trends, analyze the data and make the most important decisions by consensus. We employ data and do not minimize the relevance, but neither do we overvalue the importance.

This perspective regarding data drove us also to embrace the development of an improved general education program for selected students in our college transfer program. The idea for this program emerged from informal conversations between two faculty members who were discussing their own college experiences. As they talked, they realized that many of the educational values instilled within them materialized from out-of-classroom experiences they had with the professors and fellow students on campus. These values could not properly be measured by existing assessment tools because the faculty members were discussing the intangible benefits that education provides to students.

This discussion led the faculty to propose an enhanced program for selected students based on the educational philosophy of President Woodrow Wilson, whose birthplace is located within the college's service area. We attended a national general education conference where we discussed our ideas with many of the country's premier thinkers on the topic of general education. We are now at a stage where the program outline has been formulated and we are seeking innovative funding strategies to take a cohort through the program.

The Wilson Scholars Program will provide students with extracurricular service and learning projects that will be discussed in a seminar led by faculty members. Since our college transfer degree program, and its general education components, were designed as a discrete series of classes that students moved through without any real cohesion, we determined that the intangible culture of the learning experience provided for at four-year universities was missing from the community college experience. We feared that students were viewing community college education as a generic, course-by-course experience. Therefore, our plan is designed to work with the Woodrow Wilson Birthplace and other area organizations to create an all-encompassing educational experience based upon the educational philosophy of Wilson for the purpose of leadership and citizenship. Reliance on assessment data would not allow us to realize the real purpose of engaging in this endeavor. We hope to employ data to demonstrate student success through this initiative, but we care more about the values we seek to instill in the participants. Our goal is to have the program running next year. The results may not be truly known until those students find a way to contribute to society decades from now.

## Proposition X
## The Future Is a Creation, Not a Prediction.
## This Power of Agency Is the Distinguishing Context
## of Human Chaotic Systems.

All of what has been discussed in the response to Dr. Cutright's (1999) previous nine propositions represents Blue Ridge Community College's attempt over the last ten years to create a future as opposed to predict one. *Carpe diem* is an overused expression. However, in a chaotic context, *carpe diem* has its merits. Many colleges fear the future and, therefore, create structures to react to the unexpected. They create and live in a negative environment because invariably the unexpected presupposes the worse.

What we have learned is that the unexpected can yield incredible opportunities for innovation. Blue Ridge Community College is tied to a central system of colleges, so we do not enjoy the autonomy that other community colleges experience, let alone universities. It would be easy to accept the notion that our fate is sealed. Since outside forces contribute to the shape our future takes, it would be simple to just sit back and allow whatever happens to happen. What we have found instead is, even with these types of restraints, we have tremendous power in shaping our own future.

Our pending adoption of a massive software package (produced by PeopleSoft), which will replace our antiquated Student Information System, is an excellent illustration of how we strive to shape our own future. The Virginia Community College System selected this new system for student records centrally, but it will be implemented on each of twenty-three of the system's colleges over the next three years. It will affect everyone in the community college system, although there are few people involved in the process who clearly understand exactly what the impact will be.

Blue Ridge Community College has not been given a choice regarding whether or not to implement this software system. The decision was made at the highest level, and it is not negotiable. Yet the massive systemwide undertaking associated with implementing a modern software system for student records has created a foreboding across the system and across our campus. The enterprise is complicated and will require a great deal of training.

When the Virginia Community College System realized that the project would be implemented in stages, they approached our president and asked us to be one of the three pilot colleges needed to implement the project first. The most logical reaction, common among most VCCS colleges, was to avoid this project until other colleges could implement it first. Let someone else deal with the initial problems, work through them, and when the time comes use the models that those first-wave colleges developed. Admittedly, this same discussion took place at Blue Ridge when the president first proposed that we agree to the system office request.

In the end, the opportunity we will have to shape our own future, and possibly a portion of the System's future, was too tempting. We did not want to be stuck with someone else's model. We volunteered to be one of the three pilot programs. The type of risk associated with innovation has considerable benefits. Once again, the software will afford us the opportunity to re-think our student registration and payment processes. We will be one of the first in the system that will employ the power of the students themselves to register and manage their own enrollment, much like banks now allow customers to manage their own accounts online or by telephone. The project will allow the institution to reduce long-term operational cost by using short-term risk capital. If successful, it can solidify the institution's already impressive reputation as an innovative, technological leader. Finally, it relieves the institution's staff of lengthy periods of concern about what might happen. We consider it the equivalent of diving in a brisk pool, rather than dipping one's toe in the cold but inevitable waters. It is our experience that diving into decisions like this one has empowered our college to create the future rather than wait until the future is predicted for us. Ironically, by doing so we also help to predict the future that other colleges will inherit by following our lead.

### Conclusion

Cutright's (1999) ten propositions have considerable value as a metaphor for strategic planning in higher education. They are largely consistent with our experiences at Blue Ridge Community College. Still, they do not exhaustively describe the behavior of chaotic institutions.

Chaos theory is not simply a means of governance; it is a way of life. Thus, Cutright's (1999) propositions, while useful, are not the only dimensions that must be considered when promoting chaos theory as an institutional value to a college community of skeptics. Several other factors must also be considered, discussed, weighed, and ultimately valued if the chaotic perspective is to truly become effective in a decentralized environment.

One such factor is the demands that active participation and engagement on a chaos-oriented campus places on faculty, staff, and administrators. A chaotic institution is a decentralized institution, one where line employees are empowered. In a chaotic institution, static job descriptions are interesting vestiges of times gone by. For example, a staff member on our campus whose job description lists him as an "automotive instructional assistant" is the person who also happens to be chairing the committee that is building our next strategic directions document. We have faculty members who are actively involved in facilities design. The institution's technology plan is developed by a hodgepodge of interested individuals. Turf wars, and the blind exercise of administrative power, cannot be tolerated on a chaotic campus. All doors must be opened, and more importantly, all minds must be.

The payoff of chaos is collective vision, an institution of individuals all singing from the same sheet of music. In turn, that means all must have a meaningful voice in the development of mission, vision, values, and strategic directions. Without buy-in, there will be cacophony in execution and implementation.

All of that sounds wonderful, but it involves so much work for people who are already too busy. Chaotic institutions are places where people must work harder and smarter. Chaotic institutions are not for the faint of heart, the lazy, or those who say, "tell me what to do." They are not for those who want to work to the contract. They are for the adventurous, the bold, the committed, the visionary, those who care about their future and the future of the institution, and those who see themselves as leaders from the line.

Since the chaotic environment is demanding on employees, another factor chaos theory-oriented colleges must consider is the recruiting and retention of quality employees who can assimilate successfully into the participatory culture. The type of people needed to staff chaotic institutions are in short supply. Routine hiring practices won't find them, and routine retention strategies won't keep them. The recruiting process must clearly demonstrate for prospective employees our expectations, including the provision that the job description is a polite fiction and that conflict is a necessary part of the process. Unlike linear organizations, the hiring process must also create buy-in across the institution for the prospective hire. We require public presentations by candidates in order for them to demonstrate their interactive style. Selection committees often include people far outside the nominal domain of the job openings.

Burdens on new and seasoned employees are matched by the demands placed on students in a chaos-oriented college. Many students, used to the structure of traditional institutions, may become confused by expectations of who does what to whom—expectations that will not be met in a chaotic institution. Some students will have a difficult time figuring out things as mundane as who signs a form, to whom one might appeal a grade, or who to ask for special dispensation. An even greater surprise for students may be the perceived inconsistency in the manner that policies are applied to individual circumstances. Empowering employees at the lowest organizational level means allowing them to decide about how and when individual circumstances ought to override policies. Students, who are taught all sorts of things about institutional cultures, can also be taught how to live and interact in chaotic cultures.

Another factor that chaos-oriented colleges must consider involves the demands the culture places on the external community. Chaotic institutions operate differently, including how they relate to their external boards and community groups. For community colleges in particular, the community is the source of power and the target of the mission. Few communities will have any sense of the utility of chaos theory. Often, community leaders will prefer traditional institutions, where it is easier to figure out whom to call, and whom to call to account. It may take a community some time to become accustomed to institutional spokespersons coming from unusual places in the institution.

All of the above means that there must be a hyper-developed sense of trust throughout the institution—trust in peers, in subordinates, and superiors, and trust in our own ability to work productively toward institutional goals, in an unstable and shifting landscape. Traditional employees (and leaders) may yield to paranoia and lapse into personalities versus substance. Employees can learn to function in a chaotic environment, but paranoia and personalities come as character traits, refractory to change. Just a few such people can kill chaos.

The final factor affecting the efficacy of chaos theory as a metaphor for planning involves the demands that chaos places on a college's technology. In chaotic organizations job descriptions, the functional pattern of organization, and communication patterns do not follow traditional linear patterns. Therefore, it is not possible to run chaotically by using paper memos. The default communication pattern must be "all information goes to everyone." Using paper would mean the death of millions of innocent pine trees. Casual meetings in the hallways, often treasured in academe, do not fit the fast-paced life in a chaotic institution. Thus, chaotic institutions must have a powerful technology infrastructure.

Chaotic institutions cannot rely on obsolete computers, Internet connections that work slowly or unreliably, or software that crashes. Technology is what makes chaos possible, and technology is expensive. Chaotic institutions must make budgetary commitments to technology or give up the chaotic model. In our case, we made an institutional commitment in 1989 (initiated by the faculty) to make do with fewer full-time faculty members in order to fund our need to modernize technology. We continue to be committed to that principle. As a result, we have world-class technology and an institution that uses it as a means of operating.

It is not possible to move gently toward chaos theory. In social systems, it is not possible to change just one thing, leaving the rest of the system intact. In the case of chaos theory, that statement is true with a vengeance. Chaos in governance will create chaos everywhere. Moving gradually toward a chaotic model is like trying to light just one corner of a pan of gasoline.

Winston Churchill once said about democracy that it is the worst form of government except for all the others. Similarly, chaos theory is the worst form of institutional planning, except for all the other governance systems. It probably would never work in many institutions, and it certainly will not work with certain institutional leaders. Presidents interested merely in consolidating and exercising power will destroy chaotic processes. Defensive administrators and rigid faculty can foredoom chaotic methodology. Alienated staff can make chaos a horrid waste of time. Incompetent or egocentric employees can make chaos pointless puffery. But for those institutions that eagerly welcome chaos, the outcomes can be sweet indeed.

# References

Cutright, M. (1999). *A chaos-theory metaphor for strategic planning in higher education: An exploratory study.* Unpublished doctoral dissertation, the University of Tennessee, Knoxville.

Fisher, J. L., & Koch, J. V. (1996). *Presidential leadership: Making a difference.* Phoenix, AZ: Oryx Press.

Greenleaf, R. K. (1983). *Servant leadership: A journey into the nature of legitimate power and greatness.* Mahwah NJ: Paulist Press.

Levin, B. H., Lanigan, J. B., & Perkins, J. R. (1995). *Strategic planning in a decentralized environment: The death of linearity.* Presented at the 24th Annual Conference of the Southern Association for Community College Research. Asheville, NC, August 6–9.

Lorenz, E. (1993). *The essence of chaos.* Seattle: University of Washington Press.

Mintzberg, H. (1993). *The rise and fall of strategic planning: Re-conceiving roles for planning, plans, planners.* New York: Free Press.

Wheatley, M. J. (1999). *Leadership and the new science: Discovering order in a chaotic world.* San Francisco: Berrett-Koehler Publishers.

# CHAPTER SIX

## Chaos Theory and the Evolution of a State System of Higher Education

*Jeffery P. Aper*

### What Is Chaos Theory, and How Does It Relate to Planning in Higher Education?

Chaos theory has found substantial utility in the past decade or so, in the metaphoric or literal description of social systems. But concise and consistent descriptions of chaos theory have been relatively scarce.

Perhaps one of the most useful descriptions is from the 1990 *Report of the Commission on the University of the Twenty-First Century* in Virginia:

> A mathematical concept called, somewhat misleadingly, "chaos," holds that at certain points small changes within systems will produce great and unpredictable results. For instance, a small rock in the middle of a rushing stream may cause enormous turbulence in the water for some distance, after it passes over and around the rock. The mathematics created to conceive such "chaotic" situations is non-linear: the future does not follow trends established in the past . . . . To some, chaos theory is critical to the future of science, permitting scientists to present representations of reality not otherwise conceivable. Others are less impressed by its promise. What it represents to us is the probability that the future will not be simply a linear extrapolation of the past, that small events happening today will cause unexpected new patterns to develop downstream. (*A Case for Change*, 1990, inside back cover.)

Although chaos theory has roots and precedent in science and mathematics going back a century or more, its discovery and articulation as a set of concepts and principles coincides largely with the advent of computers and their ability to perform the multiple iterations of calculations creating patterns of system behavior. The beginning of chaos theory in its modern sense it widely attributed to the meteorological modeling experiments of Edward Lorenz in the 1960s. From this work, for example, emerged the notion of the *butterfly effect*, the idea that the flapping of a butterfly's wings could, eventually, influence the development and course of a tornado continents away, through minute changes in the weather system, changes that were changed and magnified through the repetition of system dynamics (Gleick, 1987; Lorenz, 1993). Subsequent to Lorenz's work, investigators in fields as diverse as astronomy, geology, population ecology, and quantum mechanics have verified chaotic patterns and constructed mathematical models to describe and replicate them (Newman & Wessinger, 1993).

Applications of chaos theory to the understanding and enhancement of social systems and organizations are ideas that have been advanced by many of the originators of key concepts of chaos theory within the sciences, among them David Ruelle (1991) and Ilya Prigogine (with Stengers, 1984). The "mainstreaming" of chaos theory as a tool for the discussion and understanding of organizations is generally attributed to the 1992 publication of Margaret Wheatley's *Leadership and the New Science: Learning About Organization from an Orderly Universe*. Gareth Morgan's 1997 second edition of *Images of Organization* demonstrates the degree to which the perspective had been by that point broadly considered, as he discussed chaos at some length as a strong and primary metaphor for organizational understanding.

Particularly notable about the 1990 Virginia report cited above is that it predates almost all notable and influential applications of chaos theory to organizations, at least as those perspectives were advanced by organizational scholars themselves. Very little, to this day, has been written about the application of chaos theory to the specific function of planning in higher education (Cutright, 1999). It would appear that the metaphor of chaos theory as articulated and used by the authors of the Virginia report originates almost in its entirety to reference in the physical sciences of its discovery, and represents perhaps the earliest intentional application and articulation of these concepts to organizational behavior and planning in higher education. Further, the majority of states have recently adopted or are currently considering long-range strategic plans for public higher education, and more than 40 percent now have some form of performance-based funding mechanism in place for their postsecondary institutions (*Chronicle of Higher Education Almanac*, 2000a). The experience of Virginia in the 1990s has much to tell about the ways in which states wrestle with planning, priority-setting, and funding for their systems of higher education.

In the following sections, some context and implications of the Virginia higher education policy environment leading up to and following the publication of the chaos-theory influenced report of the commission are discussed.

## Origins and Powers of Virginia's
## Higher Education Coordinating Board

Public higher education in the Commonwealth of Virginia was characterized through much of the last half of the twentieth century by a generally high level of confidence in the institutions on the parts of governors and legislators (Aper, 1989). Thus central coordination of Virginia higher education was limited through the 1950s, 1960s, and into the early 1970s (Aper, 1989). The State Council of Higher Education for Virginia (SCHEV) was created in 1956 with original responsibilities related to overall coordination of state level activities such as academic program approval and review of institutional information related to budget requests. As early as 1961 state officials had called for specific institutional studies of teaching loads, curriculum organization, noninstructional duties, and research activities with the intent of improving opportunities for more effective teaching and service. This was the beginning of ongoing state-level efforts to systematically review expenditures and practices with an eye toward enhanced efficiency. Though the legislature consistently showed a high level of interest in higher education, they also historically followed a generally hands-off philosophy with regard to the internal functions and administration of colleges and universities, apparently persuaded by the arguments of SCHEV and the institutions that one of the strengths in Virginia higher education lay in its diversity and the need to recognize institutional individuality (Aper, 1989). Many state officials, and legislators in particular, through the 1980s and into the 1990s viewed Virginia's institutions of higher education as constituting a diverse and generally healthy system with a positive and growing national reputation. The institutions were valued highly as sources of prestige and economic development for the state (Aper & Hinkle, 1991).

Formal attempts at state-level strategic planning were evident in the first edition of a publication entitled *The Virginia Plan for Higher Education*, published in 1967. This and subsequent versions of this document came to be published with some regularity through the 1970s and 1980s, and were intended to provide an overview of the current and anticipated activities of the public colleges and universities in the commonwealth. In 1972 and again in 1974 there were recommendations from some legislators and from study commissions that SCHEV assume expanded powers or be transformed into a statewide governing entity. These recommendations were not followed, although in 1974 SCHEV was given more responsibility for academic program approval, generating enrollment projections, long-range planning, and budget review. In 1976 SCHEV introduced a comprehensive data reporting mechanism that placed a heavy reporting burden on institutions, but this process was ultimately suspended in the late 1980s, at least partly due to technological advancements in data management (Aper, 1989).

In spite of SCHEV's increasing activities the agency was criticized by some members of the legislature and other policymakers in the 1970s and in the early 1980s for not providing more specific policy direction for state expenditures on higher education. The governor's guidance package for the 1980–1982 biennial budget stated specifically that the expansion of higher education had occurred "without the benefit of any budget guidelines and management systems designed to monitor their growth and make them set priorities within limited resources" (Aper, 1989, p. 45). SCHEV had limited influence over the higher education budget as a tool for shaping policy, yet was faced with expectations that it should set the higher education policy agenda. High expectations and limited authority were ongoing conditions of SCHEV's existence into the 1980s and 1990s. Thus, state-level coordination and planning were best described in the 1980s as they had been in the 1970s—a concatenation of aims and priorities of powerful legislators, governors, and the institutions themselves. SCHEV, the agency ostensibly responsible for planning, walked a tightrope trying to serve these multiple masters. At the same time state officials expressed confidence in SCHEV, the state Department of Planning and Budget (DPB) grew to include responsibilities for some budgeting functions for higher education. As one DPB analyst saw it, SCHEV was "viewed as being more of an advocate for universities" (Aper, 1989, p. 84), yet at the same time SCHEV was not seen by the institutions as an insider or ally. A former SCHEV staff member noted that the agency was caught between its multiple masters—the institutions wanted it to be an advocate for higher education, the legislature wanted it to find solutions to their problems, the governor wanted it to support his policies whatever they might be, and there was no way the agency could serve each of these purposes simultaneously.

## 1980s—Expectations, Policy, and Planning

In spite of this relative tension, SCHEV emerged in the 1980s, under the leadership of Executive Director Gordon Davies, as an agent of change in Virginia higher education. Yet in true Virginia fashion, that is, the genteel politics of what some might refer to as the "old Virginia"—in which gentlemen had discussions and reached agreements in principle, in which policies were tried out and given extended time to see how they panned out—change initiated from the state level came in slow degrees and in an intentionally decentralized way. According to one senior institutional official, the initiatives for new programs were introduced to the legislature in time for legislators to "absorb it . . . you have to throw it out there and start to work on it." The nature of this process was described by a legislative staff member: "given the way we operate in Virginia, you almost have to let something play out and give the people who are proposing it be done a chance." This process was described as often taking several years, "from the time they first start to talk about something and you let the problems work through and then you come back and look at it a different way. Then you really get things implemented" (quoted in Aper, 1989, p. 97). Specific programs related to planning in the 1970s and 1980s that were initiated and ultimately abandoned included a comprehensive institutional data reporting system; a program budgeting system that would have included comprehensive evaluation as part of the budgetary process for institutions; and statewide higher education program reviews (Aper, 1989). Each of these efforts to obtain more information about process and products of higher education were, however, ultimately deflected and even abandoned, not in small part due to the pervasiveness of traditions of institutional autonomy and confidence in the overall quality of most of the states' colleges and universities.

As an illustration, in the early 1980s SCHEV first made the case for quality as a component of the funding process; "The guidelines used to ensure equitable distribution of funds need to be changed to place less emphasis upon the size of an institution and more emphasis upon what it does and how well it does it" (Aper, 1989, p. 45). SCHEV Executive Director Gordon Davies in 1987 urged incentives for institutions to respond to state priorities, then an emerging state-level strategy in several states (Holland & Berdahl, 1990). This approach exemplified SCHEV's carrot and stick approach to shaping policy within the limits of Virginia political tradition (Aper, 1989, pp. 47–48).

The increased focus on quality was exemplified in the planning approach to the evolution of student assessment policy and practice. When in 1985 the legislature called upon all public institutions to engage in serious student assessment activities, it did not coerce or threaten institutions into compliance, nor did they follow the path of mandated measures or common approaches. By the mid to late 1980s, many states were mandating specific kinds of assessment activities and programs. While Virginia also called upon institutions to undertake such efforts, the state characteristically supported individual institutions in developing their own policies and practices in a largely decentralized and institution-oriented way, leaving the bulk of the planning and development of the programs to the institutions themselves. By the late 1980s Virginia's approach was considered to be a model for other states in encouraging institutions to engage in assessment through a combination of incentives, support, and moderate budget levers (Aper, 1989; Aper & Hinkle, 1991; Ewell & Boyer, 1988). The expectations of state leaders were aptly summarized by Gordon Davies, who asserted that what policymakers wanted to know was that institutions were "examining their assumptions and the results. They do not want to establish the criteria for accountability. They want to know that institutions are behaving responsibly. . . . I believe the institution, in order to warrant this grant of responsibility, should be willing to assure the public that it maintains a thoughtful and questioning stance toward its own standards." Davies and his staff, notably then Associate Director Margaret (Peg) Miller, described assessment more in terms of "complacency reduction" for the several institutions rather than as a specific plan for accountability (Aper, 1989).

## The Virginia Approach to Higher Education and Planning

This decentralized approach was supported by Davies, then Secretary of Education Donald Finley, as well as then Governor Gerald Baliles and key members of the legislature. The prevailing attitude within the executive branch was described by Secretary Finley, who in 1989 argued that "the results [of assessment] are going to be more long-term and better if we try to build a mechanism that allows the faculty and students to do it themselves, under a very decentralized model, and trust them to carry forth. . . . [T]hat . . . will be much more productive than trying to drive something home . . . out of Richmond" (quoted in Aper, 1989, p. 128). As political observers and insiders noted, this approach was not atypical of the ways in which higher education had historically been treated by state government in Virginia. In 1989 a state Department of Planning and Budget insider described the ways in which Virginia higher education through the 1980s was frequently treated differently in the state budgeting process than other agencies or other funding priorities. Institutions had tended to be treated with greater deference than other state entities at budget time, and there was reluctance to engage in mandatory regulation (Aper, 1989). While planning was a desired process, it was seen as general coordination of efforts and not a specific set of objectives. As Davies suggested in 1997, "what we do today is not satisfactory for tomorrow; the notion of a five-year plan is quaint; there is no end to change and possible improvement but the goal is to become 'more perfect' rather than 'perfect'" (p. 3). This reflects the ongoing evolution of Davies's view of planning strategy for Virginia higher education; centrally coordinated, but locally developed, guided by core values, not by iron-clad objectives.

It would, however, be inaccurate to suggest that Virginia state government had historically simply taken a laissez faire attitude toward its component organizational units generally, or even toward higher education, specifically. Interest in performance measures for public departments and institutions continued in the 1990s. From the uniform reporting system and attempts at program budgeting in the 1970s and 1980s to the pilot projects on performance measures for state programs as part of the budgeting process (Virginia Department of Planning and Budget, December 1, 1993), and mandated strategic planning efforts (Virginia Department of Planning and Budget, 1994, pp. 15–16) in the 1990s, state government sought to mix traditional management approaches with traditions of institutional autonomy. Budget reforms instituted in 1995 "incorporated measurement of performance" into state budget processes, in some ways a realization of unfulfilled program budgeting efforts that had been initiated in the late 1970s. As in past decades, the 1990s saw continued legislative review of higher education, and especially of SCHEV, which was the subject of a searching study by the Joint Legislative Audit and Review Committee (JLARC) in 1995. It is worth noting that the JLARC review seems to have been prompted by continuing conflict with the governor over the role and purpose of SCHEV.

## The Commission on the University of the Twenty-First Century

The notion of planning epitomized in Davies's 1997 reflections on higher education and its governance echoed the approach suggested by the report of the Virginia Commission on the University of the Twenty-First Century (1990). This report reflected the leading edge of understanding of the Virginia approach to public higher education as the decade of the 1980s came to a close. The report was a strong statement in defense of a continued process of decentralized planning and coordination, calling for greater autonomy for institutions and noting that changing environments required that institutions be given maximum opportunities for self-direction and organizational flexibility.

The *Report of the Commission on the University of the Twenty-First Century* stated explicitly that the commission rejected "preparing a detailed plan for Virginia higher education in the next century" (Commonwealth of Virginia, 1990, p. 1). The commission identified as its fundamental question: "How can Virginia cause constructive and fundamental change within its colleges and universities so they will be ready to meet the demands of life in the twenty-first century?" (1990, p. 1). Consistent with the professed views of leaders in both the legislature and the executive branch, the members of the commission observed that "the state's system of higher education has emerged as one of the most highly regarded in the nation. It has been well funded in recent years, and its colleges and universities have been left largely autonomous. Virginia is poised to lead a national movement to change perspectives, curricula, values, and behavior in American higher education" (1990, p. 2). Though, as is common in such reports, the importance of public higher education to workforce preparation and economic development were highlighted, the commissioners rejected the notion "that the major purpose of higher education is to prepare people for jobs. We believe that higher education should help all people develop their capacities to the fullest—as workers, citizens, members of families and other social institutions, and participants in the global community" (1990, p. 4).

The commission recommended rethinking a broad range of issues. Institutional administrative structure, policies on tenure and faculty reward systems, space planning, class scheduling, and even record keeping were subject to recommendations. Budgetary reform was recommended as a way for institutional budgeting to become more decentralized and autonomous, based on "post-audit accountability, exception reporting, and a clear set of expectations, rewards, and penalties [that] will put administration of higher education firmly in the control of those employed to do it: the presidents and their senior staffs" (1990, p. 13). In their final recommendations the commission praised the virtues of institutional autonomy and urged that the state "encourage creativity and discourage complacency" (1990, p. 14).

The commission commented, "Neither governance nor administrative systems necessarily need to be changed. We're concerned about something more fundamental. We're asking the persons responsible for Virginia higher education to see things as a whole: to see that everything relates to everything else, and that behaviors must change in light of that understanding" (1990, p. 15). Though praising the loosely coordinated system of colleges and universities in Virginia, the commission held that there was insufficient coordination—not because they urged greater predictability, but because they saw that extant circumstances resulted in an "arrangement [that] does not encourage or reward cooperation, risk-taking, or innovation" (1990, p. 16). Yet the commission further stated that "the planning processes of the Council appear to work well. They are flexible, relatively informal, and able to respond quickly to change circumstances and new needs. A highly pragmatic, flexible, and continuous approach to planning is what the times require. The era of the thick, long-range master plan has passed" (1990, p. 17).

Interestingly, the commission noted the substantial funding for Virginia higher education during the 1980s and made emphatic recommendations for the need to continue to be generous in public support for higher education. As events unfolded an implication of the economic downturn and changes in attitude toward governance of the following decade would seem to be that a decentralized, flexible approach to planning and policy in higher education was seen as a luxury of financially healthy governments. When the budget collapses, so perhaps does the will to permit a thousand flowers to bloom. At the height of the political conflicts over higher education policy in Virginia in the mid- to late 1990s, Davies publicly argued that political interference was symptomatic of the larger question of shifts from one intellectual tradition toward another not yet defined. He quoted Ronald Heifitz (1994, in Davies, 1997); "severe distress can make people cruel; empathy, compassion, and flexibility of mind are sacrificed to the desperate desire for order." Davies added that "to charge that colleges and universities are subversive to established values and principles of democracy finds fertile ground in the anti-intellectualism that historically has characterized Americans' ambivalent feelings about academic institutions. It leads to the conclusion that it is necessary to control who is allowed to teach or correct what is being taught" (1997, p. 10).

## The Report of the Commission on the University of the Twenty-First Century and Chaos Theory

Unlike many such reports of its ilk, the report carried little presentation of quantitative data and projection. The principal authors of the report later noted that though there was an abundance of such data available to be considered by the commissioners, the commissioners didn't find them important to the basic case. Moreover, there was a basic distrust of planning based on the linear projection of numbers taken out of full context. As Gordon Davies noted, as an example, "long-range forecasts of enrollment are notoriously imprecise." Though the members of the commission did not reject the importance of such projections where necessary, in the case of capital construction planning, for example, neither did they design a plan dependent upon particular patterns of enrollment growth, state spending, or other numerical data presumed to be indicators of the success, failure, or relevance of the plan. As the report states, "This is a vision for good, bad, or average state revenue growth" (p. 20), although as events would reveal, the spirit of the recommendations was largely abandoned in a period of poor revenue growth.

In fact, the report specifically rejected the traditional image of the detailed, numerically driven strategic plan. Coupled with this was an unwillingness to confuse the length of the report with the breadth of the vision it presented. This orientation to planning demonstrated an acceptance of a large element of unpredictability about the future, as shown in the absence of linear projections. Thus, the members of the commission saw their job as one of creation rather than prediction. As the report stated, "Looking into the future is a risky business, but we have not so much predicted what will happen as said what we think should happen" (p. 2).

In marked contrast to most state policy thinking about higher education since the 1970s, and in fact, Virginia's actions from the mid-1990s to 2000, the report showed a lack of emphasis on accountability to a central authority or set of rules. Instead, relatively more emphasis was placed on the establishment of a core set of principles that would guide institutions in their own planning and futures development. This is consistent with the historic structure of Virginia public higher education, but also relates to the chaos concept of "attractors": a relatively small set of ideas or properties around which systems organize, find patterns, and establish boundaries on purpose and actions. Equally important to the establishment of appropriate principles or attractors are the identification and modification of those elements as they exist, with or without official sanction or consideration; for example, the long-fretted practice of enrollment-driven funding that is essentially insensible to considerations of qualitative factors.

There was an emphasis throughout the report on the importance and examination of relationships, rather than formal, physical entities (e.g., the establishment of degree programs or governing boards) or their "hard" properties (e.g., quantitative performance projections or standards). These relationships include, for example, those between institutions and faculty, faculty and students, institution and institution, the public and private sectors, and Virginia and the world economy. As the report stated, "all of these relationships should be improved and carefully nurtured to ensure that old barriers do not prevent Virginia from seizing new opportunities . . . . We are asking the persons responsible for Virginia higher education to see that everything relates to everything else, and that behaviors must change in light of that understanding" (p. 15). This relates to some premises underlying chaos theory: what's important isn't so much the matter in a system, but the energy expended within it. As a system, all energy expenditure affects the system as a whole, and not just the immediate target of impact. The report further reflected its chaos influence in that its authors were not concerned with specifically predicting the future. Chaos implies that inasmuch as the future isn't perfectly predictable, planning and funding should reflect that reality.

The report suggested recognition of the chaos idea of turbulence— system disturbance—as a creative force. "We urge greater active engagement among the various parts of the education enterprise in Virginia. We prize cordiality but we want to see engagement: active, productive working relationships. This is what will really help students, businesses, and the state as a whole" (p. 20). Willingness to take risks and not expect uniform, machine-like outcomes from carefully specified and measured procedures or inputs is a further extension of this understanding. For example, speaking of state funding formulas, the commission says, "To be blunt, the present arrangement does not encourage or reward risk-taking or innovation" (p. 16). In fact, the Virginia guidelines for a general funding "formula" that were developed in the late 1960s were finally abandoned in 1990 as "unrealistic" (Commonwealth of Virginia, 2000, p. 37).

The discussion above highlights some of the most notable characteristics of the 1990 commission report and what makes it so interesting historically. Further consideration of the context of the report and its aftermath provides insight into the great difficulties such a vision for higher education faces in an uncertain policy environment that typically drives decision makers to run for the cover of more conventional and traditional planning and policy frameworks.

## The Leadership of Gordon Davies and Gerald Baliles

The report of the Commission on the University of the Twenty-First Century was reflective also of the remarkable influence of both Gordon Davies and Gerald Baliles during the 1980s. Davies consistently marshaled the arguments for higher education as an expression of the public confidence in the future, as a moral and ethical commitment to a greater civic duty on the parts of citizens, and as a cause worthy of all people linking arms to build greater opportunities for Virginia. He and Baliles shared such a vision, and saw themselves as shaping policy broadly while providing appropriate "carrots and sticks" to motivate institutions to engage in self-study, reflection, and change. In this, two important variables merit note: the nature and effectiveness of what Burns (1978) first referred to as "transformational leadership" and the role of the governor in shaping higher education in any given state. With regard to the latter, as later events demonstrated, the intent and attitude of the governor may vastly change the nature of the public environment for higher education in a state.

As suggested more than twenty years ago, "the transforming leader looks for potential motives in followers, seeks to satisfy higher needs, and engages the full person of the follower. The result of transforming leadership is a relationship of mutual stimulation and elevation that converts followers into leaders and may convert leaders into moral agents" (Burns, 1978, p. 4). That single statement is highly descriptive of Davies's efforts to shape higher education policy in Virginia during his term as executive director of SCHEV. Davies consistently viewed higher education as a fundamentally moral endeavor, stating in 1997, "education is not a trivial business, a private code, or discretionary expenditure. It is a deeply ethical undertaking at which we must succeed if we're to survive as a free people" (Davies, 1997, pp. 1–2). Even Davies's detractors acknowledged his intellectual power and leadership. One of the most striking things about the report of the Commission on the University in the Twenty-First Century is its prescience in anticipating the importance of technology in higher education, the rise of post tenure reviews, performance-based budgeting, as well as such things as prepaid tuition programs and partnerships between colleges and businesses (*Chronicle of Higher Education*, May 16, 1997, p. A29). Again true to Davies's activities and practices, Burns suggested that intellectual leaders "deal with both analytical and normative ideas and they bring both to bear on their environment. However transcendent their theories and values, intellectual leaders are not detached from their social milieus; typically they seek to change it" (p. 142).

The role of the governor in shaping state higher education policy has been well documented in the literature. The influence of Governor Thomas Kean in New Jersey in the 1980s is exemplary in this regard. Virginia Governor Gerald Baliles, who served in that office from 1987 until 1991, was also highly influential with regard to higher education. Baliles and Davies worked very well together. As one administrative staff member stated midway through Baliles's term in office, "he's a wonderful Governor for higher education, he does his homework; he understands the issues and, of course, from the insider's viewpoint, he and Gordon Davies have worked extremely well together." Another SCHEV official of the time called Governor Baliles "probably the most intellectual and academic Governor we've had in recent memory" (quoted in Aper, 1989, p. 89).

Though budgetary and policy circumstances in Virginia changed dramatically from 1989 to 1997, Davies continued to champion a nonlinear and even chaos-influenced approach to planning and governance in Virginia higher education. His 1997 essay, *Twenty Years of Higher Education in Virginia*, was philosophically quite consistent with the earlier *Report of the Commission on the University of the Twenty-First Century*. In this paper, Davies continued to urge that institutions must be agile and guided by consistent core values. He suggested that endless adaptability, rapid response, demonstrated quality, and substantial local autonomy would be needed by colleges and universities in the future. He noted, "the systems that will adapt best to the new landscape are those whose boundaries are reasonably permeable, whose conception of mission is to perform certain kinds of work rather than to preserve certain types of institutions . . . the new landscape will belong to the agile . . . to behave otherwise is to be like the Pony Express, seeking faster horses and better riders even as the telegraph wires are being strung overhead" (1997, p. 21). He recommended that the path of administrative "restructuring" and "decentralization," begun in the late 1980s, continue (p. 21). These recommendations continued to emphasize a vision of organizational planning and operation far removed from more traditional notions of mechanistic, hierarchical, command-control systems (e.g., Cutright, 1999; Morgan, 1997).

Davies's vision of the coordination of higher education by the state continued to emphasize a coordinating body that was in the business of "complacency reduction." He explained, "The new coordinating body is in the business of disturbing complacency effectively, and having engendered a sense of restlessness and healthy dissatisfaction within the system of higher education and among those responsible for it" (p. 21). He was skeptical of the possibility of success for centralized coordination, planning, and management systems, arguing that no "central administration will be able to develop strategies that are responsive to the changes that occur in the complex environments that now exist. We have to learn management techniques that do not attempt to force feed all information through a central mechanism, because such mechanisms can't react quickly or creatively. Authority and responsibility need to be dispersed throughout the system" (1997, p. 22). Such "techniques rely upon decentralization and institutional autonomy; insistence upon results; high tolerance for competition, confusion, and failure; and strategic investment. The new higher education coordinating body is a gadfly rather than a planner, an investor rather than an allocator, a mediator rather than a regulator" (1997, p. 22). This strategy, he held, is not based on the wielding of formal authority. Like Burns (1978), he suggested that the effective leadership of SCHEV required the informal authority that could only grow with "the tacit support of both the colleges and universities and state government" (1997, p. 22). He saw this informal authority as central to Virginia's approach to governance in higher education, and urged that it not be abandoned in favor of "statutory and regulatory authority" (1997, p. 22).

With specific reference to planning, Davies commented, "In the environment in which we find ourselves today, the whole notion of planning takes on a different character. Strong, inflexible systems are exactly what is not needed. We need instead systems that are deeply rooted in common values and objectives, but whose constituent parts are able to adapt quickly to unanticipated developments" (1997, p. 26). Davies suggested that while each institution should have a strategic plan, a detailed statewide plan would be "unproductively confrontational, irrelevant, or compromised to the point of banality" (1997, p. 26). Instead, he suggested that "one of most importance services the Council can provide is to stimulate imaginations and provoke consideration of where higher education should be going" (1997, pp. 26–27). This flexibility was argued to include new or unconventional partnerships with entities beyond the university, such as the recently developed Virginia Business-Higher Education Council, an example of "the alternative organizations [that] try to establish communication with elected public officials and others by circumventing bureaucratic processes that would inhibit it" (p. 28). He urged partnerships, collaboration, and elimination of barriers between traditional organizations both within and outside the academy.

Davies concluded, "American systems of higher education are complex, even chaotic. Students progress through them in a variety of ways that surprise even those of us who are supposed to be responsible for them. Our systems combine, and seek to hold in productive tension, the right of individual men and women to shape their own learning and the responsibility of government to use its revenues as efficiently and effectively as possible. There are no simple formulae for doing this, only creative adaptations to unanticipated change. The systems of higher education are as distinctively American as jazz. And like jazz, our systems of higher education thrive on improvisation" (1997, p. 35).

## Changes in Virginia Higher Education in the 1990s

The 1990s witnessed important shifts in circumstances and planning for Virginia higher education. Virginia public colleges and universities suffered the first of several devastating fiscal quakes in late 1990 when budgets were cut significantly. The chairman's prologue to the 1996 *Report of the Commission on the Future of Higher Education in Virginia* (Commonwealth of Virginia) a made note of the fact that Virginia's colleges and universities since 1990 had gone through a period of "unprecedented . . . upheaval and financial insecurity" (pp. 1–2). Davies (1997) also noted that "in 1977, the system's share of the state's general fund revenue was 14.4 percent; by 1997 it has dropped to 11.7 percent" (p. 5). He further observed that in 1995 Virginia "ranked 44th in funding per student, ahead of only Louisiana and West Virginia among the southern states. In 1987, we ranked 27th" (p. 5). In the late 1970s Virginia institutions of higher education were expected to generate about 33 percent of their operating revenues from tuition, and in the mid 1990s this proportion had reached almost 50 percent. The sobering conditions of public finance in Virginia were coupled with a Democratic governor, Douglas Wilder, and his successor, Republican George Allen, who both called upon public colleges and universities to reform the deployment of faculty, ensure academic quality, minimize administrative and instructional costs, prepare for enrollment increases, and live within the funding priorities established by the General Assembly (*Final Report of the Governor's Blue Ribbon Commission*, 2000, p. 43).

The *Chronicle of Higher Education* on January 20, 1995, reported on significant cuts in higher education funding and especially funding for the State Council of Higher Education that Virginia Governor George Allen had proposed at the time. Though these cuts were controversial, they marked the continuing overall trend in the first half of the 1990s of state reduction of financial support for Virginia colleges and universities while at the same time the state sought greater influence over the activities of colleges and universities. Ideological and political differences in Virginia government resulted in a bitter struggle over the proper role of the state in supporting higher education, as well as the role of the governor in shaping the governance of individual institutions. Davies openly resisted what he saw as an unacceptable politicization of higher education policy in Virginia, and publicly insisted that state officials "leave politics at the door" (1997, p. 8). He urged that shared core values continue to be the driving force in planning, policy, and governance, arguing that "what we need now are governing boards exemplifying the defining values we're trying to protect as higher education changes to meet the needs of an advanced technology based economy" (1997, p. 8). Additionally, he observed, "in the strong Virginia tradition of lay governance, [Board members should] mirror the defining values of an ideal citizenry: involved, enlightened, tolerant, and able to negotiate differences of opinion" (p. 8). He called upon boards to resist efforts to closely control institutions, "playing on the historical American distrust of the professional and managerial classes, board members at both the system and institutional levels may attempt to micromanage, producing a huge amount of friction that inhibits administrators who actually run things from getting their work done. Complex organizations that thrive on ideas can be reduced to shuffling bureaucracies by board micromanagement" (p. 9).

Philosophically, Davies was also consistently opposed to a simplistic human capital formation theory that considered higher education as a private good, as a personal investment in the self that would pay dividends in terms of economic productivity and higher earnings for the individual. He decried this view in 1997, observing that circumstances have "fueled a widely held perception of higher education as a private rather than public good. From a consumer standpoint, it is viewed as a service purchased at high price, with no resulting social or ethical obligation to the recipient. The notion of higher education as a public good, as one of cohesive elements of old society together, is largely discounted today" (p. 6). The move of the state toward providing more financial assistance to students while continuing to underfund institutions was noted critically as not addressing the need for fully providing the base funding for colleges and universities.

The culmination of this divergence of opinion, on one hand represented by Governor Allen and the other represented by SCHEV Director Davies, resulted ultimately in the April 1997 firing of Davies by the State Council of Higher Education. Davies minced no words in commenting on the circumstances. "If you don't believe what you're being told, you micromanage everything. You can't believe your Director, you can't believe your staff." According to the *Chronicle*, "reaction to the Davies decision has been particularly strong because college officials consider him one of the most visionary leaders in academe" (*Chronicle of Higher Education*, May 16, 1997, p. A29).

It would be simplistic to suggest that Gordon Davies's departure from Virginia was somehow the watershed event that irrevocably divorced chaos considerations from planning for higher education in that state. Yet the 1996 and 2000 commission reports intended to guide such planning do seem to illustrate movement away from such guiding principles and attempts to adopt more conventional "command and control" thinking about higher education systems. Davies's ultimate arrival as state higher education executive officer in Kentucky at a time when vision in that state is highly valued may set the stage for ongoing cross state comparisons, if indeed Kentucky adopts a chaos-influenced meta-strategy for long term planning.

## A Planning Vision in the 1990s: The 1996 Report
## of the Commission on the Future of Higher Education

The change in the higher education environment in Virginia was reflected in the 1996 report of the Commission on the Future of Higher Education in Virginia (adopted as Senate Joint Resolution 139, 1996). This report reflected a shift from the philosophical tenor of the earlier commission report. While there was still stated commitment to institutional autonomy, it was invariably linked to assertions that institutions must be efficient and effective, providing uniform, comparable data to the state for accountability purposes, and insisted that autonomy must be coupled with rigorous central coordination. There was discussion of the link between decentralization and accountability. In commenting on the assessment efforts of the 1980s the commission observed that "the Council's primary objective was to promote curricular change and improvement within the institutions, and process has produced notable but spotty results. More important from the standpoint of accountability, results across institutions are not comparable" (p. 22). The call for uniform and specifically comparable data is a particularly noteworthy repudiation of the intentional devolution of authority over choices of assessment measures, policies, and techniques in the 1980s and seemingly inconsistent with the mission-driven effectiveness approach to accreditation developed by the Southern Association of Colleges and Schools in the early 1980s (Aper, 1989). The commission praised performance indicators and descriptive data used to describe characteristics of each institution, arguing that these are the "kinds of things consumers and other stakeholders want to know about colleges and universities" (p. 22). The report called on the institutions to include the results of alumni and employer satisfaction surveys in their annual reports of indicators. They also urged the development and use of "standardized achievement examinations as a way to determine what graduates know and can do after completing baccalaureate or associate degrees" (p. 23). Tied to these recommendations, the commission suggested that SCHEV, the governor, and the legislature develop a plan for assigning "selected colleges and universities greater responsibility for their daily operations and for their long-term development" (p. 23). Even this was tied to a call for SCHEV to help develop a cost accounting procedure that would "enable policymakers to know the actual average annual cost of educating graduate, professional, and undergraduate students" (p. 21).

The report was heavily oriented toward the language of economic productivity, calling upon colleges and universities to "restructure themselves to find ways to teach more students with fewer resources, to streamline administrative operations, and to decide which activity should stay, and which should go" (1996, p. 2). Economic development was emphasized as a primary function of public higher education. Institutions were urged to work "to ensure that the needs of business and industry are clearly identified, that services and resources are in place to address these needs, that the availability of services is clearly communicated to business and industry, and that duplication and unnecessary competitive efforts are avoided" (p. 17). The report highlighted five central points that focused attention specifically on (a) issues of efficiency and effectiveness, and the public perception of both, (b) the financial procedures followed by institutions, (c) the need for additional state support and institutional productivity, (d) the unacceptably high level of tuition charged for undergraduate education, and (e) the close coupling of higher education and economic growth (1996, pp. 3–4).

The report held that teaching and research were "out of balance" in Virginia higher education, emphasizing productivity goals operationalized by "faculty teaching more courses, using technology to reach greater numbers of students, and moving away from traditional classroom formats to encourage students to learn independently and with other students" (p. 6). They urged that technology be considered with regard to "improving instruction, providing access, and avoiding unnecessary duplication" (p. 14). The commission declared support for the concept of academic freedom but denied that tenure was essential either to protecting such freedom or to the quality of higher education. They held that tenure decisions rest "too heavily" on scholarship and recommended that excellent teachers should be granted tenure even if they are not published scholars. At one point they added the interesting comment, "In our view, knowledge is not advanced if it does not reach the student"—apparently disregarding the idea that knowledge may be advanced if it is put into application, published, or otherwise disseminated within the community of researchers, practitioners, or scholars.

The report contained detailed comments on the undesirability of program duplication, a longtime primary function of SCHEV, but the authors appeared oblivious to the fact that the technological applications they urged for allowing professors to serve more students will also make the marketplace for such courses national and even international. SCHEV was, as has repeatedly been the case historically, called upon to take a more aggressive and unilateral approach to the termination of unproductive or low quality programs.

They also commented at length on academic standards, and asked seven specific questions about "what we actually get for our money" that are revealing about the consumerist/economic production approach to public higher education inherent in this and similar reports:

1.  What do students know and what can they do when they leave college?

2.  What kinds of learning experiences do students get for their money?

3.  Do alumni (one group of customers) think their investment in higher education was worthwhile?

4.  Do employers (another group [of customers]) think the alumni they hire are adequately skilled and knowledgeable?

5.  What businesses were helped, saved, or attracted to Virginia by the efforts of colleges and universities?

6.  What is the cost to Virginia taxpayers to do research supported by the federal government and industry?

7.  What are the verifiable benefits to Virginia of the research that is done? (1996, p. 13)

The report made a strong argument for colleges and universities as engines of economic development. They urged each institution to name "a director and of economic advancement to coordinate institutional support of economic development. Each institution should establish or join forces with a regional roundtable of business leaders to identify regional focal industry, identify essential educational support, and report on regional higher education actions required to support economic development" (p. 17).

The commission did "not foresee this plan diminishing in any way the active involvement of the governor and the general assembly in shaping our system of higher education. Rather, we foresee a lessened need and justification for central government to oversee and overrule daily operational transactions of the institutions" (p. 23). They pursued the possibility of institutions becoming "quasi-public" entities, yet later they noted "to further insure coordination the system of higher education, the institutions that might be assigned to the special status would continue to be subject to all other planning, review, and approval procedures of the Council of Higher Education" (p. 24). They outlined what they saw as potential advantages of decentralization: i.e., that people within the institutions would be fully responsible, that the institutions would have added flexibility to adapt, that increased autonomy would result in a greater sense of ownership, and that state government would become smaller as the institutions were assigned quasi-public status, thus "government can be downsized to realize the efficiencies inherent in flexible organizational units responsible for the results they produce" (p. 25).

The commission commented on the role of SCHEV in a manner reminiscent of similar reports in previous decades. After extolling the virtues of quasi-public entities and organizational autonomy they stated that they "want a system that behaves like a system: all of its parts working in harmony toward common objectives with minimal waste and inefficiency" (p. 26), which they then acknowledge "makes conflict inevitable." Later, they note that they "emphatically do not want the Council of Higher Education to do the kind of rigid, top down planning that would put each Virginia college and university into a straightjacket, [however] we think that policymakers would be helped by having a general sense of what probably will happen in the system of higher education in the immediate future" (pp. 26–27). This difficult path between the quest for institutional autonomy and a predictable, accountable, efficient, and productive system has continued to be a serious dilemma of policymaking, as the review of the 2000 *Final Report of the Governor's Blue Ribbon Commission on Higher Education* below will elaborate.

They went on to urge that SCHEV be adequately supported in order to "continue to be an advocate for advanced learning in the Commonwealth" (p. 27), and "should be independent of the interests of the institutions and of all the other interested parties. It should have the statutory authority and political capital to affect institutional behavior so that it serves the needs of the Commonwealth. Its advocacy should be, in the broadest sense, on behalf of the people of Virginia" (p. 27). They go on then to suggest that the Council have the budgetary authority to influence institutional behavior.

The *Report of the Commission on the Future of the University* aimed to provide a mix of prescription and calls for autonomy, of limited traditional planning and of greater power for a central agency to engage in predictive planning and greater control of budgeting and academic programs, of urging support for faculty and calling for limitations on mainstays of faculty life and culture, such as tenure. In all, the report lay the groundwork for the accountability-driven, indicator-based funding recommended by the *Blue Ribbon Commission Report* (2000), and accepted in principle by the Virginia legislature early in 2000 (*Chronicle of Higher Education*, February 4, 2000).

The tenor of the 1996 report, in tandem with the efforts of the governor and legislature to encourage members of boards of visitors (as lay institutional boards are called in Virginia) to insert themselves more aggressively into the day-to-day management of institutions, and the ultimate decree of institutional performance standards that were communicated to the institutions through the campus chief financial officers all communicate clearly that the Commonwealth had moved far from the chaos theory-influenced recommendations of the 1990 Commission report. Virginia had, in effect, in less than a decade retreated from an approach to higher education policy and planning that reflected the most current trends in thought and practice about complex organizations to a more conventional command and control model. The *Report of the Commission on the Future of the University* in many ways reflected a traditionally bureaucratic understanding of systems and organizations, an understanding that compelled its authors to make recommendations aimed at creating, or at least pulling, the correct levers that would result in desired outputs. This relatively simplistic notion of economic production and efficiency—that the aim of public policy is to maximize the ratio of measurable inputs and outputs is evident in the report and events that followed its release.

## To Infinity and Beyond: The 2000 Final Report of the Governor's Blue Ribbon Commission on Higher Education

In February 2000 the latest of the three state commission reports to shape higher education policy and planning in Virginia since 1990 was released. The report contained seventy-three recommendations for public higher education that pressed further in directions suggested by earlier documents, notably the essential role of higher education in workforce and economic development, the paramount priority of undergraduate education (in apparent disregard for the graduate, research/scholarship, and service missions of some institutions), the need for academic accountability to public entities, and most notably, heavy emphasis on the managerial role of the board in governing institutions, and explicit linking of performance indicators to the budgetary process.

The report proposed six-year "performance agreements" that would serve as a kind of contract between each institution and the state for long-term funding. Each institution would negotiate such an agreement, although there is an expectation for the collection of a significant amount of common data intended to provide for comparisons among institutions. The proposed budget process is transactional—if institutions pledge to gather and report on a variety of concrete indicators of performance, and the data indicate success, then the state will, to the extent possible, provide an agreed-upon level of funding for a six-year period. As seen in many states, particularly in elementary and secondary education, the quid pro quo is stable or increased funding in return for increased, standardized data reporting requirements.

Another notable theme in the 2000 report was the repeated emphasis on the role of the institutional boards of visitors in the governance of the colleges and universities. Board members are called upon to require detailed budget information in order to "permit them to assess the cost-effectiveness of particular degree programs, to assess the financial impact of programs over time, and to address other issues bearing on the allocation of resources to the institution's strategic goals and mission-driven priorities" (p. 48). Boards are to be the source of budget requests and must certify that they have "reviewed and considered the request, that the request reflects the priorities the board has established for the institution pursuant to its mission and strategic plan and that the request is endorsed and supported by the board" (p. 48). Further, boards are to review "decisions about what kinds of courses and programs are taught by tenured, contract, or adjunct faculty" (p. 63).

As an interesting and perhaps revealing aside, the beginning of the section on Boards of Visitors noted that "The Governor, General Assembly, institutional administrators, parents, alumni, students, and especially, boards of visitors must all understand the singular role of the governing boards of our institutions" (p. 74). Strangely absent from this list is the faculty, although it seems hard to imagine that it is not important for faculty to understand this role. In fact, virtually the only comment on the role of faculty in governance is a comment that since faculty "are responsible for the learning that occurs in the classroom . . . board members should be interested to know them and their thoughts and opinions on issues that confront the institution" (p. 83). The faculty role appears here to be one of specialized labor rather than one of partnership in the larger life of the institution.

The members of the board, it was emphasized, as appointees of the governor, are in his [or her] stead constitutionally responsible for the "management and operation" of public institutions, suggesting, perhaps, a further extension of the immediate authority of the governor over the day-to-day operation of public institutions of higher education (p. 75). In this report it was the board that was consistently identified as the source of management direction and authority for institutions. Discussion of the role of the president and certainly of the faculty in institutional governance was almost entirely absent, perhaps a troubling observation for advocates of the principle of shared governance on college and university campuses.

It is, however, evident that the authors of this report continued to struggle with the balance between a desire for institutional autonomy and flexibility and potent expectations for control and predictability. It was observed that "State-driven, system-wide policies tend to tie the hand of institutional managers [a term frequently used in the document] and boards of visitors who are best positioned to identify and address institutional priorities" (p. 43). Early in the document they stated that, "At the state level, the impulse to plan and control centrally must be resisted" (p. 8), yet there followed recommendations that appeared to contradict this assertion.

There is some irony in the claim that institutions must be freed from burdensome reporting, since the commission decried such details at the same time they recommended required new processes of very detailed reporting on every program, student achievement and outcomes; comparative institutional measures; a budget negotiation process that involves the campus, executive, legislative, and SCHEV officials; and calls for SCHEV to oversee and report on a large array of data to be collected in the name of accountability. Quality, flexibility, and autonomy were frequently suggested, yet institutions were also to be subject to constant central oversight. Even the elements of what constitute a proper general education core are detailed, almost in the same sentence with pronouncements on the importance of system diversity and institutional missions. This seeming expectation for essential, uniform outcomes again appears to be consistent with aims of recent elementary and secondary policy.

In all, the 2000 report was a blend of traditional thinking about organizations and systems, the amplification of policy themes sounded in Virginia for decades, and a desire to prepare a large and diverse network of colleges and universities for the needs and uncertainties of a new century.

At the time of this writing the ways in which these actions and recommendations will unfold in Virginia remain somewhat uncertain. Higher education in the Commonwealth is emerging from a decade of sometimes severe turbulence in the state higher education policy environment. Governor Jim Gilmore has helped stabilize SCHEV, which is gradually recovering from its turmoil of the 1990s, yet there remains much to do to restore faith in agencies and processes that just a decade ago were seen as jewels in the educational crown of Virginia. Of particular interest to those in higher education may be the appointment in April 2000 of Ms. Phyllis Palmiero as the new director of SCHEV. Palmiero is a former Deputy Director of the Virginia Department of Planning and Budget, and spent her career prior to joining SCHEV primarily as a budget analyst in various capacities in both public and private entities. The SCHEV website (SCHEV, 2000) describes her as

> A driving force for accountability in Virginia higher education, Ms. Palmiero is credited with bringing systemwide performance measurement to Virginia higher education. She also contributed significantly to making performance funding a part of the landscape in Virginia higher education finance. She conceived the Reports of Institutional Effectiveness adopted by the Blue Ribbon Commission on Higher Education which was endorsed by the Governor and General Assembly in the 2000 Session; was the architect behind several proposals which linked enhanced funding to performance results; and was the creator of the Core Performance Measures for Institutions of Higher Education, in place since 1995. (SCHEV, 2000.)

Palmiero has made her mark on Virginia higher education as a strong advocate for linking funding and performance measures. Her finance background and orientation bring to mind Readings' (1996) critical observation that in the current era, educational "accountability is a synonym for accounting" (p. 32), as cost-benefit analyses define educational quality and vague concepts of excellence. Though the now Republican-controlled legislature has indicated general acceptance of a kind of state management of higher education based on strong Boards of Visitors and a tight coupling of performance measures and public funding, it remains somewhat uncertain in its commitment to either the agency or to the performance contract funding for higher education that has been proposed. The conflicting values and philosophies evident in the 2000 Blue Ribbon Commission report may be reflective of the larger uncertainties that continue to shape Virginia's relationship with her colleges and universities.

## Postscript: Planning and Kentucky Higher Education at the Dawn of a New Century

Gordon Davies's departure from Virginia resulted ultimately in his arrival in Kentucky, where under the governorship of Paul Patton the state was poising itself to aim for major improvements in its higher education system and contributions to the well-being of the citizens of the state. After a 1996 report on the state of higher education, the legislature had in 1997 met in special session devoted to higher education reform. Davies came on board to serve as President of the Kentucky Council on Postsecondary Education (KCPE) and give substance to the development of an ambitious and far-reaching plan for public higher education. At the time of this writing, there continues to be a high level of agreement among legislators, Governor Patton, and the KCPE on these plans. The details continue to be a matter of discussion, negotiation, and implementation, with the ongoing creation of a virtual university, the disconnection of the community college system from the University of Kentucky, the creation of eight major trust funds to support public priorities, and other actions intended to enhance the flexibility, access, and autonomy of Kentucky public higher education (Kentucky Council on Postsecondary Education, 1999).

The KCPE during Governor Paul Patton's first term developed a plan called *2020 Vision: An Agenda for the Kentucky System of Postsecondary Education.* One of the things the governor did was to set up a strategic committee on postsecondary education, "bringing together state policy leaders in a Forum to exchange ideas about the future of postsecondary education in Kentucky. Its members, including the governor, legislative leaders, Council members and the Council president, and other representatives, play a pivotal role in assuring that the efforts of postsecondary education system have the long-term support of policymakers and are tied to statewide needs and economic well-being" (Kentucky 2020 vision, 1998, p. 6). The work of the commission, the governor, legislature, and the Council on Postsecondary Education was rooted in basic questions about access, participation, and success for Kentucky students in higher education, support for economic development, and the ongoing improvement and effectiveness of Kentucky institutions of higher education. The questions asked were not terribly different from those asked by similar commissions in Virginia.

Kentucky's planning approaches to higher education have not yet been pressed by economic downturns that might force a decision as to whether the state will be a stern taskmaster or a thoughtful coach for the colleges and universities. In fact, public spending on higher education in Kentucky will increase by over 8 percent in 2000–2001, to just over a billion dollars, and by just over 10 percent again in 2001–2002 to almost 1.15 billion dollars. This near 20 percent increase for the biennial period is the first time in Kentucky history that higher education will receive funding increases of such size in consecutive biennial budgets (*Chronicle Almanac*, 2000b). So far efforts at support and reform in Kentucky have been largely effective and manageable, though not without conflict. Gordon Davies and Paul Patton seem to be consistent in their efforts to reshape Kentucky higher education with a combination of modest restructuring, institutional autonomy, budgetary incentives, partnerships between institutions, business, and government, and the moral suasion that comes with a commitment to harnessing higher education to assuage society's most intractable problems, which in many parts of Kentucky are painfully evident. As one of the guiding questions of the 2020 report asks, "Have our schools, colleges, and universities become nationally respected for their progress and their commitment to helping build better lives for all Kentuckians?" (p. 7). Interestingly, however, at the same time that expectations for Kentucky higher education to contribute to the general welfare have been sharpened, Davies has expressed hope that the number of quality indicators would actually be reduced, while budgetary incentives were enhanced (Davies, 2000).

## A Final, Final Word: How Important Is Budget in Shaping Planning Approaches?

It merits noting that the *Chronicle of Higher Education* on August 6, 1999, reported on a study published by the National Center for Public Policy in Higher Education that presented projected state budget surpluses or deficits by 2008. The report predicts Kentucky with a surplus of 0.5 percent compared to Virginia, with a predicted deficit of 6.8 percent, suggesting foreseeable trends of budget shortfalls for the majority of states, but particularly illustrating a potentially crucial difference in the foreseeable future for the two commonwealths. If this bit of prognostication proves accurate, if state goals and objectives for higher education remain unchanged, and if planning approaches are, in fact, shaped by budgetary exigency, these two states may well continue to demonstrate very different approaches to the relationship between the state and public institutions of higher education. Yet simple fiscal analysis does not account for the major differences in the institutional and state culture and history that shape the dynamics of policy and planning for public higher education. As Davies (2000) has noted, in every state policymakers must be aware of the degree to which approaches to planning from the state level are congruent with the characteristics of the system and the institutions themselves. Thus, though there is apparent isomorphism between state systems of higher education, there are also a host of variables of culture and climate that must be taken into account in any attempt to plan for and to understand the dynamics of higher education in each state.

# References

Aper, J. P. (1989). *The development of student assessment policy in Virginia*. Unpublished dissertation. Virginia Polytechnic Institute & State University, Blacksburg, VA.

Aper, J. P., & Hinkle, D.H. (1991). State policy for assessing student outcomes: A case study with implications for state and institutional authorities. *Journal of Higher Education, 62*(5), 539–555.

Burns, J. M. (1978). *Leadership*. New York: Harper & Row.

*Chronicle of Higher Education Almanac*. (2000a). Nine issues affecting colleges: Roll call of the states, *47*(1), 16.

*Chronicle of Higher Education Almanac*. (2000b). The states: Kentucky, *47*(1), 79–80.

Commonwealth of Virginia. (1990). *Report of the Virginia Commission on the University of the Twenty-First Century*. Richmond: Author.

Commonwealth of Virginia Department of Planning and Budget. (1993, December 1). *Performance Measures Pilot Project*. Richmond: Author.

Commonwealth of Virginia Department of Planning and Budget. (1994, December). *A Strategic Planning and Performance Measurement Proposal for the Commonwealth of Virginia*. Richmond: Author.

Commonwealth of Virginia Senate Document Number 36, Joint Legislative Audit and Review Committee. (1995). *Review of the State Council of Higher Education for Virginia*. Richmond: Author.

Commonwealth of Virginia. (1996). *Report of the Commission on the Future of Higher Education in Virginia*. Richmond: Author.

Commonwealth of Virginia Senate Joint Resolution 139. (1996). *Matching Virginia Higher Education's Strengths with the Commonwealth's Needs*. Richmond: Author.

Commonwealth of Virginia. (2000). *Final report of the governor's blue ribbon commission on higher education*. Richmond: Author.

Crosson, P. H. (1984). State postsecondary education policy systems. *The Review of Higher Education, 7*(2), 125–142.

Cutright, M. (1999, April). *Planning in higher education: A model from chaos theory*. Paper presented at the annual meeting of the American Educational Research Association, Montreal, Quebec.

Davies, G. K. (1997). *Twenty years of higher education in Virginia*. Http://schev.edu.wumedia/gkdltr.html

Davies, G. K. (1998). *The status of Kentucky postsecondary education: Progress toward reform*. Frankfort, KY: Commonwealth of Kentucky, Council on Postsecondary Education.

Davies, G. K. (2000, October 2). Personal communication.

Ewell, P. T., & Boyer, C. M. (1988). Acting out state-mandated assessment: Evidence from five states. *Change, 20*(4), 41–47.

Gleick, J. (1987). *Chaos: Making a new science.* New York: Penguin.

Healy, P. (1997, May 16). Firing of education expert in Virginia raises fears nationwide. *Chronicle of Higher Education,* p. A29.
http://chronicle.com/daily/2000/02/2000020401n.htm

Hebel, S. (1999, May 19). Virginia panel endorses plan for performance-based financing of colleges. *Chronicle of Higher Education,*

Hebel, S. (2000, February 4). Virginia panel calls for colleges to follow 6-year plans, agree to performance goals. *Chronicle of Higher Education,*
Http://chronicle.com/daily/99/05/99051902n.htm

Holland, B. A., & Berdahl, R. O. (1990). *Green carrots: A survey of state use of fiscal incentives for academic quality.* Paper presented at annual meeting of the Association for the Study of Higher Education, Portland, Oregon.

Hoy, W. K., & Miskel, C. G. (1996). *Educational administration: Theory, research, and practice* (5th ed.). New York: McGraw-Hill.

Katz, D., & Kahn, R. L. (1978). *The social psychology of organizations.* New York: Wiley.

Keller, G. (1983). *Academic strategy: The management revolution in American higher education.* Baltimore: Johns Hopkins University Press.

Kentucky Council on Postsecondary Education. (1998, July). 2020 Vision: An agenda for Kentucky's system of postsecondary education.
www.cpe/state/ky/us/issues/2020visn.htm

Kentucky Council on Postsecondary Education. (1999). *1999 Status Report to the Governor and the General Assembly.* www.cpe.state.ky.us/data/accountability/1999StatusRpt. pdf

Kiel, L. D. (1994). *Managing chaos and complexity in government: A new paradigm for managing change, innovation, and organizational renewal.* San Francisco: Jossey-Bass.

Kiel, L. D., & Elliott, E. (Eds.). (1996). *Chaos theory in the social sciences: Foundations and applications.* Ann Arbor: University of Michigan.

Kingdon, J. W. (1984). *Agendas, alternatives, and public policies.* Boston: Little, Brown.

Lively, K. (1995, January 20). U.S. states take a tough line on budgets: Efficiency is watchword as Virginia's governor plans to cut colleges' funds. *Chronicle of Higher Education,* p. A23.

Lorenz, E. (1993). *The essence of chaos.* Seattle: University of Washington.

Mintzberg, H. (1994). *The rise and fall of strategic planning: Reconceiving roles for planning, plans, planners.* New York: Free Press.

Morgan, G. (1997). *Images of organization, (2nd ed.).* Thousand Oaks, CA: Sage.

Newman, I., & Wessinger, C. (1993, Spring). Chaos modeling: An introduction and research application. *Mid-Western Educational Researcher, 6*(2), 2–5.

Prigogine, I., & Stengers, I. (1984). *Order out of chaos.* New York: Bantam.

Readings, B. (1996). *The university in ruins.* Cambridge: Harvard University Press.

Ruelle, D. (1991). *Chance and chaos.* Princeton, NJ: Princeton University Press.

State Council of Higher Education for Virginia. (2000). *Phyllis Palmiero, Executive Director.* www.schev.edu/html/general/bios/bio-palmiero.html

Wheatley, M. J. (1992). *Leadership and the new science: Learning about organizations from an orderly universe.* San Francisco: Berrett-Koehler.

# CHAPTER SEVEN

## Performance Indicators and Chaos Theory
*Bob Barnetson*

### Introduction

It is unclear how performance indicators (PIs) and performance funding in higher education actually affect organizational behavior. For the lack of an alternative, authors most frequently conceptualize PIs and performance funding as affecting goal setting by rewarding previous outcomes—that is, they accept a rational approach to institutional decision making that is consistent with a mechanical metaphor for organizations (Barnetson, 2000). This chapter develops an alternative way to conceptualize how PIs and performance funding affect organizational behavior based upon the notion that PIs are conceptual technologies that shape what issues we think about and how we think about those issues. This approach draws upon chaos theory-derived metaphors to explain organizational behavior.

This chapter begins by describing performance indicators and performance funding. Subsequently, it examines the way in which most authors think about their effect on organizational functioning and the metaphors and beliefs that legitimate this approach. It is important to explore these metaphors and beliefs because they shape what we believe to be the nature of the world and that, in turn, shapes the policies we implement. Once we have these most basic assumptions on the table, this chapter posits an alternative set of beliefs about the nature of the world that support chaos theory-derived metaphors for organizations. These, in turn, legitimate the notion that PIs function as conceptual technologies. Finally, this chapter discusses the implications of PIs for chaos-driven organizations.

### Contemporary Approaches to PIs and Performance Funding

Cave, Hanney, Henkel, and Kogan (1997) classify indicators as simple, general, and performance. Simple indicators provide a neutral description of a phenomenon or activity (e.g., overall institutional enrollment). General indicators provide data unrelated to goals such as assessing students' perceptions of how enrollment affects the feeling of community on campus. Performance indicators possess a point of reference or goal against which an institution's performance is compared. For example, if an institution is mandated to increase its enrollment each year, the percentage change in enrollment would be a *performance indicator* because it contains a point of reference or goal against which a performance can be compared.

North American governments commonly implement PIs at a state or provincial level (Burke & Serban, 1999). Frequently, a series of PIs will be developed and funding allocated based upon an institution's performance on them. For example, Tennessee has linked institutional funding to performance indicator scores since the late 1970s (Banta, Rudolph, Van Dyke, & Fisher, 1996). Proponents of performance funding argue that allocating a small portion of institutions' funding based upon PI results can propel institutions to address government priorities without introducing damaging instability in funding (Bateman & Elliott, 1994). The literature is largely silent as to how PIs and performance funding affect institutional behavior. Those authors who discuss this issue usually adopt (implicitly or explicitly) a rational model of organizational functioning (Barnetson, 2000). That is, they assume that PIs and performance funding affect institutional goal setting by rewarding and/or punishing earlier outcomes and, subsequently, altering future behavior and outcomes (Boberg & Barnetson, 2000). Surprisingly, there is little evidence that this is how PIs and performance funding work. The expectation that PIs and performance funding affect institutional behavior in a rational manner stems from the widespread acceptance of goal-based metaphors for organizations and is legitimated by western beliefs about human nature and the nature of the world (cf. Barnetson, 2000).

## Common Organizational Metaphors and Beliefs

As outlined by Cutright in chapter 1, the mechanical metaphor is frequently invoked to describe organizations. Another common metaphor is the organization as a political system. Thinking about organizations as machines or as political systems is premised upon organizations being goal-driven. The *mechanical metaphor* assumes organizations operate based upon orderly relations between clearly defined components. This arrangement yields predictable operations facilitating the achievement of a clear goal (Morgan,

1997). Organizational stability stems from a hierarchy of authority and control that prevents deviant behavior. The *political metaphor* also assumes that organizational behavior is goal-driven as actors within the organization pursue their own goals (Birnbaum, 1988). Organizations remain stable because coalitions dominate organizations.

Both of these metaphors legitimate the use of PIs and performance funding to monitor and manipulate organizational activities. If organizations operate to some degree like machines, then it is possible for governments to evaluate and manipulate organizational behavior to achieve social goals. And, if organizations operate to some degree like political systems, it is necessary for governments to monitor organizational outcomes to ensure that internal interests are not being pursued at the expense of desired social outcomes. These metaphors also assume decision making is rational—that is, that decision makers act to achieve goals.

Our beliefs about the *nature of the world* legitimate the organizational metaphors we use. For example, the mechanical metaphor assumes that tight control over organizational components is necessary to prevent the system from breaking down. The belief that systems will eventually break down is consistent with western religious and scientific traditions. Newtonian science suggests that order is inevitably eroded by change and, over time, systems move toward complete disorder (i.e., entropy) (Halliday & Resnick, 1988). Western religions posit a similar dialectic process of truth conflicting with evil and culminating in the end of existence (Brooke, 1991; Woodcock, 1992). Delaying this inevitable decay requires control over organizational processes like that which we can exercise over the processes of machines.

Our beliefs about *human nature* also legitimate the organizational metaphors we use. The political metaphor suggests that we act in our own interests and frequently this will be at the expense of organizational goals. This metaphor finds support in the broadly accepted notion that humans are inherently self-interested and, ergo, competitive. This belief underlies ideologies such as Liberalism and Conservativism and is supported by appeals to Darwinesque notions of survival of the fittest (Pratt, 1998; Gibbins & Youngman, 1996). Preventing private interests from subverting the public interest sanctions government intervention.

## Alternative Beliefs and Metaphors

How we conceptualize the nature of the world affects the organizational metaphors we use to guide our actions in it. Traditional scientific thinking is now giving way to more complex models of the world. For example, chaos theory suggests order is an inherent aspect of systems as they shape and reshape themselves in order to facilitate their primary purpose. The patterns and boundaries of these systems are caused by attractors. *Attractors* are elements in a system with drawing or organizational power. The presence of multiple attractors establishes the boundaries of a system but also result in unstable and complex behavior (Capra, 1996).

For example, attractors such as topography, geology, weather patterns and previous behavior bound (but don't necessarily determine) the behavior of rivers. Tectonic changes can alter these attractors and this, in turn, alters the range of behaviors that the river can exhibit as it moves water to a lower point. In this way, attractors give chaotic systems the quality of self-organization—that is, the ability to recreate order and pattern (at least temporarily) despite continuous adjustments caused by internal and external shocks to the system—necessary so that systems can achieve their purpose.

Despite the power of attractors to self-organize systems, even small changes in the system or the attractors can result in significant and unpredictable results and linear extrapolations of current trends into the future that may be unreliable. This instability is a result of systems behaving in a nonlinear way. This occurs because a system's behavior feeds back upon itself and modifies the system's pattern. This suggests that causal relationships will be more complex in chaos theory-derived organizations metaphors than in the mechanical metaphor because effect often becomes or reinforces cause (Wheatley, 1992)

The beliefs we hold about human nature also affect our way of thinking about organizations and their management. The argument that evolution has made humans inherently competitive (i.e., survival of the fittest) ignores that survival is a function of adaptation to circumstances so as to facilitate proliferation. Competition and confrontation is not necessarily the best strategy to pass on one's genetic heritage (Fisher, 1982). As noted by evolutionary psychologists, the most successful survival strategy is a social one: cooperation is a more efficient and effective way to ensure the reproduction than is competition (Wright, 1994). Society itself—a social arrangement depending exclusively on cooperation—is the most obvious evidence that human nature isn't unavoidably competitive (Kohn, 1992).

This suggests that premising organizational management upon the notion that people are unvaryingly selfish may be flawed.

## Alternative Ways to Think About Organizations

If we make different assumptions about human nature and the nature of the world, it becomes possible to think about how organizations operate in different ways. For example, the *cybernetic organization* suggests organizations monitor the environment, relate that information to their operating norms and, recognizing significant deviations, initiate action in order to avoid undesirable states—perhaps by altering organizational activity, structure, or goals (Morgan, 1997; Birnbaum, 1988). This approach suggests that organizations may develop short-term goals during the process of acting and that order evolves in order to maintain the system's basic integrity.

Managing cybernetic organizations focuses on setting reference points and core values (i.e., recognizing organizational attractors) and allowing order to emerge from the process (often through experimentation and learning from failure). Effective organizations are able to question these reference points. The strength of this model is its recognition that organizations can self-regulate with the goal of avoiding undesirable states. The cybernetic model, however, presents a limited picture of the issues of power and control that often impede self-organization and monitoring. This weakness stems from the aggregate and conscious nature of social organizations as compared to the unity of function and reactionary nature of organic systems. Further, the cybernetic model also requires a degree of self-evaluation and self-discipline that is not commonly found in traditional organizations. This is advocated for, however, in learning organizations (cf. Senge, 1990; Watkins & Marsick, 1993).

Such process-based models explain the paradox of higher education as poorly managed and highly effective: loosely coupled organizations (where management control is weak) perform well because the operational components possess the flexibility necessary to adapt to changing environments (Birnbaum, 1988; Weick, 1976). Loosely coupled systems also allow the organization to manage conflicting goals by creating relatively isolated solutions to problems. While each component of an organization has the capacity to act autonomously, the pressure placed upon each unit to integrate its actions into the needs and constraints of the larger organization of which it is a part. If order emerges spontaneously and if form changes to facilitate the pursuit of organizational purpose(s), then it is not necessary to summatively monitor institutions: fluctuations signify organizational evolution rather than decay.

## Performance Indicators as Conceptual Technologies

The ideas that organizational behavior is significantly influenced by feedback and bounded by attractors differs significantly from the notion of an organization as a machine with stable and predictable ways of operating. This new way of thinking about organizations suggests that PIs and performance funding may affect organizations in a manner different than is generally assumed—perhaps influencing the attractors that are so important in patterning organizational behavior.

Barnetson and Cutright (2000) argue that PIs are *conceptual technologies* that shape what issues we think about and how we think about those issues by embedding normative assumptions into the selection and structure of PIs. Performance indicators shape *what* issue we think about by focusing our attention on specific aspects of institutional performance. For example, a PI measuring graduates' employment rates indicates that this outcome is of importance to the government. Performance indicators also shape *how* we think about an issue. They do this by specifying how the concept will be quantified and, thus, operationalize the concept (Dochy, Segers, & Wijen, 1990). For example, one might assess a system's accessibility through PIs that measure the number of student seats available. This ignores that accessibility is predicated upon both (a) the availability of seats and (b) the ability of students to afford educational costs. By excluding a PI that assesses the affordability of tuition, the government shapes public perception of an issue so as to exclude affordability from discussions of accessibility. Consequently, the use of PIs affects how institutions and policies are evaluated because the power to delineate what evidence is considered relevant is shifted to those who create and control PI-driven systems.

Framing PIs as explicitly political tools designed to shape perception (and, ultimately behavior) through embedding normative assumptions in the selection and structure of indicators differs substantially from the prevailing belief that PIs are objective assessments of outcomes. Barnetson and Cutright (2000) assert that there are six types of normative assumptions that can be embedded in performance indicators. These assumptions are outlined in Table 1.

**Table 1.** Typology of embedded assumptions

| *Type* | *Explanation* |
|---|---|
| Value: | The act of measurement delineates what activity or outcome is valued. That is, the inclusion or exclusion of PIs determines what is considered important and unimportant. |
| Definition: | Performance indicators (re)define concepts (e.g., accessibility, affordability, quality, etc.) by operationalizing them in measurable terms. |
| Goal: | Performance indicators differ from simple indicators because they include a point of reference by which a performance is judged. Performance indicators assign goals through both the value embedded in an indicator and the point of reference used in the indicator. |
| Causality: | Performance indicators assign responsibility for an activity or outcome by embedding an assumption of causality. This may confuse causality (i.e., one variable causing a second) with association (i.e., where two variables occur together as a result of a third variable) and assert that institutional activities play a determinant role in generating the performance assessed. |
| Comparability: | The use of common PIs assumes institutions (departments, individuals, etc.) are comparable. This may pressure institutions to generate common outcomes or undertake common activities which may or may not be appropriate given institutional circumstances and mission. |
| Normalcy: | Performance indicators delineate a range of normal behaviors or outcomes. This may pressure institutions to alter their activities so as to decrease a systemic disadvantage or increase a systemic advantage. |

By making explicit the assumptions embedded in a series of PIs, it becomes possible to understand the broader policy agenda that underlies the PIs and, subsequently, to knowledgeably approve of, alter, or critically challenge their implementation. This is important because the use of PIs shifts the power to set priorities and goals to those who create and control these documentary decision-making systems (Newson, 1994). That is, when PIs act as conceptual technologies, they provide a means for those outside of higher education to influence the organizational attractors that pattern a system. The importance of these attractors suggests that attempting to influence them can have significant (but unpredictable) results.

## Performance Indicators and Chaos-Derived Metaphors

Performance indicators and performance funding are paradoxical: while their use has little ability to affect organizational behavior in the short-term, they can substantially and fundamentally change higher education over the long-term. This paradox emerges when we answer two questions: (1) how do PIs affect organizational behavior? and (2) what impact can they have in the short- and long-term?

### How Do PIs Affect Organizational Behavior?

Attractors are an important determinate of systems' boundaries and patterns. If PIs and performance funding alter organizational behavior, it seems likely that they interact in some manner with these attractors. As discussed above, they do this by shaping what issues we think about and how we think about those issues. The impact of interaction may manifest itself in two ways: PIs may create/strengthen attractors or PIs may suppress existing attractors.

In chaos-derived metaphors, organizational behavior is shaped by attractors such as the environment, important values, and resource availability. The introduction of PIs may alter organizational behavior by, for example, increasing the strength of one value relative to another or introducing an entirely new attractor. If PIs operate by creating or strengthening attractors, linking a PI to funding may further reinforce the strength of the attractor. For example, a college's purpose may be to teach students. The way it organizes instruction and develops curriculum may be guided by key values (i.e., attractors) such as preparing students equally for employment and to be good citizens. The introduction of a PI measuring employment rates of graduates may increase the strength of the "employment outcomes" attractor (by shaping what issues faculty think about and how they think about those issues) and, therefore, cause a relative de-emphasis of activities that prepare students to be good citizens.

A second way in which to think about how PIs affect organizational behavior is that they may artificially constrain the natural behavior of an organization by acting as rules. Rules differ from attractors. Attractors tend to be few in number, are internal to the system, and have power beyond their initial articulation or origin. Rules are external constraints imposed upon a system that are introduced by playing down the importance we ascribe to a particular behavior or altering how we think about it. Because rules frustrate the natural behavior of a system, they lead to resistance and/or minimal compliance. For example, many universities espouse the importance of teaching, spend substantial amounts of money to improve instructional quality, and may even implement (or have imposed upon them) PIs that measure and reward instructional quality. The frequent failure of such systems to significantly affect behavior change beyond initial and minimal compliance stems from the attractors in universities that link professional prestige and tenure to research activity. In this case, individual actors continue to pattern their behavior based upon the system's attractors while demonstrating minimal compliance with new rules. This dynamic is an example of how difficult it is to thwart the drawing power of natural attractors through the imposition of rules.

It is conceivable that PIs and performance funding can operate in both of these manners. For example, a government may seek to curtail activity in some spheres while increasing it in others through the introduction of PIs that constrain and encourage respectively. In the absence of research about which way PI-driven systems most often operate, I would conjecture that PI-driven systems are primarily constraining (i.e., act as rules). I say this because, in the short timelines of most government policies, it is easier to constrain existing behavior (by making its outcomes less appealing via performance funding) than it is to encourage institutions to increase the level of existing behavior (through inducements). Similarly, it is easier to encourage existing behavior through inducements than it is to encourage people to undertake entirely new activities. That is to say, it is easier to act upon an existing attractor than to introduce new ones.

## The Long- and Short-Term Impact of PIs on Organizations

If PIs act to constrain in the short-term, then institutions will most likely engage in compliance behavior (i.e., minimal observance and lip service). But it is important to remember the nonlinear nature of organizations in chaos theory-derived metaphors and the implications this has for the long-term impact of PI systems. Metaphorically speaking, long-term constraint by PIs may poison the environment that gave rise to the existing pattern of organizational behavior. As resource dependence theory suggests, if some behavior is no longer rewarded and rewards for new behavior are available, then institutions will change their behavior in order to maintain the flow of resources (Pfeffer, 1992; Pfeffer & Salancik, 1978). This is consistent with Capra's (1996) suggestion that systems remain stable until (a) they grow too complex for the environment to sustain or (b) their environment changes in a way that no longer sustains them.

The nonlinear nature of organizations makes it difficult to predict how or when institutions will react to this sort of feedback. It may be that actors within the organization will resist the change (at least initially) and a PI-driven system will have no immediate impact on organizational behavior. Over time, however, political, moral, and/or financial pressure may build until a bifurcation point is reached and a substantial change in structure, personnel, and/or programming occurs as the system attempts to a achieve new order that is sustainable in the new environment. That is to say, while institutions may not immediately or consciously change their behavior, PI-systems may make one pattern of action (e.g., focusing on vocational programming) more acceptable or possible. Over time, the accumulation of incremental changes may effect a substantial change in institutional behavior—so much so that, in effect, the basic attractors of an institution may change. How this change manifests itself in organizational structure and purpose, though, may be difficult to predict.

### The Utility of PIs

As explored above, the use of PIs and performance funding may result in changes to organizational behavior but those changes may be difficult to predict. Performance indicators may, however, be useful as a planning tool. Cutright's (1997) summary of chaos theory as applied to higher education planning suggests long-term predictability is elusive; therefore, the outcome of planning should not be a plan, but rather planning. Flexible and detail-free strategic planning leads to the development and execution of operational plans as needed. In this approach, PIs can be used to monitor the environment (i.e., act as tin-openers) and trigger an examination of an issue whenever a PI indicates an anomaly. Recognizing anomalies and engaging them means institutions are better able to adapt to their environment. This approach also takes advantage of the efficient way in which PIs can be used to simplify large amounts of data.

Cutright also suggests that the widest possible universe of information should be made available to all members of an institution in order for the institution to recognize and adapt to environmental changes. When PIs act as conceptual technologies, they constrict information flow by designating what data will be collected and how it will be interpreted. This goal is achieved by quantifying data, thereby decreasing the importance of context and limited institutions' ability to infer causality. Performance indicators also constrict information flow by embedding assumptions about goals, values, definitions, causality, normalcy, and comparability into the structure and selection of indicators. This reduces organizational conflict over interpretation. Reducing conflict is not necessarily healthy because organizational turbulence (debate over mission, environmental pressure, appropriate responses, etc.) signals that an organization is actively engaging its environment. Suppressing organizational turbulence through domination or compromise delays dealing with turbulence until the threat it poses to an organization reaches a higher level. This suggests that imposing conceptual agreement and rewarding only success may reduce the utility of PIs in planning by stifling the experimentation that leads to adaptation and innovation. This stems from the mechanistic notion that deviation and failure represent systemic decay and, therefore, must be prevented.

Performance indicators may also be useful to those seeking to influence planning because they may telescope the policy agenda of those who create them. For example, Atkinson-Grosjean and Grosjean's (2000) survey of performance funding in the United States, the United Kingdom, Australia, New Zealand, the Netherlands, and Sweden notes that the systems tend to focus on efficiency, centralize management, and ignore traditional social or moral imperatives. This focus on the quantifiable (often utilitarian or instrumental) aspects raises fears that the intrinsic values of education may be lost. Determining what assumptions are embedded in the selection and structure of the indicators (as demonstrated in Barnetson & Cutright, 2000), make it possible to oppose indicators that run contrary to the basic attractors of higher education. In this way, PIs act as tin-openers for organizations by placing government policy objectives in the open for examination. This, in turn, allows institutions to consciously react to (and possibly mitigate) this agenda. This provides a way to reduce the possibility of long-term changes (caused by PI-driven systems) that are antithetical to the values of higher education.

## Conclusion

The notion that PIs and performance funding affect postsecondary institutions in a rational manner has wide currency in the higher education literature. This chapter posited an alternative way to think about the impact of PI-driven systems on organizations by drawing upon chaos theory-derived organizational metaphors. Instead of altering goals in a Pavlovian manner, PIs operate as conceptual technologies. That is, they shape what issue we think about and how we think about those issues and in doing so, have the power to substantially alter the attractors that pattern organizational behavior. This chapter also suggests that PI-driven systems most often act to constrain attractors (i.e., act as rules). The nonlinear nature of systems means that this can unpredictably destabilize the systems created by attractors and cause organizations to change in order to regain stability. As suggested by Atkinson-Grosjean and Grosjean (2000), frequently the systems that emerge from this change ignore traditional social and moral imperatives of higher education. By being aware of the impact that PIs can have when they act as conceptual technologies, academics can better resist this erosion of their values.

# References

Atkinson-Grosjean, J., & Grosjean, G. (2000). The use of performance models in higher education: A comparative international review. *Education Policy Analysis Archives.* 8 (30). Available online at http://epaa.asu.edu.

Banta, T. W., Rudolph, L. B., Van Dyke, J., & Fisher, H. S. (1996). Performance funding comes of age in Tennessee. *Journal of Higher Education, 67*(1), 23–45.

Barnetson, B. (2000). The metaphors and beliefs underlying performance funding. Unpublished paper.

Barnetson, B., & Cutright, M. (2000). Performance indicators as conceptual technologies. *Higher Education, 40*(3), 277–292.

Bateman, M., & Elliott, R.W. (1994). An attempt to implement performance-based funding in Texas higher education: A case study. In R. M. Epper (Ed.), *Focus on the budget: Rethinking current practice, state policy and college learning.* Denver: Education Commission of the States. 41–52. ERIC Document Reproduction Service. ED 375 790.

Birnbaum, R. (1988). *How colleges work: The cybernetics of academic organizations and leadership.* San Francisco: Jossey-Bass.

Boberg, A., & Barnetson, B. (2000). System-wide program assessment with performance indicators: Alberta's performance funding mechanism. *Canadian Journal of Program Evaluation.* Special Issue, pp. 3–23.

Brooke, J. H. (1991). *Science and religion: Some historical perspectives.* New York: Cambridge University Press.

Burke, J. C., & Serban, A. M. (eds.). (1999). Performance funding for public higher education: Fad or trend? *New Directions for Higher Education, 97.*

Capra, F. (1996). *The web of life: A new scientific understanding of living systems.* Toronto: Anchor.

Cave, M., Hanney, S., Henkel, M., & Kogan, M. (1997). *The use of performance indicators in higher education: The challenges of the quality movement* (3rd ed.). London: Jessica Kingsely.

Cutright, M. (1997). Planning in higher education and chaos theory: A model, a method. Paper presented at Education Policy Research Conference. March 15. Oxford, England.

Dochy, F. J. R. C., Segers, M. S. P., & Wijnen, W. H. F. W. (1990). *Management information and performance indicators in higher education: An international issue.* Netherlands: Van Gorcum.

Fisher, H. E. (1982). *The sex contract: The evolution of human behavior.* New York: Quill.

Gibbins, R., & Youngman, L. (1996). *Mindscapes: Political ideologies towards the 21st century.* Toronto: McGraw-Hill.

Halliday, D., & Resnick, R. (1988). *Fundamentals of physics* (3rd ed.). Toronto: John Wiley & Sons.

Kohn, A. (1992). *No contest: The case against competition* (2nd ed.). Boston: Houghton Mifflin.

Morgan, G. (1997). *Images of organizations* (2nd ed.). London: Sage.

Newson, J. A. (1994). Subordinating democracy: The effects of fiscal retrenchment and university-business partnerships on knowledge creation and knowledge dissemination in universities. *Higher Education, 27,* pp. 141–161.

Pfeffer, J. (1992). *Managing with power: Politics and influence in organizations.* Boston: Harvard Business School Press.

Pfeffer, J., & Salancik, G. R. (1978). *The external control of organizations: A resource dependence perspective.* New York: Harper & Row.

Pratt, A. (1998). Neoliberalism and social policy. In M. Lavalette & A. Pratt (Eds.), *Social policy: A conceptual and theoretical introduction,* pp. 31–99. Thousand Oaks, CA: Sage.

Senge, P. M. (1990). *The fifth discipline: The art and practice of the learning organization.* Toronto: Double Day.

Watkins, K. E., & Marsick, V. J. (1993). Sculpting the learning organization: Lessons in the art and science of systematic change. San Francisco: Jossey-Bass.

Weick, K. (1976). Educational organizations and loosely coupled systems. *Administrative science quarterly, 21*(2), 1–19.

Wheatley, M. J. (1991). *Leadership and the new science: Learning about organizations from an orderly universe.* San Francisco: Berrett-Koehler.

Woodcock, G. (1992). *The monk and his message: Undermining the myth of history.* Vancouver: Douglas and McIntyre.

Wright, R. (1994). *The moral animal: Why we are the way we are.* New York: Vintage.

# CHAPTER EIGHT

## The Impact of Technology and Student Choice on Postsecondary Education: *Plus Ça Change . . .*

*Adrian Kershaw and Susan Safford*

### Introduction

Two significant and interacting phenomena impinge on higher education in the early twenty-first century. The first is the ubiquitous availability of online learning opportunities, opportunities that can free learners from the time and place constraints of traditional face-to-face instruction. The second phenomenon is the increasing tendency for students to act as consumers, picking and choosing programs, courses, and institutions to meet their needs and to fit their particular constraints at their own convenience. These two dynamics serve to turn the context in which higher education operates on its head. Hitherto, postsecondary institutions largely set the curriculum and content of learning and then students were invited to the party—but only if they followed the learning dress code!

Nowadays, many students shop around for courses that meet their needs for content, skills development potential, timing, and delivery format. Essentially, learners are inviting institutions to *their* party, setting the rules in terms of delivery and content according to their own idiosyncratic needs. They are also developing expectations about how organizations like ours should be using information and communications technologies to provide them with services.

This new environment is dynamic and challenging for institutions attempting to plan the future. To accommodate to the flux in demand patterns of the new learner/consumer, universities and colleges can look to chaos theory for clues as to how to plan for teaching and learning and for student services in a technology-mediated environment. In particular, they can find new patterns emerging from changing enrollment behavior of students, private/public and public/public partnerships, from new kinds of services, and from new administrative systems.

## The Student as Consumer

Typically, the pace of change in our institutions has been glacial. Our quality assurance systems, governance structures, budget development processes, and curriculum approval processes usually are characterized by significant lag time between the input of new ideas and the transformation of those new ideas into policy, curriculum, and service. So long as the input/output budget of new ideas balanced the rate at which our old ideas and practices melted away, our institutions have stayed in rough equilibrium with our environment. However, we are now in the midst of very rapid changes, changes that will cause institutions to worry about the future.

These changes are brought about by a number of significant, interrelated phenomena:

1. The emergence of information technology as the principal driver of economic activity in advanced economies.

2. A relative decrease in that portion of the costs of postsecondary education which is covered by government.

3. The marriage of information technology to teaching and learning.

4. Work environments that are increasingly complex and competitive and that require employees to engage in perpetual learning.

While these phenomena are by no means all of the issues with which higher education is struggling, they do resolve themselves into three significant shifts in the environment for colleges and universities. First, there has been a relative shift in the burden of financing higher education from government to the student. In most advanced countries, students are having to bear a larger portion of the costs of their educational opportunity than was the case in the past. This has meant that most students find it necessary to work as well as study. Second, because of the marriage of information technology to teaching and learning it is now possible for working students to take courses online, and at times and places that fit their schedule. This means that students are better able to juggle the responsibilities of university or college life with employment, in more effective and flexible ways than in the past. Finally, many of us attempt to manage personal and work lives driven by fifty-hour workweeks—often for multiple employers. Whatever the nature of the multiple and extensive demands on our time, we still need to keep our skills and knowledge current and we look to postsecondary courses and programs to meet those needs. The advent of technology-mediated teaching and learning has meant that we have a better chance of ordering our lives so as to provide a balance between work, play, and study.

Because of the high cost of postsecondary education and the frequent need to balance work with study and play, students have come to act more as consumers and less as passive recipients of institutional services and programs. At the undergraduate level, many students are now choosing to take a mix of online and face-to-face courses. Freed from the requirement to be in a face-to-face classroom for a significant portion of the week, they can be gainfully employed and still complete a full program of studies. In British Columbia, the role of "student-as-consumer" is played out against the backdrop of a robust transfer system at the first- and second-year levels. It is now commonplace for students to be enrolled in a degree program at one institution and to be taking one or two online courses from another. The driver for this behavior is convenience, supported by a province-wide formal transfer system that provides academic quality assurance.

But note that the undergraduate student is behaving as a consumer in the face of a limited number of choices. She has already made the commitment to a particular program of studies but is choosing to structure those studies in ways that are convenient to her. In the past, there were two options available to a student who chose, or needed, to work to finance her way through university or college. The first was to shoehorn whatever work she could manage into her full-time studies. The second was to elongate her program of studies by taking less than a full load of courses each semester. Nowadays, there are growing opportunities for a student to take a full program of studies and still maintain significant employment. However, students are still constrained by the form and structure of the program in which they are enrolled. This is not the case for those individuals who are employed full time and who are seeking professional or academic advancement by attending a postsecondary institution.

The size of this latter group will only grow as the predicted "post-boomer" shortage of workers at all levels will encourage students to blend study with well paid employment. However, thanks to the marriage of information and communications technology with teaching and learning, this group of students has—and will have—a wide range of opportunities, opportunities that are not constrained by the friction of distance or time. Given the realities of online learning, working students are often making choices in the context of a large, differentiated marketplace. They can shop around for the course or program that best meets their needs at the price they wish to pay. It is these behaviors that have led many in academia to be concerned about "diploma mills" and to rail against the notion of "student-as-consumer." Indeed, the mere mention of this last notion is almost guaranteed to raise the hackles of most academics and to drive many to extended fulminations concerning slippery slopes to low standards, tawdry dealings, and academic hucksterism. Nevertheless, students *are* beginning to act more like consumers and to view themselves as the customers of institutions. They are, however, consumers with expectations about the quality of what they purchase, about its thoroughness and reliability, and—particularly if it is an expensive good or service—its ability to continue to confer a benefit over long periods of time. As consumers of postsecondary education, most students (and especially those who are seeking professional upgrading) are aware that they are purchasing the opportunity to learn new things and/or to develop new skills that, they hope and trust, will confer a benefit upon them—be that economic, cultural, or intellectual. They are also purchasing the reputational assets of the institution whose courses or programs they are taking.

These reputational assets have value to the prospective learner. They are built upon the history and tradition of the institution and upon perceptions of the institution's quality assurance mechanisms. In significant measure, the value of the credential or other record of learning that the student is selecting is dependent upon the reputation of the issuing institution. The achievement of whatever the student seeks—employment opportunity, professional advancement, personal satisfaction, or some combination of these—will be determined in the first instance by what the wider community and the student himself believe about the quality of the institution. Added to this mix is the prospective learner's assessment of the value he or she is likely to derive from the curriculum. Does it match their personal and/or professional needs? What kinds of trade-offs are there between the amount of redundant material in the course or program and the material that is relevant to their needs? Are the opportunity costs associated with taking the course of study too high? Is there value for money? All these are questions that were always there in the past, but prospective learners had limited choice, often dictated by geography, and nearly always constrained by what their institution of choice had to offer.

For the consumer of the past it was "take it or leave it." Nowadays, that is changing.

As we suggest above, institutions bring considerable value to the customer/supplier relationship. They are not, nor should they be, driven by customer demands to the extent that they turn into diploma mills, dispensing matchbook credentials. Slavish response to the specific needs of "student-as-customer" is in the long-term interests of neither the institution nor the student. Apart from a few students who may choose to accept paper over substance, most have no desire for poor quality credentials. As consumers, students seek value for the money they spend on their education and for the time and effort they put into their studies. However, universities and colleges need to recognize that the climate in which they operate has changed and that there is a need to respond to a context in which prospective students have a much greater degree of choice.

Then how do we plan in an environment characterized by rapidly changing demand patterns, and at the same time maintain the academic standards and rigor that give value to our activity? Chaos theory gives us clues, in particular through the use of the notion of strange attractors. As we've suggested elsewhere, "student demand patterns at individual institutions will surge and recede, driven by program reputation, by public perception of employment opportunities conferred by training or education, by economic conditions, and by what is seen as being 'hot' at the moment" (Kershaw & Safford, 1998, p. 292). The trick is to develop systems and ways of planning and thinking about institutional activities that enable short-term planning and reaction to emergent demands to be coupled with the long-term development and support of disciplines and quality assurance systems.

One way of thinking about this is to conceive of technology-mediated curricula and their associated service delivery from the perspective of evolutionary theory. The traditional Darwinian view of evolution is one of slow but steady change driven by selective development of genetic variations that enable organisms to be more effective or efficient in interactions with their environment. This Darwinian, evolutionary change, marks most institutions. A slow, measured rate of change is the bedrock of the reputation and quality assurance mechanisms in most institutions. In times when the rate of change in the external environment was relatively slow, this evolutionary approach to change was sufficient to keep pace, for the most part, with changing demand patterns. Nowadays, however, that sufficiency no longer applies. While it is highly desirable to maintain that Darwinian rate of change in order to protect the mechanisms that support the reputational assets of institutions, the rate of this change must be increased somewhat to reflect the impact of the knowledge revolution and globalization, forces that appear to be accelerating change rates in the environment external to the academy. At the same time, we suggest that we must look to other models of change that are situational and revolutionary and that are reflective of the sudden and often unforeseen changes that are characteristic of chaotic systems. Again from evolutionary theory, the notion of "punctuated equilibrium" is a useful model here.

Eldredge and Gould's (1972) theory of punctuated equilibrium points to the extremely rapid, and seemingly spontaneous, emergence of new species from within the backdrop of the slower Darwinian model of evolutionary change. The new life forms are often revolutionary in their morphology and life habits. These rapid evolutionary shifts are analogous to tips into chaos in certain sections of the Darwinian record. It has become clear that the evolutionary record does not involve an "either/or" dichotomy. It seems that both Darwinian and punctuated equilibrium can exist at the same time. This "both/and" situation fits well with the realities faced by most contemporary postsecondary institutions: our educational and service plans must be both evolutionary in nature and yet capable of undergoing rapid revolution in certain areas.

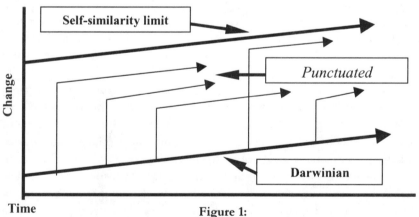

**Figure 1:**
**An evolutionary view of change in postsecondary institutions**

As Figure 1 suggests, in the academic environment the punctuated/chaotic evolutionary events eventually settle down and parallel the Darwinian development patterns as they become subject to the inherited values and mores of the institution and its governance structures.[1] This mirrors the self-similarities found in successive layers of a Mandelbrot set–computer generated fractal images reflective of natural phenomena that are apparently chaotic but that display repetitive patterns. It does not reflect the truly chaotic picture depicted in the more lurid and apocalyptic foretelling of institutional futures suggested by such writers as Drucker (2000) and Scott (1999). This view would have the punctuated equilibrium elements flying off in different directions with no underlying order being conferred by strange attractors.

The self-similarity of fractals suggests the existence of a meta-dynamic that is supportive of the Darwinian view of change in institutions. This fundamental dynamic is driven by the inherited values of our universities and colleges and it leads us to be optimistic about the future of most institutions. It also leads us to disagree with those who talk of the imminent demise of the university/college system as we know it. Provided institutions retain an external orientation, change with the structural shifts of the society, and adjust to the rapid situational shifts that occur in certain areas of the economy, they can remain in equilibrium with their environment. This requires that institutions retain their traditional commitment to scholarship, research, and teaching and to their civic responsibilities but, at the same time, develop mechanisms that enable rapid response to episodes of seemingly chaotic change occurring in particular, defined contexts.

In chaos theory terms, one of the adjustments that universities and colleges must make is to develop means by which strange attractors can be identified and appropriate changes made that reflect the impact of those underlying patterns. The phenomenon of "student-as-consumer" can be seen as a strange attractor that, as we have suggested, is causing many institutions to rethink their approaches to the development, delivery, and support of curriculum and to the provision of student services. We are witnessing universities and colleges making sometimes-difficult adjustments to the more instrumental view that students bring to their learning. Over the past decades, institutions have accommodated broader shifts in society and the economy in the slow development of such instrumentalist subjects as business studies, education, nursing, pharmacy, biotechnology, tourism, and computing science. The addition of these "new" disciplines helped the academy remain in alignment with its social context. Current pressures are not so much on the "what" of postsecondary education (though there will always be some impetus to shift program offerings), as in the "how." The means by which students will access education is a point of major choice for students and, therefore, challenge for institutions. Because of the personal financial circumstances of students and the burgeoning of online curriculum choices, students are now making choices that are based on their personal needs, convenience, and constraints. We now want to turn to a discussion of how institutions can plan and organize themselves in this kind of environment.

### Planning and Organizing for Action in a Chaotic Environment

Malcolm Gladwell, in his book *The Tipping Point* (2000), identifies numerous examples of political, sociological, criminal, and consumer behavior where a rapid shift has occurred in patterns of human activity or decision making. While Gladwell does not specifically cite chaos theory, much of the empirical and anecdotal evidence he presents can be explained through the lens of chaos theory. What these examples bring home, however, is that the wise institution will develop systems that enable it to monitor the environment—and react—in effective ways. The trick will be to recognize those meta-processes or trends that will result in chaotic behavior before the tipping point is reached. Clearly, this presents universities and colleges with a challenge. How do we marry our traditional linear deterministic governance and planning structures with systems that allow for situational complexity?

We can get clues as to how to organize ourselves for an increasingly fluid and chaotic environment from emerging practice in the health care field. Health care, like higher education, is dominated by a group of professionals—physicians—who are essentially self-regulating and have a high degree of freedom to act within administrative structures. At the same time, the physicians, like faculty, are embedded in a complex set of physical, administrative, and social structures. Building on work by Stacey (1996), Zimmerman, Lindberg, and Plsek (1998, pp. 138–143) develop a typology of management practice that maps out ways of dealing with planning and action in areas that verge on chaos. They provide us with guideposts toward an enhanced means of organizing the academy so that we may recognize and respond to the emergence of strange attractors in an apparently chaotic environment while maintaining our traditional structures.

To begin with, Zimmerman et al. (1998) identify three decision-making environments in health care organizations that are reflected in universities and colleges:

1. Environments where there are high levels of certainty and high levels of agreement in the organization on how to proceed. This is the realm of rational decision making, wherein clear paths to the achievement of goals can be laid out and the outcomes are predictable. In the academy, the development of new curricula and their approval by senate would fit into this context.

2. Environments characterized by certainty about how goals are to be achieved but little agreement on the desirability of those goals. In this context, the debates that raged in universities and colleges in the late 1990s (and in some institutions continue to rage) about the introduction of technology-mediated teaching and learning are instructive. In most cases, there was agreement about how it had to happen—it was clearly the responsibility of faculty. But often there was little agreement on whether or not it was desirable. In such settings, decision making is the product of coalition building, negotiation, and compromise. In short, the academy makes decisions in a somewhat more political rather than rational context.

3. Environments where there is a high level of agreement on where the organization must go, usually expressed in strong support for a shared mission and vision for the future. However, there is little certainty about how to realize the mission and vision. Here, decisions about curriculum and services in higher education are made in the context of comparison with the mission and vision. Are the new developments going to lead us to our goals? Which of these alternatives will get us there faster?

These three contexts are those in which the Darwinian model of institutional change prevails. They are contexts that honor and respect the traditions and inherited values of the academy. They are the contexts from which spring the reputational assets of the university or college. They are contexts that, we believe, are critical for the future viability of universities or colleges. They are not, however, sufficient any longer in and of themselves.

Our environment has become increasingly complex. We've seen how increasing consumer behavior on the part of students will challenge many institutions. We are all beset by increased competition from new providers in postsecondary education, many exploiting the use of information and communications technology to enter the marketplace. Government funding has shrunk throughout much of the developed world and developing countries continue to bootstrap themselves up the league table through the use of education and training. Many institutions or segments of institutions are faced, therefore, with a fourth decision-making environment that Zimmerman et al. (1998) characterize as "anarchy." In this environment, there are no touchstones, no guideposts as to what is happening and, consequently, no agreement on what to do in the face of change. The traditional methods of planning and approvals no longer apply and faculty and administrators have not been able to develop social technologies that enable decision making and choices in the face of change. Individuals and groups often resort to avoidance, pretending that nothing has changed, and continue to do what they have always done. This strategy, though, is a short-term at best. What is needed is a different way of organizing that allows for both the traditional decision making environment and a means by which the punctuations of rapid change can be accommodated.

Zimmerman et al. (1998) suggest that a "zone of complexity" exists that mediates between the traditional, linear planning environments and the anarchic decision-making environment. They posit a number of different decision-making and heuristic techniques that are characteristic of complex adaptive systems. We suggest that a similar system of decision making needs to be developed and sanctioned within the context of the traditions of the academy. Senates and administrative structures need to recognize that the pace of development and approval for new initiatives is too slow for those areas of the academy faced with punctuated equilibrium rates; they are simply incapable of moving fast enough to cope with the tip into chaos. A system that would permit the early identification of strange attractors and the responsive development of curriculum or service delivery models would be one that had the following characteristics:

1.  Ability to create and support, with appropriate resources, self-directed work teams that form and fold according to emergent needs
2.  Establishment by Senate, or where appropriate by administrative policy and procedure, of a set of rules of

interaction that focus on quality assurance and compliance with the mission, values, and goals of the institution

3. Routine reporting requirements on actions and progress to the sponsoring agent

4. Commitment from the appropriate approving body or bodies to permit rapid implementation that would be followed by *post hoc* evaluation of the outcomes.

In chaos theory terms, senates and other academic bodies need to become comfortable with the notion that fractal self-similarities embedded in the academic enterprise will result in reasonable outcomes, that there are meta-processes in operation that will guide actions. In short, they need to develop a level of comfort that the world as they know it is not going to end if they but trust their colleagues to do the right thing in the realm of technology-mediated educational delivery.

This kind of organizational structure would be, obviously, a challenge to many faculty and administrators in higher education. It calls for a letting go, for a level of trust that is often absent. However, it finds a mirror in many universities and colleges in integrated self-directed work teams involved in everything from research to administrative functions. The key difference is the handing over of authority by governance structures in areas that have traditionally been their purview.

## Partnerships in a Dynamic Environment

Just as we can think of consumer-driven decision making as being a strange attractor that underlies much of the apparent chaos facing higher education so can we think of the concept of partnership as being a strange attractor. Hardly a week goes by without some new announcement of a partnership being struck between postsecondary institutions. The vast majority of these partnerships are being formed to exploit the new markets for online education. The partnerships can be formed at the state jurisdictional level such as can be found in Washington State in the United States. Moreover, they can be national, such as the United Kingdom consortium comprising University College London, the London School of Economics, the London School of Business, Imperial College, and, possibly, the universities of Oxford and Cambridge, which is being assembled to bid on the development of the country's "e-university" (Goddard, 2000). They also can be international in nature, a good example of which is the recently announced African Virtual University that will deliver programs developed by partner institutions in the United States, Canada, and Europe ("Virtual university bridges," 2000). All these partnerships have one thing in common: they were created in order to develop, deliver, and support technology-mediated teaching and learning vehicles.

The concept of "partnership" is new to most institutions, however. In general, higher education organizations have guarded their autonomy, eschewing collaborative activity in all but the most specialized of activities. Lately, however, faced with growing competition on national and international levels, institutions have banded together to create, deliver, and support online courses. In the struggle to maintain the traditions of the academy in the face of an increasingly chaotic competitive environment, and driven by private sector organizations intent on creating and selling information products, universities and colleges have shown themselves willing to engage in partnerships with rival institutions (indeed, some have even formed alliances with private sector organizations). While the concept of "partnership" can be seen as a strange attractor, the particulars of the rapid evolutionary events that give rise to these alliances are situational. The strange attractor sets the underlying dynamic for a response to an apparently chaotic environment. The interplay of the aspirations, flexibility, and negotiating tactics of the various partners will determine the specific nature of the evolutionary spurt. Each institution must decide on the limits it sets on the "three Gs"—what it hopes to *get* from the partnership, what it expects to *give* to the partnership, and what it intends to *guard* from encroachment by the partnership. It is early yet, but we expect that once in production and delivery mode these partnerships will settle down to a rate of change that approximates traditional operations. In other words, the drivers of self-similarity in academic organizations will begin to assert themselves.

## Student Services and Information and Communications Technology

In 1995, at the dawn of mass access to the Internet, who amongst us guessed that the technology would drive changed course and program selection behavior by students and the abandonment of centuries old traditions of institutional autonomy in the development and delivery of courses? Similar sea changes are washing over the services we offer to students to support them in most aspects of their academic activities. Indeed, our libraries were among the earliest of our support functions to embrace the implications of the new information and communications technology.

Partnerships in postsecondary education have probably been around longest in the area of library support. Many institutions have formed consortia aimed at driving down the purchase price of materials through bulk buying practices. In addition, networks have developed that facilitate interlibrary loans. Now, institutions are banding together to confront publishing houses in an effort to contain the annual increases in the cost of journal subscriptions, increases that in Canada were in the double digits throughout the 1990s. But perhaps the most far-reaching effects will come from the melding of these social technologies with the information and communications technology. With the digitization of text has come the opportunity for most institutions to switch from collections development that focused on "just-in-case" to one that focuses on "just-in-time." Absent copyright issues, students (and scholars) can routinely get access to a large selection of journals at their desktops. Interlibrary loans of journal articles can now be digitally transmitted. Technologies such as "e-books" promise to provide digitized texts to students that—in theory if not yet in practice— can be downloaded from the Internet. These and other developments reinforce the new behavior patterns of students. They no longer have to come to the library each time they need reference material. They can choose the time most convenient to them to access the materials, independent of the opening times of the library.

However, what is going to be the impact of these rapid changes on libraries? Over time, their physical presence will not grow as it has in the past. Bricks and clicks will displace bricks and mortar as "just-in-case" collections are limited to core materials and access to virtual repositories becomes the norm for the highly specialized and the esoteric materials. But the library without walls will still need professional librarians and support staff to assist students and scholars and the physical collection will still exist in a building—even if it contains, as many libraries now do, banks of workstations for user access. The point here is that the fundamental functions of libraries will remain the same, just as the functions associated with teaching and learning remain the same in the online delivery of courses. The element that has changed is the technological context. Again, in chaos theory terms: self-similarity reasserts the fundamental identifying and unifying pattern.

Student support in the online environment is also changing yet retains the underlying principles and concepts found in traditional teaching settings. Our experience at the University College of the Cariboo (UCC) is instructive here. Our 100 Mile House operation is a storefront, community-based facility serving a catchment population of about 12,000. Located in a rural area, several hours' drive from a full service campus, the center serves the citizens of the region through a combination of face-to-face and online delivery. Some of this latter instruction is provided by UCC but most is delivered by other institutions. Supporting the learners of other institutions may strike many colleagues as unconventional. However, in terms of serving the needs of a community where the demand patterns for post-secondary education are broad but shallow, it makes sense. UCC builds value for itself in the community as the portal to education and training opportunities provided by others, and at the same time uses its expertise to assist students be successful in a learning environment that is unfamiliar. In both these contexts we play a critical role in the social, economic, and cultural development of the community we serve. The center provides quiet study space, access to the technology for those who lack it at home, library resources, tutorial support, examination invigilation, course and program advising, and progress tracking support. This latter element is critical for we have found that without someone providing prompting to online students their completion rates match those for correspondence courses— approximately 30 percent. These kinds of support services (and UCC is not unique in their provision) mirror those available to students in traditional face-to-face settings; that they are available to students from other institutions is only possible because of the technology of online learning. In chaos theory terms, this kind of service provision could be seen as a fractal phenomenon, mirroring other service provisions but not quite identical.

This same kind of phenomenon can be seen in the trend to web-enable many student service interactions. In institutions across North America, the Internet (and associated Intranets) is revolutionizing the way in which we interact with students. Admissions and registration functions, timetable construction, tuition payment, transcript requests, drop/add functions, and more are being turned on their heads. Processes are being slimmed down and speeded-up and front line staff are being freed of the need to deal with routine inquiries on a face-to-face basis and are now able to spend more time with those who need or desire such support. Students are routinely interacting with the administrative systems of the institution through the Internet in ways that are time and location independent. Again, we have self-similarity of services but the frame has changed. What is happening in the student services realm is that the nature and scope of services have evolved over time but now are being subjected to a rapid rate of evolution driven by technology. Nevertheless, the services remain very similar—they are just being delivered differently.

## Conclusion

So what does this tell us? In the arena of technology-mediated teaching, learning, and student support service—endeavors that go to the heart of the academic enterprise—chaos theory is a useful mental construct to guide our approach to planning. It tells us to expect the unexpected, to have short planning cycles, and to be prepared to change in radical ways over short periods of time in specific areas of our activities. But we must also expect that institutions concerned with remaining relevant must continue to evolve services and curriculum in a measured and steady fashion, albeit at a somewhat faster rate than in the past. This bimodal change pattern—a steady rate of change, punctuated by very rapid change periods in specific functions and areas—is conditioned, however, by the inherent values and mores of the academy that impose a self-similarity on our activities. In other words, our social technologies display fractal behavior.

And what does this tell us about how we should conduct ourselves? Academia has a reputation for being a disputatious and sometimes nasty environment when it comes to changing the way we do things. In an environment that allows for, indeed protects, debate, the conflict between those eager to embrace what's new and those slower or suspicious of change is certain to be noisy if not downright acrimonious. For those of us immersed in these disputes, patterns are invisible—but they are no less real and potent. Change we must and change we will, trusting as much in our tradition as in our imagination. *Plus ça change, plus c'est la même chose.*

## Note

1   In a sense, these inherited values are themselves a strange attractor that provides structure and direction to institutional endeavors in curriculum development and services to students.

# References

Drucker, P. (2000). Putting more now into knowledge. *Forbes 156*(11), 85–88.

Eldredge, N., & Gould, S. J. (1972). Punctuated equilibria: An alternative to phyletic gradualism. In T. J. M. Schopf (Ed.), *Models in Paleobiology*. San Francisco: Freeman, Cooper, & Co.

Gladwell, M. (2000). *The tipping point: How little things can make a big difference*. New York: Little, Brown.

Goddard, A. (2000, June 16). Big brands key to e-university. *The Times Higher Education Supplement*, p. 1.

Kershaw, A., & Safford, S. (1998). From order to chaos: The impact of educational technology on postsecondary education. *Higher Education 35*(3), 285–298.

Scott, P. (1999). Massification, internationalization and globalization. In P. Scott (Ed.), *The globalization of higher education*. Milton Keynes: Open University.

Stacey, R. (1996). *Strategic management and organizational dynamics*. London: Pitman.

Virtual university bridges digital divide. (2000, May 19). *The Times Higher Education Supplement*, p. 12.

Zimmerman, B., Lindberg, C., & Plsek, P. (1998). *Edgeware: Insights from complexity science for health care leaders*. Irving, TX: VHA.

# CHAPTER NINE

## Reshaping Higher Education in a Post-Fordist World: Chaos and Collingwood

*Bryant Griffith and Lynn Speer Lemisko*

Exhilarating and empowering ways of thinking and doing in higher education could arise out of a combination of seemingly random strands: new technologies, post-Fordist economic influence, constructivism, and the notion that chaos theory can be applied to social institutions. The convergence of these strands creates the possibility for a bright future for higher education—a future where students are part of the process of discovery, planning, and reshaping along with faculty, administration, and boards of governors.

While the reshaping of the university appears at first glance to be an action which takes place in the present aimed at influencing the future, it is our contention that this action is part of a historical process. By exploring the past, we can enhance our insight into the multifaceted possibilities that exist in the present and that lie in wait for the future.

This particular point of view regarding the importance of the past to understanding the present arises out of a particular conception of history. If history is conceived as "the past, dead and gone," then the examination of it cannot help us see into the present. However, if we hold that the past is not dead and gone, that remnants of it are still alive in our present in the form of ideas or ways of thinking—that these past notions interpenetrate our present or are the precursors, or "determining conditions" of our present notions (Collingwood, 1993, pp. 225–226, 420; 1939, pp. 97–98)—then we can argue that the past is relevant.

This conception of history was expounded upon and philosophically supported by R. G. Collingwood, an early twentieth-century English historian and philosopher. It is from this point of view, as Collingwoodian historians, that we plan to explore how the apparently unrelated strands mentioned above combined to create conditions that hold possibilities for a dynamic reconfiguration of higher education. In addition, we will argue that

R. G. Collingwood's conception of historical knowledge gives both theorists and planners in higher education another perspective that could enrich their ways of thinking about the relationship between theory and practice/planning and doing. As the political world seeks to influence higher education through theories such as post-Fordism, and as the uncritical use of new technologies multiplies, it is incumbent on us as postsecondary educators to clarify why we think and act as we do. This discussion will offer some suggestions about how our particular historical view might aid in forming a well-thought-out set of presuppositions for higher education. The aim throughout is to build the argument that the world is much more complex than generally supposed, and that developing deeper understanding is difficult, as is the application of ideas to higher education planning and policy in an increasingly results oriented world.

To explore how post-Fordism, new technology, and chaos theory could come together to present new ways of thinking in higher education, the chapter will briefly examine the following: a) the dominance of positivism in Western ways of thinking and its influence on higher education in North America; b) positivism and Fordism, and how Fordism "turned into" post-Fordism; c) problems, issues and concerns confronting higher education which arise from positivist and post-Fordist ways of thinking; d) how a scientific theory—that is, chaos theory—along with new information technologies and Collingwoodian thinking, could become tools to counteract the dominant mythologies of positivism and help higher education institutions deal with the challenges.

However, as unabashed Collingwoodian historians, our examination is clearly grounded in Collingwood's philosophy and historical approach. Therefore, we must begin by briefly outlining several salient features of Collingwood's thought to make clear the point of view from which we work.

Collingwood developed his arguments as a challenge to positivism. He argued that because there was a fundamental difference between history and the natural sciences, there must be different approaches taken to the construction of knowledge in each realm. The observation of phenomena, or the perception of the outside of events, and the measuring, classifying, and generating of laws based on the observations was, according to Collingwood, a legitimate way of knowing the natural world. He argued that this is so, because events in the natural world have no "inside." In other words, the "events of nature are mere events, not the acts of agents whose thought the scientist endeavours to trace" (1939, p. 31). However, the object of thought for history has a fundamentally different character in that the events are not merely events, but past human actions that have both an outside, or observable part, and an inside which can only be "described in terms of thought" (1993, p. 213).

Collingwood (1939, p. 31) asserted then, that knowing anything in history must involve knowing both the outside and the inside of past events. The historian's "work may begin by discovering the outside of an event, but it can never end there: he must always remember that the event was an action, and that his main task is to think himself into this action, to discern the thought of its agent." Collingwood called this task "reenactment" and claimed that it was possible for historians to "re-think" past thoughts because, although ways of thinking change and evolve, they never completely die out. Historians can reconstruct the past because they can recover ways of thinking by examining documents which have survived into the present, and re-think the thoughts of the people who created them. Reenactment is not some mystical process, but a method we commonly use in trying to understand what people mean when we read their words.

Collingwood did not believe that history or philosophy could or should aim at producing or finding universal and necessary truth. He argued (1939, p. 63) that "truth" is "something always needing to be recreated by an effort of thought." In other words, Collingwood challenges us to think, not simply accept, or deliver given facts, laws, or rules. He argued that historians should try to get "inside other people's heads, looking at their situation through their eyes, and think for yourself whether the way in which they tackled it [their problem] was the right way."

Historians live in a constant state of uncertainty. As Simon Schama wrote in his book, *Dead Certainties* (1991, p. 320), ". . . historians are left forever chasing shadows, painfully aware of their inability ever to reconstruct a dead world in its completeness, however revealing their documentation. . . . The certainty of such answers always remains contingent on their unavoidable remoteness from their subjects. We are doomed to be forever hailing someone who has just gone around the corner and out of earshot." As Collingwoodian historians, we not only live with, but also embrace this uncertainty. When history is the study of particular-to-particular, not particular to the general, the process of historical thinking moves away from positivist influences. Historians re-think the action, learn how the human mind operates by asking particular questions of particular ideas in the past, and understand that history is an ongoing process where one can uncover knowledge by tracing the preconceptions which underlie each age. History becomes an autonomous form of knowledge, a form of self-knowledge but not of positivistic certainty—and this should be celebrated.

What is also pertinent about Collingwood is his metaphysical analysis of how we think and reason. He argues repeatedly that all historical thinking is present thinking and that we make sense of the past by first understanding how we think, and then by analogy reasoning, how others thought and acted in a specific past. This means that the questions that we ask are the key to the knowledge we have. The key to historical understanding, Collingwood claimed (1943, p. 134), is that it teaches us how to think and act in the present, how to uncover self-knowledge so that we can make good judgments to ensure a free future. Collingwood asserted, "By the end of the nineteenth century, people who were studying the philosophy of history . . . had come to an agreement that history was knowledge of the individual, and this conviction had in most cases enabled them to reject . . . the later attempts to confuse history and science."

Our discussion in this chapter will focus on the ways in which post-Fordism, new technology, and chaos theory could affect ways of thinking in higher education. As Collingwoodians, we presuppose that thought influences action, that ways of thinking arise in the past and continue to circulate in the present, and that if we are to address the problems of planning in higher education in an era plagued by uncertainty, we must understand the historical process by which we reached this place and develop or utilize alternate ways of thinking, planning, and doing. In the next section we will examine some aspects of the historical process, which brought us to our present set of problems, issues, and concerns in higher education in North America.

## The Dominance of Positivism in Western Ways of Thinking

While it is always difficult to know how far back to go in tracing the emergence of a particular way of thinking, most historians agree that the European scientific revolution of the seventeenth century was nothing less than a revolution in the way Westerners perceived the world. By 1700, science had become an issue of public discourse in Europe, providing a worldview which helped people make sense out of the natural world and their experiences using human reason; replicable, experimental methodology; and mathematics, rather than relying upon the authority of the church. One of the major contributors to this way of thinking was Isaac Newton, who offered mathematical proof that nature had order and meaning. This worldview, which became known as the "Newtonian World Machine" (Gooch, 1970, p. 11), held that the entire universe acted according to basic laws, which were everywhere and always the same. The laws existed, and all humans had to do was discover them.

The application of reason to the understanding of the natural world appeared to be amazingly effective. Soon, thinkers of the Enlightenment began to attempt to apply the same scientific, rational approach to understanding society. It was believed that the laws of society and government would eventually be well understood, which would mean that all would live happy and fulfilling lives, resting in the certainty of science. In Europe, the new faith in reason and science produced the notion that anything was possible, and this gave an immense boost to the belief in human progress.

During the nineteenth-century industrial revolutions in Europe and North America, the application of science and reason brought about new systems of economic production based on new technologies and techniques. This contributed to the sense that human beings had increasing control over the environment. Links between science and technology and prosperity and progress only strengthened the belief that the methods of natural science provided the principal, even the sole, model for the attainment of true knowledge. This belief is the basic tenet of positivism—the philosophical position articulated by Auguste Comte during that time period.

Rationalism and positivism had an impact on academia during the nineteenth century. In many circles, it came to be believed that scientific method could and should be applied to understand human interactions both in the past and the present. Understanding could be developed through the simple processes of observation, categorization, and labeling, which would lead to the discovery of another "law" of human interaction and behavior. In history and sociology, adherence to this approach meant that scholars began to look for single, unifying causes to explain all human behavior. For example, Marx used the notion of class struggle as the primary cause to explain the past and forecast the future. Although the discoveries of the new scientific revolution, circa 1890 to circa 1920, such as the theory of relativity, and the uncertainty principle, created some unease among academics and the public, the general belief was that correct or true answers were to be had and that the cause and effect correlation of human events could be uncovered.

Much of this modernist thinking came to a crashing end, however, in the trenches of France between 1914 and 1918. The Great War caused a sense of profound dislocation for Europeans who were involved in the conflict. Faced with the overwhelming destruction of modern total warfare in their homelands, European thinkers reworked their presuppositions through Marx and later Sartre. Other European thinkers, including R. G. Collingwood, argued that while reason is indispensable to civilization, the search for universal laws of human behavior is the basis of totalitarian thinking.

The impact of the Great War was different in the United States, however. Insulated from both the physical and psychic devastation of the war as a result of distance and limited involvement, Americans generally perceived the positive aspects of applied science. While Europeans experienced first-hand the horror of new technology in the form of modern weapons, most Americans experienced increasing access to consumer products such as automobiles, wrist watches, radios, and other gadgets before, during, and directly after the war, as well as benefited from the scientific discoveries in areas such as orthopaedics and rehabilitation medicine and immunization, which arose directly out of the laboratory of the western front. It is not surprising, therefore, to find that Americans embraced rationalism and the scientific method.

In American institutions of higher education, where rapid growth was also particularly influenced by Social Darwinism and pragmatism, there was often little tolerance at the administrative level for the uncertainty of thinkers such as Collingwood and Whitehead. American positivists continued to argue that they should be able to uncover a series of rules for human behavior similar to those found in natural science.

While Anglo-Canadian intellectual life had been most heavily influenced by various forms of philosophic idealism throughout the nineteenth century, the influence of positivism and pragmatism became increasingly evident (McKillop, 1994). World War I then created that sense of dislocation in Canada. Faced with the upheaval of the Great War, which undermined their sense of tradition, English Canadian thinkers responded in two ways—some attempted to shore up old ways of thinking, while others searched for ideas that could help build the country along new lines (McKillop, 1987, 1994; Owram, 1986). While elements of idealism persisted throughout the inter-war years, pragmatism and positivism clearly began to exert an increasing influence on English Canadian ways of thinking. After all, it was believed that industrial might, and not the power of ideas, had won the war. In English Canada, World War I had promoted ideas of efficiency, scientific management, and industrial training, and the contribution of research in the areas of medicine and munitions, for example, undertaken by universities during the war contributed to the notion that these institutions should have some practical value (McKillop, 1994; Owram, 1986).

World War II seemed to provide further evidence of the power of applied science for both Canadians and Americans. And, by the end of World War II, international economic, political, and diplomatic power were firmly entrenched in the United States. Because of this, Americans inherited the role of reconstructing the myth about progress and explanation, in and through their institutes of higher learning. Basking in financial success and the scientific successes of various Cold War initiatives, such as the "space race," it is not surprising that the myth of progress constructed by American institutions glorified logical positivism and pragmatism until late in the twentieth century.

This brief journey into the origins and dominance of positivist thought has taken on a rather linear progression. Positivism was not the only way of thinking in circulation in Europe and North America between the seventeenth century and the Great War. For example, philosophic idealism, romanticism, and irrationalism were all part of the mix. In turn, rationalism and positivism did not completely disappear in Europe after the war, nor were all Americans positivists. The point here is to simply provide an insight into the power and persistence of the rationalist, positivist perspective, so that we have insight into one set of assumptions which are influencing efforts to re-shape higher education.

This "universe as a machine" worldview has led to the belief that "scientific" management techniques, ascertained by gathering empirical data about organizational structures and human relationships, can be applied in planning and policymaking in higher education. This, of course, presupposes that empirical data is "evidence" and that cause and effect are fixed and predictable. As Collingwoodian historians, we argue that this approach does not take into account the "inside"—that is, the thought that lies behind the action—and, therefore, that positivism is not proving to be a satisfactory approach in addressing issues in higher education in a time of increasing uncertainty.

## Positivism, Fordism, and Post-Fordism

We would like to turn our attention now to a dynamic factor in the ways of thinking emerging in the late twentieth century, which is having an important impact on higher education, namely post-Fordism. The characterization of post-Fordism is not an easy task as it is not a coherent school of thought but rather a series of descriptions of actions from varying points of view. However, as Collingwoodian historians, we know that understanding and describing the set of ideas from which post-Fordism arose—that is, Fordism—we can develop some sound insights into the "post" way of thinking. In other words, the best way to understanding post-Fordism is to describe Fordism.

Fordism takes its name from the production techniques developed by the automobile manufacturer, Henry Ford. Understanding of Fordism begins with the image of the Fordist assembly line, which was based on the rationalization procedures of logical positivism as applied to manufacturing techniques. However, as a concept, Fordism takes in all of the ways of thinking—social institutions, structural forms, and strategies to implement them—which go along with the notion of mass production.

Fordism presupposes economies of scale and supply driven production—that is, the more that can be supplied, the lower the cost to the consumer, who will then purchase that which is produced. Production is carried out by semi-skilled assembly line workers, who require protection through trade union organizations and state intervention into conflicts between labor and capital. With this as part of the dynamic, we can see the relationship between Fordism and the Keynesian welfare state. As Fordism thrived, the role of the state in managing factors such as the balance between supply and demand and wages was established. National governments invested in the process through the nationalization of key areas of their economies, the encouragement of mass consumption, the construction of infrastructure, and the development of social welfare and full employment policies. The welfare state and Fordism are intimately related. National expansion was planned and executed with Fordist and positivist thinking presupposed.

With the understanding that Fordism includes all the ways of thinking, doing, and organizing related to mass production, we now know that post-Fordism has something to do with a different kind of production or labor process, and, of course, with all the ways of thinking, doing, and organizing that go along with this. In order to broaden our conceptualization of the term, we must also explore some of the forces that drove and are driving the emergence of post-Fordism.

Beginning in the late 1970s there developed a growing sense that Fordism was in crisis (Tremblay, 2000; Jessop, 2000). The development of new modes of production and consumption and new information and computer technologies, along with increasing international competition, engendered the belief that new approaches to economic organizations were required. In addition, the welfare state had become a creature unto itself, amassing enormous debts and deficits. States reacted by turning to classical liberal strategies, attempting to reduce government spending by privatizing and deregulating. This induced high rates of unemployment, the antithesis of the Keynesian ideal. Thus Fordism was threatened by the uncoupling of social and economic policies (Mishra, 1985), and post-Fordism became a reaction to what was seen by many as the excesses of the liberal welfare state.

Post-Fordism can be defined as "just-in-time" economics, based upon flexible production process, machines, and workforce. Under this system, mass production is replaced by production on demand—that is, products are distributed "just in time" to meet a consumer's demand. Workers need to have flexible specializations to enable companies to move rapidly to newly emerging market demands. Instead of local economic markets, post-Fordism is based upon serving worldwide demands. It is believed, therefore, that worker wage demands can be met in very different ways. In a nationalist, Fordist economy, wage structures are designed to foster growth by encouraging consumption in their own market areas. In a post-Fordist economy, it is worldwide consumption that matters; therefore, both wages and prices of commodities in North America become a matter of international policy. Workers in a post-Fordist society would be rewarded for being flexible. Under post-Fordism, management of the economy would be undertaken by leaner and more flexible bureaucratic structures, including international, pan-regional, and multinational bodies and national governments, as well as local and regional organizations. Success in this system is defined in terms of responsiveness to customers.

It seems very clear that Fordism, with its reliance upon rationalized mass production procedures and notions of planned government intervention, has a close relationship with logical positivism. However, it is yet to be seen whether or not the post-Fordist system will counteract positivistic presuppositions. Although post-Fordism presupposes degrees of uncertainty that are unfathomable in the positivist lexicon, we know, as Collingwoodian historians, that "old" ways of thinking do not simply disappear as alternative ways arise. We will argue later that post-Fordism, along with new technologies, chaos theory, and Collingwoodian historical thinking, might be used as an antithesis to what has been the dominant positivist planning models used in both America and Europe. However, prior to this, we need to lay out some of the problems, issues, and concerns facing higher education in this era of increasing uncertainty.

## Problems, Issues, and Concerns Confronting Higher Education

In the last decades of the twentieth century most academic disciplines have been engaged in conversations aimed at trying to make sense of their past and present, and at laying plans for the future. Each, in its own way, is conducting a very basic self reexamination. This reexamination should be going on at the broader, institutional level. One of the major challenges to the university as an institution of higher education is to confront its own view of itself.

Universities have held positions of high esteem based on their traditional role as educators of the elite. In this capacity, universities were the arbiters of change, defining both the processes and the outcomes. These organizations have a rich and powerful international tradition that has outlasted depressions, revolutions, and world wars, but the stability and time-honored practices of the university have been encroached upon by the fact that they have generally become publicly funded institutions. While this has brought the positive result of exposing a wider population to a university education, it has also meant that universities found it necessary to react to pragmatic government policies. Public funding has meant that universities have been challenged with regard to how they see themselves— that is, as refuges of free and critical thought, unaffected by more mundane material considerations.

In addition, the fact of public funding has opened the university to the claim that it must be responsive to the perceived needs of business and society. In the pragmatic world of just-in-time, flexible economic thought, for example, universities are seen by many as dinosaurs. It is believed by many that their graduates spend far too much time thinking about the reasons *why* people act and about the long-term consequences of actions. In other words, it is believed that university graduates spend far too much time on theory rather than practice. Beyond offering the challenge to universities to redefine themselves—which we argue is necessary—this demand for focus on practice has worrisome implications. Implicit in this approach is a questioning of the value of many academic disciplines. For example, if practice is a present problem that is unrelated to the past, of what value is the study of history? As Collingwoodian historians, this question is disturbing for several reasons: First it implies that the past can be separated from the present. Secondly, it implies that human action can be determined by positivistic rule-making. Thirdly, and most perhaps most frightening, is the implication that theory can be separated from practice. This distinction takes away one of the fundamental *raison d'etre* of liberal higher education, that is, its ability to interweave theory and practice in a critical way and provide its students with what Socrates might have called "ways to know yourself."

When we examine some of the ways in which universities have reacted to the various intrusions into their "turf," several other particular problems and issues facing higher education become evident. In response to this new world, universities have and are reacting in a variety of ways. In Canada, between circa 1945 and the recent past, it was possible to obtain a sound liberal arts and science degree at any of Canada's postsecondary institutions. However, in the 1990s, the university system began to move away from the basic general liberal education model. Canadian universities are now divided into various categories, including small, comprehensive, or research based. Canadian universities are now publicly reviewed in the national news magazine *Maclean's*, and students vote with their dollars and feet by attending the institution they believe best suits their future needs. With the growing belief that universities are dinosaurs, many multinational corporations have established their own institutes for higher education where their own values and skills can be taught. For all of these reasons, universities must now take into consideration ways of enticing students because these "consumers" are now shopping, not waiting passively to be accepted. This is an issue that universities have not had to deal with in the past. In addition, higher education is having to deal with the issue of new technologies. As the political and business world, driven by post-Fordist assumptions, seeks to influence higher education, the uncritical use of new technologies multiplies. Institutes of higher learning must clarify and develop sound epistemological reasons for incorporating information technologies, or they will be doomed to the role of mere reactionaries.

This, then, is the major challenge to higher education—to reexamine and redefine itself as an institution that is responsive to legitimate societal demands, while retaining those valuable aspects of its tradition. Peter Senge (Kofman & Senge, 1993, p.5) argues that building a learning organization requires that we carefully examine our preconceptions about how we think and interact and that "we need to invent a new more learningful [sic] model through regaining our memory of the community nature of the self and of the poetic nature of language and the world . . ." (Kofman & Senge, 1993, p. 20). The question is, however, from what source should this more "learningful" model emerge?

If planning in higher education is based upon positivistic thought, and if positivistic thought is correct, then things can be fixed with "more and better" planning. We suggest that this approach does not help us "regain our communal and poetic memory." In fact, by playing with positivism we are more likely to lose any ability to plan in ways that conform to the historical presuppositions of higher education and would rather be planning for "assembly line" production. We also argue that while post-Fordist thinking offers notions that encourage more flexible approaches to planning and doing, it also embraces a pragmatic philosophy, which presupposes that only that which "proves useful" is worthwhile. This utilitarian approach might not encourage development of reflective and critical thinking skills, which have been part of the tradition of higher education. While it is clear that higher education must speak to the issues of rapid change, flexible work, and world markets, we suggest that the thinking required to address these human issues is more closely tied to "chaos thinking" than to positivism or pragmatism. We will argue in the following section that if higher education embraces notions arising from chaos theory and Collingwoodian thought and incorporates new technologies based on sound epistemological reasons, a more "learningful" planning and doing approach could emerge. This would allow higher education to argue that outcomes-based thinking might be useful but is not the whole answer, as well as allowing the re-shaping of the institution into a place best suited to debate political, economic, social, and ethical issues in a time of increasing uncertainty.

## Dealing with the Challenges:
## Chaos Theory, Information Technology, and Collingwood

In its simplest form chaos theory is based on the understanding that while both natural and human systems/organizations appear to have stable or consistent patterns which allow some degree of accurate prediction, these systems are, in fact, unpredictable because they are unstable: "Make a slight change to the way a system is by a small amount at one time, and the later behavior [sic] of the system may soon become completely different" (Hawking, 1994, p. 143). While this notion might at first glance lead to the frightening conclusion that there is no use in attempting any type of planning at all, we propose that such a realization actually could help higher education adapt to a world that is truly in flux. Arising from the positivist explorations of the physical world during the late nineteenth century, and the more recent findings of computer-driven models aimed at deriving explanations, chaos theory has the potential to free us from the dominance of positivism—an ultimate irony of the use of analytical thought. By recognizing that slight changes can cause enormous differences in planned outcomes, we can come to understand that it is the planning process, not "the plan," which is important; and, when the process is seen to be more important than the "outcome," we have a circumstance wherein we can respond to change and uncertainty in a flexible and accommodating fashion—unpredicted outcomes are expected, rather than perceived as "ruined plans."

As Collingwoodian historians, we see positive benefits if chaos theory were to be embraced. While it might seem odd to suggest that chaos theory is similar to historical thinking, we argue that recognizing the similarities allows thinking in higher education and historical thought to be seen as distinct but not separate parts of the same process of uncovering the nature of the human mind. Chaos thinking is a nonlinear way that the mind works. This description is similar in many ways with some forms of historiography, which date back to Greek times. While we will stipulate the ways in which chaos theory and Collingwoodian thought agree, it is as important to point out that a rich historical inheritance was already in place which viewed the world as self-reflective, complex, interactive, and process oriented. In other words, chaos theory is another in the ongoing process of attempting to free us of our positivistic presuppositions.

In order to make our case, we will turn to a very brief exploration of the relationship between Collingwoodian thinking and the ways of thinking about planning and doing in higher education that are being developed by theorists who have applied chaos theory to social organizations. For our example, we turn to Marc Cutright's work and provide some analysis of four of the points he makes in his discussion of the application of chaos thinking to strategic planning (1999). To demonstrate the similarities between Collingwoodian thought and chaos theory, several ideas proposed by Cutright are laid out and discussed.

When Cutright (1999, p. 7) claims that "The ideal outcome of planning is planning not plan," he argues that plans should be general, flexible, and relatively detail-free. Collingwoodian historians understand this approach intuitively. Because we approach a problem by asking questions, and know that those questions usually lead to even more questions, not fixed or ultimate answers, we have a "built in" sense that it is the process, not the outcome, that is important.

Cutright (1999, p. 7) also argues that "planning begins with a distillation of the institutions' key values and purposes." Collingwoodian historians would call this uncovering the institute's presuppositions. In the case of higher education, we argue that uncovering the institution's presuppositions is requisite to understanding why universities developed as they did, as well as being essential to understanding the thinking that lies behind present action. Similar to Cutright's claim that planning must begin with a clarification of values and purposes, we argue, as Collingwoodians, that thought affects action, and, therefore, assumptions must be revealed.

While Cutright (1999, p. 7) argues that "the widest possible universe of information should be made available to all members of the institution," he is not claiming that information should be shared simply for its own sake. When he claims that "this universe of information includes ongoing, rich, and current *feedback* [emphasis added]," he is arguing that information should be relative to a specific context, and that information becomes important in relation to the effect it has on the organization—in other words, when it becomes feedback in the planning process. These notions strike a cord with Collingwoodian historians. First, for the historian, information or "facts" only become important in relation to the context. For example, the Rubicon River is of itself unimportant, but when related to Caesar's crossing, the river becomes very important. In addition, we acknowledge the importance of information as something more than data "dropped on a table." Collingwood argued that there is an intimate relationship between historians and their object of knowledge—that is, past human action—because they reenact thought. During this process historians do not simply gather "information" about past action, but in fact become intrinsically affected by their "information gathering." Collingwood (1939, p. 114) argued, "If what the historian knows is past thoughts, and if he [sic] knows them by re-thinking them himself, it follows that the knowledge he achieves by historical inquiry is not knowledge of his situation as opposed to knowledge of himself, it is a knowledge of his situation which is, at the same time, knowledge of himself. In rethinking what somebody else thought, he thinks it himself. In knowing that somebody else thought it, he knows that he himself is able to think it." When historians reenact the thought of historical agents involved in past action, they are, in effect, involved in a "feedback loop" that leads to self-knowledge. Hence, we claim a relationship between what Cutright claims is the appropriate use of information in a chaotic system and Collingwoodian thought.

As Collingwoodian historians, we also find ourselves in sync with Cutright (1999, p. 7) when he states that "dissent and conflict are creative, healthy and real. The absence of conflict is reductionist, illusionary and suspect." Collingwoodians know that knowledge construction is the result of the tensions or "conflict" between thesis and antithesis and that this is not a simple dialectic, but a "trialectic" thinking process wherein the synthesis does not resolve the conflict, but merely serves to set up a new tension from which new ideas can emerge. In other words, the synthesis is not the "outcome," but part of the process. This is the case because thought is a process where one idea is not separated from the next but flows with it. To assume that ideas are separate is a positivistic fallacy. As Collingwoodian historians, we claim, along with Cutright, that institutions of higher education must honor dissent and be open to challenge if their response is to go beyond a reaction where change is an illusion of the moment.

In fact, we propose that Collingwood equips us to deal with the post-Fordist, uncertain world that is intruding into higher education. Out of Collingwood's insistence that all action arises out of presuppositions, that all knowledge is self-knowledge developed through the process of questioning and answering, and that this entire process is actually based on the idea that knowledge must constantly be recreated through the effort of thought, we can devise a methodology which allows us to deal with the unpredictability posited by chaos theory. Both Collingwood and chaos theorists recognize that uncertainty is the only unwavering constant. Both provide to higher educationists ways of looking at the world that hold potential for a dynamic reconfiguring of postsecondary education.

As Collingwoodian historians we are clearly intrigued by the origins and impacts of thought. However, we are not oblivious to the impact and potential benefits of the new "post-Fordist" technologies. We take the position that well-reasoned use of information technology also provides an opportunity for a dramatic and positive change in higher education. New technologies have given students a unique opportunity to voice their views and concerns about higher education. Students are unbound by normal convention as to the questions they may ask, the limits they may explore, and the sources they may contact in their quest. They have become what R. G. Collingwood might call "true historians." In this quest they have the opportunity to re-shape higher education by asking questions and demanding answers which might not normally be confronted by faculty and boards of governors. Students can offer the voice of dissent that creates those healthy conflicts from which arise the opportunity to engage in debate and rethink the aims and procedures of higher education. This is an exciting possibility, if higher educationists begin to embrace the notion that the world is complex and chaotic, and adopt, for example, a constructivist epistemology. The need for new ways of educating seems intensified by post-Fordism: " . . . whereas the Fordist production line demanded a robotic, compliant worker, reproduced through a 'traditional' authoritarian pedagogy, the new post-Fordist production line, with its stress on flexibility, decentralization and worker autonomy, will necessarily imply the adoption of a progressive form of education which lays the emphasis on pupil autonomy" (Hickox & Moore, 1992, p. 96).

This returns us to the ideas surrounding the potential benefits of the new technologies. Traditionally, the university was driven by a "top-down" epistemology where there was little or no recognition of constructivism. However, with the development of technology-rich environments, it has become almost impossible to ignore constructivist learning theory. At institutions of higher learning where Information Technology (IT) has been embraced, a different equilibrium between teacher and learner is being established where both teacher and student become learners; both ask questions and interact with each other to discover how IT can be used most appropriately, or how information found on the world wide web (or Internet) is best applied to the specific setting. In other words, there is a new autonomy, creating a chaos-like order. Any information may be useful and it is up to the individual to construct meaning.

This position is supported by a study (Cutright & Griffith, 2000) that examined experiences in a laptop university, demonstrating that students became assertive and more open about the process of learning in these technology-rich environments. They ask questions of their teachers about recently published sources they found on the Internet and expect answers about their accuracy and why they should or should not be used. The relationship between teacher and learner is thus blurred or redefined.

Good postsecondary teachers are and will be those individuals who recognize that we live in a chaotic, post-Fordist world of process, rapid change, and evolving contexts. Good postsecondary institutions are and will be those that support these teachers. This, in turn, entails a reconstruction of postsecondary curriculum and contributes to the re-shaping of higher education. Curriculum is being rewritten as we write, because of the present technology-rich environment. This demonstrates the way in which new technologies have influenced the epistemology of higher education, which in turn is contributing to new ways of thinking about planning and doing.

Constructivism allows both students and teachers to become part of an ongoing learning process. The outcomes become a fact of input in a different, somewhat chaotic manner, so that the process becomes the central focus. Post-Fordism becomes a contributing factor because the new economy focuses on "right here, right now" answers to "just-in-time" questions. Accountability becomes an important touchstone. The seemingly random combination of constructivist learning with chaos thinking and post-Fordist economic influence and technology is leading to the possibility of a very exciting future for higher education. This is a future where students are part of the process of discovery along with faculty.

This all entails new leadership models for a chaotic and process oriented world. The leadership in higher education institutions will, by necessity, be more horizontal rather than vertical, and leaders will not rise based on the "Peter Principle," but rather on the basis of qualities such as openness and ability to help the organization along in the process of reconstruction. It is most likely that career administrators will emerge from the academic sector, along with academics that will become short-term administrators attempting to achieve specific visions. Both will be needed. Continuity of purpose and historic institutional record need to be coupled with the creative input from those who perceive the opportunities to move teaching and learning forward rapidly. Thus, as new leadership models emerge, they will embrace the developing trends described in this chapter.

As Collingwoodian historians, we will not lay claim to calling this a "new" era. The period through which we are living may simply see yet another reconfiguration of modernism and positivism. While post-Fordism does include more flexible thinking, its pragmatic view is contiguous with positivistic assumptions, demonstrating a continuity with modernism. However, the implications of information technology and the Internet, when tied to chaos theory, present the possibility of the emergence of an exciting and perhaps very different set of presuppositions than we now hold. Only time will tell which possibility will be embraced and if the face of higher education will change to meet the new millennium.

## Last Thoughts

We have made much reference to the importance of the historical process, arguing that Collingwood's conception of historical knowledge gives theorists in higher education another perspective on the relationship between theory and practice. Collingwood's lifelong struggle against the influence of positivist thought in social, political, and academic thinking was an attempt to place self-knowledge at the center of epistemology. His rejection of our ability to know the past with the kind of certainty claimed by the positivists led to a conception of human thought based on self-knowledge and analogous thinking as applied to specific questions and centered on process rather than outcome. Simon Schama has made similar claims in *Dead Certainties*. While not all historians hold this view, we believe that it is helpful to higher education theorists who have traditionally been forced to react rather than propose. Chaos theory and the impact of information technology on higher education are also major factors that, if coupled with a historical epistemology, might allow for an innovative approach to these rapidly changing and uncertain times. By asking its critics to think about the process by which higher education emerged and the impact of change from a historical advantage, a clearer conception of the epistemological basis of higher education should come forth. The implications of chaos theory provide a substantial basis for freeing the field from positivism. Likewise, technology-rich environments provide both students and educators the opportunity to rethink the relationships between learning and teaching. The application of a historical analysis provides a substantial addition to the equation used to rethink the aims and processes of higher education. Thus higher educational theory collapses into historical thought and its philosophical implications. Collingwood would be pleased.

# References

Collingwood, R. G. (1939). *An autobiography.* London: Oxford University Press.

Collingwood, R. G. (1993). *The idea of history, revised edition with lectures 1926–1928.* Edited with introduction by Jan Van Der Dussen. Oxford: Clarendon Press.

Cutright, M. (1999). Planning in higher education: A model from chaos theory. Paper presented at the annual conference of the American Educational Research Association, Montreal, Quebec, Canada, April 1999.

Cutright, M., & Griffith, B. (2000). The "Acadia Advantage" and a new vision for education in Canada. The Technology Source http://horizon.unc.edu/TS/vision/2000-03.asp.

Gooch, B. D. (1970). *Europe in the nineteenth century.* Toronto: The Macmillan Company.

Hawking, S. (1994). *Black holes and baby universes and other essays.* New York: Bantam Books.

Hickox, M., & Moore, R. (1992). Education and post-Fordism, a new correspondence. In P. Brown & H. Lauder (Eds.), *Education for Economic Survival.* London: Routledge

Jessop, B. (2000). Post-Fordism and the state. [Online]. Available: http://www.geo.ut.ee/inimtool/referaadid/krap/referaatpalhus.html.

Kofman, F., & Senge, P. M. (1993). Communities of commitment: The heart of learning organizations. *Organizational Dynamics, 22,* 4–20.

McKillop, A. B. (1987). *Contours of Canadian thought.* Toronto: University of Toronto Press.

McKillop, A. B. (1994). *Matters of mind: The university in Ontario 1791–1951.* Toronto: University of Toronto Press.

Mishra, R. (1985) *The welfare state in crisis.* Brighton: Harvester.

Owram, D. (1986). *The government generation.* Toronto: University of Toronto Press.

Schama, S. (1991). *Dead certainties.* New York: Knopf.

Tremblay, G. (2000). The information society: From Fordism to Gatesism. *Canadian Journal of Communications.* [Online]. Available: http://www.cjc-online.ca/backIssues/20.4/tremblay.html.

# CHAPTER TEN

## Chaotic Systems: Confounding or Confirming the Leadership Role in Higher Education?

*John T. Dever*

The metaphor of chaos theory, as applied to the environment within which higher education currently functions and to the organizational processes by which it habitually operates, is highly instructive for understanding the institutional interplay between strategic planning and leadership. Insofar as planning has evolved from the old long-range model, producing dense documents of detailed and usually inoperable steps for five years out, to a genuinely strategic mode, it has largely been because of the recognition of the turbulence in the external environment that now impinges so acutely upon what was often before conceived of as the relatively self-contained world of college and university life. Keller (1997, p. 169) pinpoints "Darwinian attention to the external environment and its needs" as the critical shift that has occurred in higher education planning. Whether on the cultural, economic, or technological fronts, few stable assumptions can be made except that unanticipated change will occur and only those institutions capable of responding creatively to the threats or opportunities associated with such changes will thrive or survive. Chaos theory, with its explicit rejection of linear extrapolation from the past as a way to predict the future, aptly captures the sense of uncertainty that undermines the Newtonian premises of direct cause and effect that shaped earlier planning efforts. At the same time, because the theory does not simply posit randomness but points to ways (e.g., feedback loops and attractors) to identify and harness complex, replicated patterns, it holds out promise for situating the planning process in some workable context.

Likewise, given the well-recognized loose coupling (Weick, 1976) that characterizes the internal operational and decision-making processes of academic culture, chaos theory offers a more usable model than a dysfunctional hierarchy and a more hopeful one than the dyspeptic "garbage can" or "organized anarchy" (Cohen, March, & Olsen, 1972).

Rather than rail against the lack of clear command and control or bemoan the fickleness of institutional politics, one can use the rich descriptive resources of chaos theory to chart the significant formative effects of small beginnings (the butterfly effect), the highly revealing fractal similarities throughout organizational layers, and the eventual self-organization that occurs even among the most self-directed of professors. If there is any hope for planning to become a true engine driving intended institutional change, it must occur within a framework of assumptions that effectively accounts both for the inherent uncertainties within and without the college or university and for the principles that allow some predictability and productive order to emerge. As a scientific model metaphorically applied to organizational systems, chaos theory provides such a framework.

Assuming the applicability of chaos theory to current conditions of higher education, the question remains of whether such an understanding leaves any room for leadership as traditionally understood, particularly by the college or university president. Is the only choice for a president aspiring to lead to be one of the multiple "strange attractors" that provide counterpoint against environmental turbulence and institutional trepidation, with a resulting series of momentary equilibriums that are not necessarily intended or desirable? To what extent, if any, can qualities of character, commitment, and vision at the top still make a difference for the better in institutional growth and development?

Most fundamental in responding to this question is the correct grasp of chaos theory as a metaphor applied to social systems. Although much more accurate and useful than conceiving of organizations in mechanistic terms, the embrace of a new metaphor and the understanding that comes with it should not blind us to the fact that tenor and vehicle inevitably have as many, if not more, differences than similarities. As Morgan (1996, p. 5) notes: "Metaphor is inherently paradoxical. It can create powerful insights that also become distortions, as the way of seeing created through a metaphor becomes a way of *not* seeing." However remarkable a job chaos theory does in accounting for and helping to foresee to the extent possible the course of natural phenomena and however clarifying and helpful it is to apply comparable analysis to social organizations, weather systems and higher education remain entities of fundamentally different stripes.

The key difference to keep in mind, of course, is the role of human agency. Colleges and universities are founded and sustained with distinctively human ends and means in mind. Their operations are manifestly influenced by the whole gamut of human reason, emotion, and will: intellect through ignorance, aspiration through anxiety, and determination through lassitude. To the degree that the lower end of the spectrum (misunderstanding, apprehension, and disempowerment) is prevalent, the more the social system is like a natural one, vulnerable to unanticipated forces from beyond and within. To the degree that knowledge, goal setting, and commitment are ascendant, the more likely the institution is to maintain effective control of its destiny. Leadership is the tried-and-tested means of bringing the higher range of human faculties to bear productively on the processes of social organization. But leaders who act as if misunderstanding, fear, and failure of nerve do not remain ever ready to assume dominance will prove ultimately foolish and subject their institutions to the vicissitudes of internal turmoil and external turbulence. One must understand how systems work and how they deteriorate if one is not to become the victim of them. The value of chaos theory is that it helps conceptualize a complex social system in a way that allows the creative forces of human agency to be applied efficaciously.

However, the model undercounts the potential of leadership if presidents are relegated to the relatively passive roles (e.g., strange attractors) assigned by a metaphorical conception devoid of personal instrumentality. To risk another metaphor, let me propose the garden and its keeper as a vehicle that accounts for human agency responding in a foresightful way to a plenitude of forces that threaten disruption or offer grounds for purposeful growth. In *Richard II*, Shakespeare (1597) provides the *locus classicus* for metaphorically describing how a world awash in disorder can be brought to purpose by a grasp of the forces at play and by pursuit of a plan for productive design. The gardener addresses his assistants:

> Go bind thou up young dangling apricocks,
> Which like unruly children make their sire
> Stoop with oppression of their prodigal weight;
> Give some supportance to the bending twigs.
> Go thou, and like an executioner
> Cut off the heads of [too] fast growing sprays,
> That look too lofty in our commonwealth:
> All must be even in our government.
> You thus employed, I will go root away
> The noisome weeds which without profit suck
> The soil's fertility from wholesome flowers. (3.4.29–39)

In the play, the point is soon made that the king could have avoided the troubles that beset him had he tended to his kingdom as a well-kept garden (explicitly identified as "a model"). For us here, the point is not to displace chaos theory with an allegorical garden as a guide for planning and leading in higher education, but to stress the danger of how too heavy an emphasis on any single metaphorical construction can distort as well as enlighten. In the case before us, the chaos model may be seen to describe well the dynamics of internal and external organizational environments that enlightened leaders must contend with, but not necessarily the methods they employ to fully exploit the resources of their role.

Planning and carrying through on the plan are touchstone activities that put leadership to the test. Planning and execution assume the ability to apply intelligence in the direction of a desired outcome that is actually realized. However, as Mintzberg (1994) has amply demonstrated, planning in its strategic mode has often gone awry, the results being far less than satisfactory. What lessons from chaos theory can the successful educational leader put to good use? First and foremost, the president is in the best position to keep prominent before the college and university community that complacency is unacceptable in the current and foreseeable environment for higher education, that solutions that have been serviceable in the past are rapidly being displaced by competitive forces from within and beyond the academy. At the moment of writing, this circumstance is nowhere more acute than in the changes being wrought in the teaching and learning processes by web based and enhanced instruction. Former monopolies held by higher education on the delivery of knowledge and the credentialing of skills are rapidly disintegrating. Those pretending otherwise put their institutions at grave risk. The lesson to be learned is not just that another strategic plan must be developed for distance education but rather that all must be on the alert for other transforming forces that may have seemed small at first (the prevalent use of e-mail is still less than a decade old) but which escalate, combine, and separate at speeds heretofore unimaginable. The president can use the position of office and the authority to recognize and promote the efforts of others to perform the indispensable service of keeping the organization alert and responsive through continual adjustments in planning.

The president becomes then the institutional exemplar for maintaining a sense of carefully considered and consistent purpose and direction while accommodating and adapting to the ever-present flux. By distinguishing between, on the one hand, an overall strategy designed to move the college or university forward, in effect, a set of broad goals and proposals that can hold their own despite the vicissitudes of the moment, and, on the other, a set of operational plans that inevitably will be modified in view of varying circumstances but remain consistent with strategy, the president shows how to move beyond mere control as a dominant value. Shifting operations without a strategic framework breeds institutional cynicism about the ability to follow through; holding firm to an objective whose time has passed proves even more disserviceable. The president can model the behaviors that inform truly responsive and evolving adaptability while not losing hold of core values. The degree to which this is successful can often be seen in the self-replications occurring at various levels of organizational life, not in the sense of blind adherence to the president's dictum, but in a similar capacity for agility matched with steadfastness. Fairweather (1997, p. 41) has put his finger on a major insight when he advocates leaders seeing "the handling of small problems as an opportunity or lever to bring about movement towards fulfillment of an overall strategy." Example nearly always trumps exhortation as a motivator for enduring change.

As suggested earlier, the extent to which higher order human capabilities play the dominant part in organizational processes, the more likely the institution is to maintain its ability to successfully navigate turbulence from within and without, to exercise strategic agency as a virtuous mean between a misguided estimation of its own autonomy, on the one hand, and a resigned sense of abnegation to the exigencies of the moment, on the other. The president is in the best position to promote the governing role of enlightened, beneficent, and resolute approaches to whatever issues beset the college or university. He or she can insist on the comprehensive gathering of institutional data and information, particularly as related to key performance areas, and its open and widespread dissemination. He or she can model decision-making processes heavily informed by such research, while showing that the influence exercised by other pressures, such as campus or community politics, is acknowledged, even respected, but not determinant. At the same time, the president can help dispel the myth that all decisions can be data-driven, and openly show how frequently intuition and judgment grounded in values and vision ultimately determine outcomes.

Extending leadership beyond the immediate administrative domain, the president can use such occasions for broad-based consultations that draw upon the learning and expertise present at all levels of the organization. Bringing such knowledge sources to bear upon critical decisions not only strengthens the basis on which they are made, but it goes far in building the relationships and trust that dispel the apprehensions capable of derailing the effective exercise of leadership and planning. The learning organization model advanced by Senge (1990) possesses a natural affinity for attempts to conceptualize how a vibrant and responsive institution of higher education ideally functions (Dever, 1997). The greater the degree to which a president is committed to fostering the application of the disciplines characteristic of learning organizations, the more likely the institution can chart its own destiny because it will have fully made use of its considerable human capital (the personal mastery of its faculty and professional staff) and will have rigorously tested its operating assumptions against challenging scenarios (building mental models). On the side of cohesion, an engaged collegiality among faculty (team learning) can be directed toward the strategic advancement of the institution if all have contributed to what they see as constituting its future (shared vision). Overarching all is the principle shared with chaos theory about the nonlinearity of the cause-and-effect relationships, the need to account for feedback and its capacity to significantly modify intended outcomes through multiple loopings, with the resultant need to take corrective steps (systems thinking). The well-tempered leader who guides the organization by informed precept and worthy example can count on it to respond successfully to most challenges.

In the face of external imposition or internal disruption, the one indispensable quality of self-management that the president can preeminently bring to the institution is "will." Organizations may excel at learning: the collective understanding of their members through disciplined activities and processes far outstrips the capacity represented in the mere sum of knowledge possessed by individual members. But left to themselves, the self-regulation that eventually emerges for most colleges and universities is notoriously disposed toward complacency at one extreme, and unproductive and often self-destructive conflict at the other. Here, the analogies between weather systems and higher education may become too close for comfort, droughts alternating with monsoons. The critical difference that allows human intentionality to exert meaningful influence is the executive function. Although it cannot *control* an outcome without paying a terrific price in terms of demoralizing others and undermining their capacity for genuine agency, it can *shape* the way things play out, exercising the legitimate prerogative to set the terms between what is acceptable and what is not. It can go further and insist on forward movement in accord with planned strategy when other forces are seeking the comfortable familiarity of the status quo or ill-considered reaction to ephemera.

All in all, the chaos model does not displace the need for strong and principled personal leadership in higher education. Rather, it suggests some areas in which leadership is indispensable and others where a president may deftly move with, and strategically guide, the forces impinging upon and emerging within the organization. If planning is framed not as a rigid blueprint, but a set of agreed upon guideposts providing direction and continuity in the midst of ever-increasing flux, then it can become a principal vehicle for purposeful institutional advancement. Armed with knowledge, confidence, and commitment, the president may even see himself or herself as the keeper of the well-tended and well-designed garden, directing as needed the propping-up of the productive fruit and the pruning of the inefficient growth, while reserving to self the task of purging what has become actively harmful to cultivation. Mixing metaphors in the current environment may well be not a sign of inconsistency but a strategy for successful adaptation.

# References

Cohen, M. D., March, J. G., & Olsen, J. P. (1972). A garbage can model of organizational choice. *Administrative Science Quarterly, 17*(1), 1–25.

Dever, J. T. (1997). Reconciling educational leadership and the learning organization. *Community College Review, 25*(2), 57–63.

Fairweather, P. (1997, Spring). Using small problems to make big changes. *Planning for Higher Education, 25,* 39–43.

Keller, G. (1997). Examining what works in strategic planning. In Peterson, M. W., Dill, D. D., & Mets, L. A. (Eds.), *Planning and Management for a Changing Environment* (pp. 158–170). San Francisco: Jossey-Bass Publishers.

Mintzberg, H. (1994). *The rise and fall of strategic planning: Reconceiving roles for planning, plans, planners.* New York: The Free Press.

Morgan, G. (1996). *Images of organization,* 2nd edition. Thousand Oaks, CA: Sage Publications.

Senge, P. M. (1990). *The fifth discipline: The art and practice of the learning organization.* New York: Doubleday.

Shakespeare, W. (1974). *The Tragedy of King Richard the Second.* In Evans, G. B. (Ed.), *The Riverside Shakespeare* (pp. 805–841). Boston: Houghton Mifflin Company. (Original work published 1597).

Weick, K. E. (1976, March). Educational organizations as loosely coupled systems. *Administrative Science Quarterly, 21,* 1–19.

# CHAPTER ELEVEN

## Leadership's Natural Ally: Applying Chaos and Complexity Theories to Academe

*Barbara Mossberg*

*"A rich and beautiful book is always open before us. We have but to learn to read it."*—J. B. Jackson, *Landscape*
*"It is a wonderful feeling to recognize the unity of a complex of phenomena that to direct observation appear to be quite separate things."*—Einstein
*"There is nothing people hate so much as a new experience"*—D. H. Lawrence, *Classics of American Literature*

### Introduction

#### Chaos Theory as a Therapeutic Literacy

I may be the only college president whose inauguration featured the song "Cockeyed Optimist" from the Rogers and Hammerstein musical *South Pacific*. As president, when I am asked how I can or even should maintain optimism and poise in the constant turmoil that swirls like Jupiter's climate, I give a scientific explanation. I say, "I have chaos."

Many people would agree with chaos as a diagnosis of today's educational climate—and therefore, as a reason for hopelessness. Long throughout history, we have used the term "chaos" to write off a situation as resistant to our best efforts and knowledge. The assigning of the category of "chaos" interprets the environment as so out of control that intervention is irrelevant; nothing anyone can do could remedy the situation. A diagnosis of "chaos" justifies apathy and breeds despair—and renders leadership irrelevant. Therefore, citing chaos as a rationale for optimism seems paradoxical if not downright eccentric.

However, by "chaos" I am referring to a set of revolutionary scientific discoveries of order in the universe. These discoveries refute the premises on which we humans historically have understood this age-old category of ultradisorder, whether referring to a global catastrophe or a teenager's closet.

In the last thirty or more years, science from many disciplines has challenged the logic of pessimism concerning situations that seem chaotic. Based on revelations of how the "real world" actually works, "chaos theory" shows how chaotic behavior defines natural orderly systems. There is meaning and order and success in what appears to be chaos: this makes obsolete a fearful and defensive attitude toward the chaotic environment in which we live and work.

Science's rehabilitation of chaos into a grand theory of orderly behavior in systems defined by complexity and change makes chaos, the theory, resonate deeply with leaders of today's academic organizations. To leadership of academic organizations undergoing fundamental and traumatic change—in other words, which experience themselves as chaotic, a theory, which provides a new way to assess chaotic situations more hopefully, is encouraging news.

Thus in this essay I will propose an idea about a use of chaos *theory* as a new and therapeutic way to read—and lead—a chaotic environment. I will advocate the strategic knowledge of chaos (and other related theories of order including "complexity"[1] and "consilience"[2]) as a vaccine for the debilitating and demoralizing sense of hopelessness, however rational it seems, that attends a diagnosis of chaos.

Using chaos theory to reassess the condition of higher education as well as to provide new leadership paradigms seems especially appropriate when I think of the challenges facing higher education leadership today. The analogies for higher education come from the natural world.

First, like the geological structures on earth's surface, American education is under continual pressure to reform. Currents and winds of society's needs reshape our structures of learning. Tectonic shifts and collisions and mergers of mandates cause upheavals, rifts, compression, expansion, quakes, and explosions from our deep structure, the core elements of our history and experience and psychology as a people. The need to provide the kind of education that negotiates and makes intelligible the changing environment forces higher education to be dynamic, and to play within the ground rules for chaotic systems. The Grove was not like this.

Second, the complexity of higher education today, resulting from the internal and external pressures on institutions, makes them expand in time and space like supernovas. Today's institutions are becoming larger, more diffuse, more porous in their borders, more distributed, sowing new schools and practices and complex new educational formats. The original hydrogen and helium of academe, religion, and philosophy, bundled as ethics, have become an expanded disciplinary periodical table of elemental ways of knowing about the world. And our new elements of knowledge have taken on new formats, some explosive, so that institutions replenish the universe with new complex and essential components for continuous learning.

Emergent technologies and increased demands for a different kind of learning challenge the assumptions by which people practice the art and science of education. Public doubt accompanies increased pressure for "accountability" to public needs. This turbulent climate is seen as the cause for leadership upheavals occurring with frequency. "Interim" is increasingly becoming a fixed title in any organization chart. Institutions are "downsizing" or "rightsizing" and changing the rules for who comes, on what terms. People are insecure and look for new structures of permanence, even as calls for change originate in the workplace, with parents, with people in "the real world" who have urgent needs for a learning to take place, which is more relevant and enables people to negotiate complexity and change with confidence.[3] Within the institution, things seem fragmented in curriculum, organization, and agendas of diverse groups. There is a loss of confidence in our ability to develop meaningful education in the current structures.

The analogies of higher education to powerful chaotic systems defined by change express my sense of the magnitude of academic leadership's challenge: to transform and transition learning institutions through a revisioning of the nature of organizations, leadership, and learning itself.

The very ground beneath our feet shifts and trembles, as the old verities of "course," "canon," "faculty," "requirements," "campus," "curriculum," "classroom," "distance learning," "continuing education," "organization chart," "power," and other modern and traditional elements are undergoing renovation or revolution.

We can call this state of affairs "transition," or "continuing process," or any other name, but the climate of doubt, fear, and pressure from within and without defines the leader's environment. There is spiritual suffering in academic organizations undergoing change. Such an environment makes especially urgent the leader's role, yet the cultural context in which academe operates means that while leaders are accountable and responsible for the destiny of their institutions, the fates of its members, and those affected by the institution, they do not have the traditional organizational direct power to effect change and bring about action. The climate of doubt and fear makes the leader's role both more critical and more difficult.

In this high stress, high stakes, uncertain and volatile ethos, higher education leadership can be considered an extreme profession equivalent to extreme sports. What qualities of mind and heart, what knowledge, skills, attributes, and attitudes can enable and sustain leadership in cultures undergoing rapid change and challenge? What ideas are genuinely helpful to changing organizations? What ideas can strengthen one's capacity to evoke the triumph of the human spirit, resilience, creativity, and hope, out of isolation, struggle, and adversity? What would foster the belief in ourselves, as Faulkner said in his Nobel Prize acceptance speech, "not only to endure but to prevail?"[4]

Leadership has always been about a farsighted ability to identify and evoke as yet unrecognized potential in individuals and entities. A leader's optimistic vision can sustain people's belief in the institution's capacity to transform, reform, and move forward. Chaos serves leadership by providing a vision that enlarges our sense of what is possible organizationally—a vision of the institution's capacity to act chaotically as we now understand Nature to act. That ability of the leader to hold and convey a view of the organization as orderly and coherent is more important in a climate of change. If chaos theory can help us see disorder on grand scales as "order," then we can imagine that the organizational challenges that look chaotic can also be *not as bad as it seems*. We need to think this, or we will give up or come up with solutions that don't help in the short or long run.

A view of the organization as dynamic, whole, and full of continuous and infinite energy and renewal is a vision which sustains both the leader and the organization. Neither leaders nor the organizations they serve can flourish with a sense of fear or defensiveness of, and without a full sense of trust in, the capacity of the environment to act in productive and meaningful and ultimately *organized* ways for long-term sustainability.

Therefore, what I think of as "the order theories" or "whole systems theories" can serve us as an antidote for a counterproductive pessimistic interpretation of chaotic happenings and experience. These theories can be trusted. They are experientially based, a tried and true type of practical knowledge that can serve academic leadership as a particularly inspiring and frequently consoling perspective, for those conditions that specifically are thought of in terms of *things going wrong*.

Applied consistently, chaos theory works as a transformative interpretive tool for leadership. In this transforming theory, we find evidence for the need to rethink our sense of helplessness and fatalism in the face of apparent chaos. Instead we find encouragement to be proactive, to approach challenges with renewed energy that is not inhibited by fear. Such encouragement can sustain our daily and long-term efforts. Appreciating chaotic complex natural systems can foster the effort to reassure and to guide organizations enduring the turbulence of change. We can have more confidence in our institutions and ourselves as we consider our mandates and options, and assess what needs to be done, and what can and must be done. We can have a far different approach to problems, which otherwise would make us fearful, resigned, or just dismiss them.

Leadership's gifts of vision, energy, enthusiasm, and hope are transformative for an organization in the same way that chaos theory enables a rereading of the environment. In this rereading, what appears as "meaninglessness," "mess," "disorder," and "going nowhere" is valued as the flowing look of a system at work, an intrinsic expression of the universe's order and meaning and even beauty. Even as higher education must change continually how it organizes learning, and thus is inescapably chaotic, to say that is to recognize that higher education has a natural and enduring vitality that not only withstands change but also requires it to fulfill its ultimately responsive mission. In the face of institutional change, leadership can play a key role in helping the college or university keep intact and coherent its essential purpose, values, and organizing principles.

Of all the tactical knowledge that chaos theory gives to organizational and academic leadership—and chaos theory is a most practical tool for daily administration—I find its most indispensable aspect for leadership in its basis for transformational revisioning. Understanding chaos—even recognizing that such a science exists, which refutes the superficial impressions of disorder—can help reassure and guide organizations enduring the turbulence of change. And appreciating chaotic and complex systems can justify and sustain the optimism of anyone trying to make a positive difference in a learning organization, whether in a classroom or a program, an institution or system, or government or planet.

Leadership, which reads the chaotic environment as a whole, as an orderly, meaningful, and hopeful construct, results in greater trust in the environment, and greater care for it. Such perspective, or literacy, I would argue, which bestows greater reverence and trust in the environment and one another is what the "world needs now." Like love, it is a view that can sustain both leadership and our organizations. If we approach whatever we see, however chaotic it appears, with the attitude that it expresses a system that works, our leadership will be suffused with uninhibited energy and confidence and hope. My premise, then, is that solutions and strategies we need as leaders shaping learning environments, and the answers to the questions that have always turned us to education—what it all means, whom we are, why we are, where we are and where we are going, how we can get there—are all around us, orderly and beautiful, wherever we look.

Using chaos theory as a transformative diagnostic tool makes possible a sense of optimism and hope that I would argue is not only realistic, but also essential for leaders and their organizations. As a science-based interpretive analytical lens of environmental and organizational behavior and meaning, it provides an expanded vision of John Keats' "truth and beauty," which keeps confidence grounded and optimism credible.

A leader's ability to inspire hope and confidence in the enterprise must be rooted in a faith both in the organization's capacity and its surrounding ethos—its ability to operate in and serve the social infrastructures. If such faith in the institution and in the ethos is shown to be grounded in "reality"—how things operate in the "real world"—the leader's vision can shore up confidence in the institution, the sustaining belief in ourselves that Faulkner was sure would enable us to survive and prevail.

## Part One:
## The Mechanisms of the Whole

"If you do not expect it, you will not find the unexpected, for it is hard to find and difficult."—*Heraclitus*

An ordered universe, a "behaving" universe, may be part of the "unexpected" universe, which Loren Eisley referred to in his book of the same title (1964). Seeing the universe as intelligible and meaningful has been identified as a critical need for society by the work of educational visionaries such as John Stilgoe (as in *Outside Lies Magic: Regaining History and Awareness in Everyday Places*, 1998) and J. B. Jackson (as in *Discovering the Vernacular*

*Landscape*, 1984). The vision advocacy work of Jackson and Stilgoe, added to the rich array of thinking on environmental education, from David Orr (in *Ecological Literacy: Education and the Transition to a Postmodern World*, 1992) to E. O. Wilson (as in *Consilience*, 1998), urge an education for our relearning "how to see" the environment, the goal of which, I believe, is our ability to value it.

It is in this educational context that chaos theory has enormous consequences for those who work to preserve and protect the environment and those who work to increase the quality of humanity's experience through education that creates a greater consciousness, understanding, and appreciation of our world. We would act very differently toward each other and the earth if we could read the environment as intelligible and meaningful, and just as importantly, more trustfully, as *not* randomly alienating and monstrous. We could be more open to what we can learn from it and each other. We could fulfill the potential of our brain's evolution to its present size and complexity.

For academic leadership, the tactical and strategic vision chaos theory makes possible, an environment both meaningful and orderly, depends upon an overarching sense of the organization as a whole, a vision on which the organization depends to survive. My understanding of chaos theory as a re-visioning tool sustains me in emotional, intellectual, and professional ways, especially in providing me an understanding of the potential of the environment to be meaningful, and the resulting tolerance and trust and expectation with which I can see it. I believe that a long-term vision of possibility and capacity of an organization may be one of the most fundamental ways a leader serves an organization. A leader has to project confidence in the institution, its capacity, its prospects, its purpose, and its future. A leader has to be able to see, and to communicate, that in spite of how things look from within or without, the institution is sustainable, is in momentum, is doing all right, is surviving and can move on. These are the questions everyone wants to know, inside and out of the organization. Knowledge of chaos theory enables a leader to visualize the institution as a dynamic whole operating according to natural laws, and to exercise leadership from this trustful perspective. For me, the perspectives of chaos theory provide an intellectual and spiritual framework for leadership's requisite perseverance and hope.

### Look All Around: Or, Chaos, a Beautiful Global Vision for Leaders of Transition: The Lessons of the Sphinx for Leadership's Literacy

The intellectual, cognitive, and spiritual dimensions of leadership that can invoke this life-sustaining belief are a function of vision. There is a direct relationship between how we see and the resilience, flexibility, tolerance, long-term strategic thinking, and ability to deal with complexity and rapid change (and the confusion and fear transition causes) with optimism, courage, and hope. This set of attributes is essential for the organization struggling to maintain stability even as it transforms itself surely but unrecognizably into new forms and formats.

The organization in transition has specific needs for a coherent vision of itself, even and especially in transition. This need defines today's leadership.

But the need for such leadership is not new. It long has been identified in cultural wisdom as essential to our preservation. For example, in the ancient myth of the Sphinx, upon which Sophoclean and other early forms of Greek drama were based, we learn that a coherent vision of an entity in transitional growth is held explicitly as leadership's role. The story concerns a community suffering, in a state of siege, perishing because of its isolation from the outside world. Travelers were not permitted to enter unless they could pass an "entrance exam" administered by a monster, the Sphinx. To each would-be member of the community, the Sphinx asked: *What walks on four legs in the morning, two legs at noon, and three legs in the afternoon?* The failure to come up with the right answer does not result in another chance at the question (or a Kaplan course), or simply being rejected. The person who gives the wrong answer is put to death. No one could answer. Inside and outside the city walls, people were dying.

What knowledge is considered of such fatal importance? The answer, a human being *(man)*, requires a holistic, integrated ability to see a coherent vision of an entity changing over time. A life is described metaphorically as a day: as the earth turns, infancy is early, middle age is mid-day, and old age is afternoon. Thus, a baby crawls, adult strides erect, and an aged person uses the "third leg" of a supportive cane. The same human being experiences these changes.

What is extraordinary in this story is that except for an otherwise unperceptive Oedipus, who was "blind" to obvious realities in other ways, no one can "see" the meaning in a description of the most common and significant aspect of human experience—our own change and growth and that of everyone around us. How could this be? How can we not recognize a vision of ourselves?

This question builds upon the significance of the fact that the person who *could* answer the question became the "king" of the community. His ability to "read" the complex whole in terms of coherence not only saved his life but was inextricably connected to the community's self-preservation: this vision was the basis of his leadership.

If we return to the riddle itself, a dynamic portrait of human experience as a whole in time and space, we gain insight into a cultural understanding of the importance of the ability to see coherence in complexity. The story links this ability with the ability to live and to participate in community. For me, the story's meaning centers on the consequences of the lack of what I think would be classified as a "visual literacy" (Stilgoe, 1998[5]; Gardner, 1993) or "environmental literacy" (Orr, 1992[6]). Essential, life-saving, community-preserving literacy is the ability to see coherence, pattern, and meaning, in a dynamic complex manifestation (in this case, the formal connections between three life stages experienced by one coherent entity— the human being).

Such vision recognizes experience and an environment, which is shared and witnessed by every human being. The fact that the punishment is death for cognitive failure, inability to recognize how things connect and interrelate, suggests ancient wisdom's value of the ability to identify coherence and meaning in entities undergoing natural change. This is a literacy equally necessary to the individual and to the community: if one cannot answer, one cannot live with others, nor live at all. The story of the Sphinx contains the insight that such understanding of stability and wholeness in ourselves and the world around us, even as we change every day and the earth turns every moment, is an elusive, difficult ability. In fundamental ways, understanding how diverse things link and interrelate, things that seem to come in different formats and to change over time, does not come naturally.

I would submit that the leadership demands on today's organizations of higher learning require the same vision of the organization as the developmental model of the transitioning "human being" in this myth. The college or university, and higher education in general, in perpetual process, need a self-image that is coherent over time and space. This unified and unifying vision must be inclusive of a multiplicity and fluctuating velocity of missions and mandates with a recognizable past and a plausible future.

As theologian Martin E. Marty or ecotheologian Thomas Berry present national and global spiritual needs of cultural community in terms of a narrative or "story" (Marty, 1968, 1981, 1992; Berry, 1988), I would apply these ancient critical insights to the transitioning organization, which urgently needs a coherent sense of itself. Our organizations need a story, such as Oedipus gave Thebes (the answer "man" gave a dignified and consoling "plot" and meaning to the fragmented phenomenal situation of various developmental stages which did not "add up"). Organizations need to understand their own meaning, most of all when they seem fragmented, exceptional, spiraling out of control, and to lack a sense of productive order and direction. A story which can include as essential to the character and destiny or any organization the condition of continuous change, and which can show that this change does not diminish or erode or destroy the organization's purpose and identity, can help that organization find its sources of resilience and courage and creativity.

The mystery at the heart of the power of the Sphinx myth is that people could not recognize an image of what they themselves personally had experienced: in Eliot's words, they "had the experience but missed the meaning." The paradox points to the role of education as well as leadership: we must be enabled to see the whole within and beyond surface incompatibilities and disjointedness. We must develop the ability to see in diversity the whole dynamic being from the perspectives of time and space.

My reading of the Sphinx myth, then, is that the community or organization, however complex and changing, needs a vision of itself as a meaningful "whole," as a continuously transitioning entity modeling and acting in relation to a larger and dynamic ethos.

The organization, like the "walker" in the ancient Theban myth, needs to understand itself in order to envision how it belongs in the world, how its purpose fits into the larger scheme of things. It needs to understand how external forces shape it, even as it contributes to shaping the ethos of its environment. The organization needs a sense of itself as a viable, orderly, sturdy, sustainable and resilient enterprise, linked physically to other viable organizations and the economic, political, cultural, and social infrastructure on which all depend.

## Chaos Theory as Deus Ex Machina

This is where chaos theory comes to the fore. Just as the word *assessment* comes from a root word meaning *to stand aside*, the word *revelation* comes from the Old French *revelare*, meaning *to lift* or *raise*. The roots of the two terms for kinds of recognition and evaluation that determine value suggest the role of perspective in discovering a meaningful reality. One needs to be *above*, *beside*, or otherwise get sufficient distance on a situation to really see and evaluate it. From chaos theory comes the knowledge that the farther one steps back in time and space, the more one can discern the order and patterns that are there, whether on galactic or molecular scales, in every sphere of existence and mode of dynamic behavior. This is how knowledge of systems dynamics can serve leadership, which grapples with enterprises that experience themselves in various states of disorder and stasis. The counterintuitive promise of chaos theory is that situations that appear chaotic are not: our vision is crimped. Chaos provides a perspective that is so long and comprehensive that it enables us to see patterns in systems that are invisible up close. At this range, order is disguised as "mess," "irregularity," "confusion."

The revelations about chaos's laws and order in dynamic systems are based on scrupulously wrought analyses of years of observation on macro and micro levels, over time and projected through computer modeling, in physics, mathematics, and other scientific disciplines.[7] Those "proofs" have survived decades of doubt and disbelief about the claims for chaotic order as great as that which attended Galileo's discovery about earth's movement. The "hard" proofs have resulted in Nobel prizes. The science-based ability to recognize meaning and order inherent in chaotic systems is reassuring in today's transitional environment of higher education.

The corrective lens of the laws of long-term behavior in complex nonlinear systems illuminates encouraging signs in seemingly the most hopeless situations. In this lens, a situation or behavior appearing disorderly, irregular, random, meaningless, hopeless, fragmented, or out of control actually turns out to be part of a process that is profoundly orderly. Four legs, two legs, and three legs turn out to be not only connected, but *the same thing*, developed over time (and for a successful model, we all wish to experience all three stages). Things once discounted as insignificant or "wrong" emerge, in this lens, as relevant and important signifiers.

In its ability to reveal the possibility of the existence of such patterns in what seem like isolated phenomena, chaos theory unveils and recovers narrative meaning in events that otherwise seem fragmented blips. Garden-variety chaos becomes a revelation of interconnections and relationships across scales of time and space, making possible certain predictability based on laws for how things happen. The more we learn about chaos theory, the more it is apparent that being discouraged by a chaotic situation turns out to be shortsighted, a function of a lack of knowledge about how systems operate. Despair results from a critical lack of vision.

Viewing an event through chaos theory's lens of natural systems behavior, we learn to see things differently than they appear up close and as isolated phenomena. We see essential relationships among entities that seem to have nothing to do with each other in time or space. We see systems in action governed by laws of interdependence, rather than individual entities defined by autonomy and necessary boundaries and exclusion. We see cause and effect (how do things happen as they do?) appear in a way that changes our notions of power and control. Chaos theory generates expectations of significance, of what there is to observe and value in the environment. It reveals and recovers across scale and function an entity's relevance and its claims for belonging and even centrality to kinds of experience that were considered too insignificant to count: "trash," waste, irrelevance, marginality, and "noise."

Thus, in systems of diverse, competing, conflicting, even contradictory entities, chaos theory enables us to see coherence, or in Wilson's term, consilience.[8] Chaos theory turns our notions of chaos inside out, so that where we saw mess and confusion we see meaning and beauty. We see in chaotic situations what is essential for our own and our organization's success. Instead of a rationale to dismiss or negate, and reason for defensiveness and fear and lack of respect, we approach these situations with confidence. Surely this is magical. And surely our institutions need this wizardry.

Yet such transformative reading of environmental behavior is realistic. Gaining courage and encouragement instead of being discouraged, or seeing value in what traditionally has been devalued, is a therapeutic literacy.[9] Chaos theory provides the interpretive framework in which we can imagine or believe in the good and best in the most problematic of situations. This knowledge brings out the spiritual quality of leadership: based on scientific breakthroughs, optimism is proven to be a more realistic assessment than pessimism. "Getting real" means, literally, an imaginative and reasonable and necessary hope.[10]

## Part Two:
## Now That We See the Whole

Chaos is a theory about how change and process occur in "the real world." In such a world, transition must be understood as the normal ongoing activity—entities going from one state or stage to another in a ceaseless flow of "phase transitions." The theory draws its power for transformative revisioning from its purview of "the whole." The way that systems operate as a whole—governed by laws of interdependence—can be applied to academic organizations as "wholes" in and of themselves.

Since leadership's unique role is responsibility for "the whole," the application of systems theory to academic leadership provides a new way of thinking about structures for learning and community in terms of dynamic systems, and offers new understanding about how and why things happen as they do.

### *Chaos as a Lunar and Solar Set of Perspectives*

Chaos theory provides a leader of a "whole" enterprise a vision of its coherence. This perspective is as transformative a vision as the radically, even heretically, challenging view of the earth first seen from space. The analogy of chaos theory's view of nature to the astronaut's view of earth is helpful to understand the transformative perspective that chaos theory gives leadership, which by definition is occupied with framing the meaning and direction of a "whole" system or enterprise.

By going to the moon, we could see the earth "whole" for the first time. The earth was revealed as truly round, exquisitely defined, shaped, and self-contained as a cell (to invert Lewis Thomas' analogy in *The Lives of a Cell* [1971]), each of its parts interdependent and simultaneously coexisting. Diverse states of existence can be seen as physically coherent, comprising a singular "whole." What is experienced on earth as fragmented, isolated epiphenomena, a hodgepodge of competing, conflicting, and contradictory elements, is revealed as an infinitely and intricately connected ecosystem in which every part belongs and behaves in relation to every other part. An orderly interdependence is the rule governing this newly revealed "whole."

The radical transformation in our thinking enables our understanding of the dynamic, complex meaning and reality of being "whole." Thus, from a distance, the relationships, connections, patterns, and beauty of diverse states are readily apparent. Boundaries blur in a constant process of form and reformation: clouds, water, land.

We can see before our eyes, from space, even so-called "opposites" which "don't belong together" coexisting harmoniously or interacting in a shimmering blue and white image. Regarding earth at any one moment from space, we can see a "rounded" or "curved" sense of time and space as both relative and simultaneous. Thus, in the moment you are reading this sentence on earth, we now see that it is day and night (and every stage in between), wet and dry, cold and warm, low and high, calm and storm, water and land, foliage and sand, cloudy and bright—all at once. Only close up is it possible to experience each of these states as diverse and "opposite." Each is "right," "true," valid.

We see that the states of existence are not static, nor self-contained. Boundaries between land and water and air blend, blur, bend, bleed, overlap, and "morph," in a constantly flowing series of interactions over time and space. They not only spill over into each other (as light becomes darkness, storm becomes calm, cloud evaporates, water becomes shore), but they are superimposed (water over land, cloud over water), and change each other (land's heat creates winds which stir water and speed clouds, water's evaporation creates clouds which rain and cause rivers and lakes, which create more moisture which creates clouds . . .). Electromagnetic charges of a serene afternoon create imbalances that result in late afternoon thunderstorms and lightning. In turn these disturbances restore calm.

### Chaos Theory's First Gift to Leadership: Evidence of a Coherent Organization

The leader's perspective of an organization, akin to the astronaut's view of earth from space, in which everything in the system belongs, has enormous implications for institutions. What appears in an organization as irreconcilable agendas, purposes, styles, values, and even language, differences as profound as night and day, can be understood as a system of interrelationships governed by natural laws.[11] Although the various parts may change, form, and reform, the essential elements are there which comprise the "whole." The application of this to organizational leadership translates into practical and realistic views of conflict within a dynamic organization, as both inevitable and as workable.

In this respect, I liken the leader's situation at an institution to a family car trip. The destination; what music is worth listening to; what is funny; the make and year of the car; the temperature; the planned time in the car before the next stop; what is worth noticing along the road: there may be as many points of view on these matters as people in the car. That may be why Dave Barry (1991) observes that on a family car trip, the size of the car shrinks in inverse proportion to the length of the trip, so that at the end of a long trip the car has shrunk to the size of a mailbox (only not as comfortable). However, we can add to Mr. Barry's experiential observation by pointing out that in the majority of cases the family does reach its destination, even if it revises its goals about time and place. From the point of the enterprise, the family institution as a traveling unit, the goal is reached. At all times, at least from the perspective of Mars, the family is moving as a coherent entity within the car in relation to its goal, even as simultaneously, various behaviors coexist (driving, sulks, screams, sighs, getting lost, detours, nausea, pokes, and obliviousness).

To extend the analogy of the institution to the family car trip, chaos theory is a long-term view of phenomena based on observation that like the astronaut's view of earth sees connections and patterns in time and space between and among those things that do not seem related. Through chaos theory's lens, any event is perceived in context of the whole. It is a perspective that is contextual and relational: one thing is seen in terms of another. Thus, one could argue that the fundamental concept of chaos theory is the metaphoric insight that the Sphinx wished to enforce on Thebes for its own good. Our developmental insights into our own dynamic processes extend to the insights of how we are related to others. The patterns in human development link us, even as we each follow distinct, erratic, eccentric orbits and courses, and feel that "we are the only one" in our miseries and our joys, our challenges and our solutions.

The unifying view of earth from space, which the leader adopts toward the organization, points to another aspect of chaos theory that relates to the human mind's way of constructing coherence out of chaotic experience. John Briggs and David Peat, in their book on chaos theory called *Turbulent Mirror: An Illustrated Guide to Chaos Theory and the Science of Wholeness* (1989), provide an image we can develop for a critical understanding of our greatest cognitive challenge as human beings: the process of making meaning out of our experience.[12]

I would use Briggs and Peat's description of the universe as a "turbulent mirror" as a basis for support for Lifton's and Damasio's arguments that the psychologically constructed sense of self and the conception of the human body and brain provide equivalent images of the coherence and stability that prevail in an atmosphere of change and chaos.

Over the course of our history we have learned from our external environment, replicating what we see. We have seen birds and invented airplanes, seen fish and invented submarines. In this way we have used an understanding of "the other" to enlarge our sense of possibility of our own existence. But not everything we observe in our environment seems relevant or even hospitable to our sense of needs or possibilities. The environment can seem alien. If, however, we understand all we see as a "mirror," even a "turbulent mirror," we can gain a larger and more complex understanding of "ourselves" and our own capacities. Our possibilities for learning from the environment are infinitely expanded if "the whole" is considered a kind of mirror reflecting back truths about the universe, truths which provide insight into our own natures—and as Lifton and Damasio each argue, a positive sense of their stability and resilience.

In such a view, the environment can be considered a "text." We can "read" it to discover revelations about ourselves that, as the root term *revelare* suggests, are not apparent from our vantage points in time and space without the aids of computers, history, spacecraft, microscopes, and other arts and sciences. The environment is a key to our own self-knowledge. It is inextricably related to "us"—in fact, it *is* us—in ways we can decode once we expect that meaning and relevance are there if we only look. Understanding that one kind of system functions like another, we increase our capacity for creativity, invention, and discovery, each of which is rooted in an ability to perceive relationships of diverse entities. Analogy, metaphor, equations: we comprehend one thing in terms of another. The more we learn about the cosmos, the more we see cosmic processes replicated in one form and another. Chaos theory gives us astonishingly diverse examples of forms of behavior in natural systems that operate according to the same fundamental laws. Awareness of these laws enables us to see how knowledge about one system can inform our understanding of another system, no matter how different one may appear in size or location or function (this principle is termed "similarity across scales").

For leaders, the knowledge that one can look about in the natural world and see a "mirror" of what is happening in our organizations[13] as Margaret

Wheatley has shown (1999), gives us realistic organic ways to assess and understand where organizations are in their processes and how they are doing. Viewing the environment as a model of ourselves as a complex dynamic organization also provides a more empathic understanding of what we see, however different it may look. Feeling more connected to the environment, we gain a greater sense of what is at stake for what happens to it.

For organizational leadership, this point of view is very constructive. If the environment seems chaotic, or irrelevant, we can feel threatened or indifferent to its fate and ignore its relevance. But if we have a way to understand and to value what seems most *un*related and a source of greatest fear, we open ourselves to whatever we can learn. Knowing that natural systems reveal sources of stability and persistence, what we "see" can keep us from not giving up on our institutions or each other. And just as important, we will not try to destroy the environment that is essential to our own survival.

## Part Three:
## Some Introductory Examples of Some Ways
## Chaos Theory Could Be Applied to Academe

If institutional leadership uses the "real world" model of chaos theory, what is basically incorporated into the leadership paradigm is a perspective that affects the leader's outlook on everything from crisis management and institutional strategic planning to curriculum reform issues. Institutional leaders will find chaos integral to assessment:

- A long-term view—a basis for optimism
- A view of the diversity characterizing the whole—a basis for realizing coherence
- A feedback system—a basis for continuous learning
- Structures for collaboration—a basis for integration
- A view of change—a basis for planning

Once a system is understood in terms of change and complexity, then leadership can be proactive in supporting those structural and cultural initiatives which promote such principles as diversity, assessment through feedback, collaboration across discipline and organizational role, and so on. To say that leadership presides over chaotic organizations opens the way to show how other insights from chaos theory apply to the academic enterprise.

## Some Practical Applications

- the role of leadership in the academic culture
- strategic and long-term goal-setting and planning
- problemsolving and policymaking
- understanding and managing conflict
- assessment
- crisis management
- diversity initiatives
- curricular reform and faculty development
- organizational structures

Each of the above depends upon an attitude informed by knowledge of the actual "according-to-chaos" way in which things work. As a diagnostic and interpretive tool, chaos theory is most useful in all of these enterprises of academic leadership.

## Examples: The Role of Leadership in the Culture

Energy initially destabilizes a system. If we understand action as the expression of energy in a dynamic system, then any action in an organization is linked to, and causes changes over time in, other entities. Any action by an individual or group is an intervention in the constant flow of interactions. In this respect, any person or unit in a system can exert a dynamic leadership role. Having influence in a system does not depend upon one's location or "power" within the organization. In a dynamic system, any and every unit is a "mover," with power to both initiate and respond to other actions. Formal leadership's role, with purview of "the whole," is to assess the general patterns of interactions and to be proactive about the nature and timing of interventions which can stabilize—or perhaps, bring into a creative disorder—a system undergoing transformation.

Turbulence can be generated with a new person entering an institution, a policy change, an award of a grant or a gift, a new student, an outside speaker, a new law influencing student aid. Each of these bring needs for increased "energy" and change (new support staff, more meetings and events, increased spending, more staff time, more resources, new equipment, more supplies, new and challenging ideas to the status quo, unanticipated needs) which will initially destabilize an institution and cause further changes and stress and confusion. However "called for," positive, necessary, or inevitable the changes, in leadership or financial gifts or policy, there will be turbulence as the institution adapts to and absorbs the new energy, whether in the form of human or material resources, or new ideas challenging academic policies and practices, curriculum, or investment.

If leaders understand the effects of implementing planned changes or of events that influence the institution as interventions, then resistance, stress, counter-initiatives, and other responses in the system to the changes will make sense as "orderly" and "natural" forms of behavior from a systems point of view. Leaders can learn from dynamic systems to expect and even to plan for such responses, not to be destabilized or "thrown" by them, or to feel in need of defensive responses.

In planning for institutional turbulence with any new changes in policy, no matter who initiates it, we learn from chaos theory's dictum that slight actions can make a big difference over time. Even as the system will stabilize on its own, modest interventions can keep a situation from "getting out of control." While chaos theory shows how total control is not possible over the long-range, just as it is not possible to make predictions over a long period of time for behavior in a dynamic system, we also learn that continuous interventions enable an equilibrium and stability. An analogy is steering on ice. When the car starts to skid, the lightest response will keep the car from veering out of control, while a hard and violent jerk of the car in one direction or another will put the car into a chaotic spin. Thus for "crisis management," it is helpful to know that a situation that seems chaotic is going to "self-organize," and can be managed responsibly with a lighter touch if one realizes the sensitivity of the institution to any intervention. Given the interdependence of elements within a dynamic system, an earlier, lighter approach to an issue helps keep the level of turbulence down, and promotes stability.

## Curriculum—and the Case for the Liberal Arts

Chaos, and other high-cognitive order theories, was not a recognized field of research and knowledge even thirty years ago. Chaos was a "trash" fish of data, which were to be thrown out not only as unusable when caught up in the nets of traditional research forays into the reality of the universe, but as "error," a rebuke not only to the quality of research but to the areas in which people were fishing in the first place. People looking at unorthodox topics such as how clouds move, water falls, smoke rises, gas expands, and earthquakes or volcanoes shake saw evidence of "turbulence," which in their fields was discounted as not significant.

As James Gleick eloquently chronicles in his book *Chaos: Making a New Science* (1987), questions on the nature of "the whole" in dynamic systems were considered "off track" and unscholarly. Scientists lost grants, positions, graduate students, prestige, publication opportunities, and other forms of reward for their focus on a topic which was not recognized to be "in the canon." People were penalized for developing models that contradicted assumptions about how things work and what matters to understand. In other words, a significant percentage of the evidence of reality in abundance from the environment was being ignored, discounted, and not considered important enough to "read."

Carol Gilligan's work on gender difference is one example of this exclusionary process in the field of psychology. In a *Different Voice* (1982), she points out that our understanding of ethical development patterns in girls and boys was based on data which excluded the experience of girls because such experience changed the models of the researchers based on a sense of a boy's outlook as "the norm." Similarly, in the field of literature, Emily Dickinson was left out of significant studies of American literature in the 1950s to 1970s, such as F. O. Mathiessen's classic *American Renaissance* (Mossberg, 1982), because her work and biography formed a troublesome bulge in otherwise neat literary theories and models. Using J. B. Jackson's advocacy of the vernacular landscape as a "text" (1984, ix–x), where meaning and significance lie at every glance, we can see that chaos theory also opens up the universe as a "book" which gives to the whole of experience a new significance.

There is further significance for the national questions of liberal arts curriculum in putting chaos on the academic "map." For any person undertaking to understand the necessity of arts and sciences, humanities and technology, as the foundation for any lifelong education, I always recommend James Gleick's book on chaos (1987) as a starting point. Understanding that our institutional structures and policies which contribute to the separation of fields and disciplines pose obstacles to discovery has import for how we organize learning and institutional reward systems for collaboration and integration of learning outcomes. A deeper implication is in the fact that even a cursory study of the thinking and research and knowledge that have gone into major scientific breakthroughs in the past several hundred years reveals the extent to which arts and humanities and social sciences are instrumental to the ability of scholars to generate and communicate insights in the first place. Gleick's narrative of the use of Wagner, Goethe, Wallace Stevens, and others, by chaos theory's founders, is reinforced by reading the work of scientists themselves, such as Murray Gell-Mann (1994), Damasio (1999), or Richard Feynmann (D. L. Goodstein & J. R. Goodstein, 1996), who cite as a matter of course philosophy, literature, art, music, history, and other disciplines as basic to the workings and expression of their discoveries.

The understanding of the role of integrated arts and sciences has tremendous implications for how colleges and universities and all schools of learning approach issues of curriculum—options and requirements for courses of study.

We can extrapolate from the lessons of the development of chaos theory, which is a successful model to emulate: after all, it has a happy ending, in that the insights have held water and created exciting new fields, founders have received Nobel prizes, research centers on chaos theory have sprung up in the private and public sectors, major scientific breakthroughs have occurred based on the theory, and so on. When there are aspects of experience, in history or in any other field, that traditionally are left out of formal academic studies as "insignificant" and "minor" or "marginal," we can remember that the mission of advancing knowledge will not be served by leaving out essential evidence in the accumulating "story" of the human experience. There needs to be an expansive, inclusive approach to what is studied and taught, an experimental and imaginative vision which tries to model "the whole."

It is mandatory that academic research and teaching be given the resources for development that are needed to continually expand. Furthermore, it is mandatory that access and exposure to different ways of thinking and knowing are made possible throughout the disciplines and in terms of cross-cultural studies, and that the institution creates success in academic achievement through continuous evaluation of fields. Rigor, which traditionally was defined by keeping the fields "pure" and "uncompromised" or "uncontaminated" by other fields and ways of knowing, now can be supported by leadership in terms of the injunction to continuously assess and keep open the research channels, and respect the emergence of new fields. Thus, in a successful academic organization, fields should continually be challenged, opened up, expanded, merged, realigned, focused, reformed, and developed. Curriculum reform must be continual. The role of the academic leader is to ensure that a value system expresses the story of the relationship and significance of all the elements in the dynamic system,

On the basis of the findings of chaos theory, academic leaders can encourage interdisciplinary and transdisciplinary curriculum. Reading any accounts of the development of complex adaptive systems theory, beginning with Prigogine & Stengers (1984) and Gleick (1987) and Waldrop (1992), we see solid evidence for academic administration to reevaluate the structures which discourage interactions, the sharing of data, and the profiting from access and exposure to each other's fields. Thus opportunities for research and faculty development can be a way in which institutional leadership can express sustaining values and meaning, as questions, language, and insights from other fields to one's own encourage mergers, collisions, fragmentation, and wildness in the evolving curriculum. Team teaching, organizational and cultural exchanges, and consortial, grant, foundation, federal, state, community, and other programs can be chaotic forces that bring out the natural capacity for growth in the academic environment.

## Long-Range and Strategic Planning

Many institutions take one to two years to develop a five-year strategic plan. After the considerable effort and stress of coming up with a plan that has had input from multiple and competing constituencies, there is a lot of pressure for the "plan" to be implemented, and for it to be used as the primary tool to organize and guide the institution forward. However, the creation of the plan, and its very existence, are interventions in the system, and amplify sources of turbulence in calling for changes—no matter how positive—in how the system operates. These changes in how business is done, and how learning make take place, cause initial turbulence which can derail the entire planning process if resistance to them is not understood as a natural consequence, one which will not ultimately threaten the success of the plan if it is regarded as expected and dealt with as feedback.

In my experience, institutions strive boldly to reform according to collaboratively developed strategic planning processes. They are quite justly proud of these processes. Then, within the first six months of long-range planning and strategic plans, criticism of the plan is voiced by many entities in the system, including those who participated in the planning process, causing institutional dismay. A common and logical response of institutional leadership and of the institution as a whole is to second-guess the process, to doubt the wisdom or practicality of the plan after all, or the capacity of the institution or its members to carry it out. The institution can become demoralized if the plan is considered a divisive and disorganizing force, especially if the decision is made to give up on the plan for practical reasons.

My conclusion in such instances, born out by the lessons of chaos theory, is that in the face of resistance and turbulence, institutions probably give up on plans and projects prematurely. If we recognize that implementation of any plans or projects are interventions in the system which naturally cause initial turbulence, which will be followed by the system "self-organizing" and stabilizing, we do not have to give up on plans, which took considerable institutional resources to develop. Instead, we can give the projects a systemic benefit of the doubt, translated as more time to develop and stabilize. Also, using the lessons of systems dynamics, we can use institutional "feedback" to make continuous modifications in the plan. We can imagine a different model than the Deist's conception of the world (a clock which was begun ticking with no further divine intervention ever since). Instead, we can be flexible, using feedback to constantly monitor and adjust the plan. In this way, the plan continues as a responsive element within the institutional system, and serves as a stabilizing and organizing force. In the lexicon of chaos theory, we can understand a strategic plan as a "strange attractor" which organizes dynamic elements in the turbulent and complex environment.

A related lesson from system dynamics in evaluating our efforts to produce positive change refers to our overall notions of success and failure. Let us consider a plan or project that seems to have failed or is no longer working. When we try to do something new, the result by definition looks and feels different. We may not be able to tell right away the signs that something is working in an improved way. It may be that the inevitable interruptions, delays, disruptions, fits and starts, or generally uneven sense of progress that accompany getting a project going do not correlate with a quarterly report or periodically structured strategic indicators. This turbulent beginning may lead to an impression that it is "not working." But the project's natural growth and long-term stability within the organization may require this pattern of movement. We know that growth in natural systems occurs in spurts, and that fluctuations occur. Growth patterns in natural systems are seldom linear and periodic. The vocabulary of chaos includes the terms "nonlinearity" and "aperiodic" to describe the flow of natural system behavior, *as things were designed to go in a naturally organized manner.* There is timing in natural systems growth, but it is not a lock-step affair.

A simple example from nature that I like to use with organizations to illustrate this point is to imagine an alien who does not have the cyclical long-term experience on earth with our seasons. A seed is planted, watered, and grows gradually into a tree. So far so good. The tree grows leaves and flowers and fruit. All seems to be going as planned. Then "suddenly" things start to go "wrong." The leaves turn color, flowers disappear, and fruit falls to the ground. Things go from bad to worse. The branches are now barren. The tree is pummeled with hail. Branches break off. If one did not know from a long-term perspective of having seen this pattern before, one would write this tree off as a failed project. And this would be a tragic mistake, for what we know from having been on earth a few decades is that this battered and barren stage is essential for the tree's growth. The tree's "off season" restores its energy reserves for the flowering and fruit that will come again in its continued cycles. Not knowing this, one might decide to be practical and "cut one's losses," in this case literally cut the tree down for firewood.

Chaos theory, constructed in part by computer modeling of long-term behavior, provides this kind of perspective that conserves energy in systems. Any initiative—a new program, course, set of requirements—may seem to be going "nowhere," to be stalled for lack of momentum, or because of the internal or external turbulence it is causing. But the endeavor may be at a critical growth stage for the project or the institution as a whole, as it evolves into the next stages of "progress" and "success."

In other words, chaos theory's lessons on system dynamics provide strong evidence for a more forgiving, optimistic, and hopeful way of recognizing stages of progress and forestalling assessments of failure that ultimately waste an institution's time and resources and spirits.

I would submit that failure is an incompatible concept applied to complex adaptive systems such as dynamic learning organizations. If all is continuous flow and reformation, and no energy in any physical system is lost, then there is no "end" result but only more reformations. In a learning organization, assessment constitutes "feedback." Feedback enables the institution to be flexible and resilient, by being responsive to information from internal and external constituencies. In a system governed by physical laws and by properties of interdependence, there must always be "reaction" to any action. Any action is an intervention. Such action/reaction/intervention/feedback can be structured into any plan as an integral part of its processes. Project design that elicits feedback ensures continuous response within the organizational system. Organizational plans, which draw forth continuous feedback and use it to make modifications and adaptations, strengthen the stability and long-term vitality of the system. In these structural ways incorporating participation in planning, the turbulence of criticism, resistance, and doubt becomes transformed into institutionally facilitated and constructive feedback. If the organization sees that its feedback is used as a means of continually modifying a project, and if any endeavor is regarded as "under construction" or "in flow" or "in process," there is no "failure." There is only learning and new efforts and new thinking. The concept of "no failure" removes the motivation for blame and dismay from institutional assessment, and enables an institution's leadership to help the organization not "give up." This is why an encouraging and optimistic viewpoint is so essential for an institution. Grading projects as failures instead of using information to adapt strategies depletes the organization. Realistic and long-term assessment of projects and plans can help an institution become far fairer to itself, and more productive, in an atmosphere in which vital intellectual and professional experiment and growth flourish.

Chaos theory helps us to become wiser planners and assessors in another way: it humbles us in our rush to judgment. We know from chaos theory that however bleak we may find a situation, we may be wrong in our negative assessment. What looks like "error" turns out to be "right." Give things more time, after initial resistance, and they "work out." Assessment of programs, personnel, learning outcomes, initiatives, and other indicators of institutional and organizational progress need to take long-range behavior patterns into account. Applying the lessons of chaos theory for assessment of all types, including for accreditation and certification of programs, may very well be a way that institutional leadership can help higher education to begin to identify new and more realistic strategic indicators for long-term academic and organizational success.

Finally, the organization needs a robust sense of self-trust in its resilience. This sense of vitality is necessary for a willingness on everyone's part to trust the organization enough to allow each member the vulnerability on which every learning organization depends: to take risks for intellectual and professional growth. To use feedback creatively and resourcefully, responses have to be tried out, and new ideas have to be given a chance. We cannot predict how they will work given the various ongoing rhythms of other actions in the system. We know that first appearances may be deceiving. Projects may appear to be working, but they may have some error in the initial calculations that over time will become apparent. In this case the project needs to be modified. Projects may need more resources, time, thinking, collaboration, and partnerships.

The use of continual feedback for modification for institutional assessment can create an overall attitude toward projects, planning, and new thinking that encourages innovation and risk. It can help the overall goal of systems, which reward effort and risk. If we give up on projects too soon, or devolve into blame and accusations for what or who caused the failure, we will see less willingness to be vulnerable and open to new ideas on the part of students, faculty, and staff. When feedback is encouraged as helpful, and risk is encouraged, there are increased levels of contribution and vulnerability that the learning organization requires for long-term success and continuity of its academic mission.

## Conflict of Diverse Kinds

As Wilson (1998, p. 8), Orr (1992, pp. 101 ff), and other philosophers of education such as Alfred North Whitehead (1967/1929) and John Dewey (1981) would argue, academic institutions are unnaturally "organized" into separate divisions, in terms of operations and academic ways of knowing. Internal divisiveness can occupy an institution's and leader's and manager's time and spirit more than any other thing. Faculty in one discipline or school may criticize or dismiss the importance of another discipline or school. There are perceptions of incompatibilities between faculty in liberal arts, education, and professional studies. There are different views about curriculum, compensation, workload, and the role of each kind of education in today's market for "essential" education. Bitter disagreements can occur over what courses and experiences should be required for a degree. Differences occur over how to allocate resources, market programs, or spend alumni gifts. Within institutional categories, there can be profound disagreements among members of the governing board, faculty, student groups, and staff to the point of a demoralizing institutional paralysis and sense of "disorder." Any single problem appears to have multiple and mutually exclusive properties which may make any single solution improbable and unacceptable to the "whole."

On any issue, senior staff may experience themselves at odds specifically because of their particular and necessary purviews. Thus, vice presidents for development, marketing, student affairs, academic affairs, business, human resources, and environmental services, including maintenance, appropriately have differing and possibly conflicting ideas about a policy issue. Faculty working to create curriculum requirements differ among themselves about the roles of technology, foreign language, math, classical literature, business, theater, art, gender studies, area studies, or even interdisciplinary or international studies in a student's learning. The Board of Trustees may have multiple views of mission, priority, and fundraising goals. Divisions break down further. Within any department, different points of view occur over how to teach a subject, what texts belong in the course, how many papers to assign, what questions are fair to ask for teaching evaluation, who to ask to be a guest professor, or the role of discussion in determining a student's grade for the course—or the terms on which a faculty member is evaluated. Within any organizational division there is further fragmentation among individuals and groups into different and distinctive ideas, agendas, styles, and attitudes.

On any given afternoon at an institution of higher learning, there is bound to be a "crisis" due to conflicting points of view. Faculty, students, administrators, and staff may feel alienated from the institution and each other because of the presence of the different viewpoints, language, values, and agendas within each organizational category and in the role each plays for the institution.

The impression of "chaos" occurs when these seemingly irreconcilable diverse states coexist in an organization. If the leader recognizes that this "chaos" is his or her terrain, more a field in a successful ecosystem than a battlefield, and that the very nature of the organizational structure itself creates divisions within divisions, each with its own mandate and culture, a positive attitude can go far to help people to see that the differences do not constitute crisis per se. It is helpful to point out that systems of learning require academic and operational diversity, and that diversity is built into the system, so that each unit operates according to its own rhythms, time frames, values, and measures of progress and success. Even when all these entities "get along" in various coalitions, the reality is that these coalitions shift into new (however temporary) alliances and new organizational units are formed which change the nature of interaction and operating modes of all the other organizational units.

Even during times of internal stability within and among these entities, basic conflicts must be resolved on a level that satisfies "the whole" even as they cannot be resolved to satisfy every single constituency or advocacy group. However, given the interdependence of systems, often a complex issue can be resolved by bringing *more* and diverse points of view into the process, creating new balance and equilibrium.

The lack of coherence in the way the institution is often experienced by its members, even as it is a result of built-in structures, is not only the leader's terrain, but the leader's issue, which must be addressed. Unresolved, such conflict leads to a sense that the institution and its members are not congruent, focused, or functional—or even belong. This impression leads to a lowering of morale, and contributes to erosion of confidence in the institution's capacity to solve problems and create solutions for itself. It also undermines society's confidence in the organization as a model of "know how." How can we claim to prepare students to serve communities torn by lack of understanding of how and why we all belong, if we ourselves cannot construct a coherent community? Institutional credibility is at risk. Also at risk in such a demoralized climate is the climate for risk-taking itself that is the heart of learning and discovery. Creative collaborations across division and disciplines require a willingness to be vulnerable, to fail, to be misunderstood, which cannot flourish in an environment of distrust. Therefore, in frightened and divided institutions without a sense of stability, coherence, confidence, or unified purpose supporting diversity, the academic mission itself becomes at risk. As we learn from the example of chaos theory, creativity and discovery *require* access and exposure to diversity, a respect for and knowledge about different ways of knowing. The organization needs a positive way to experience its own diversity, and to build upon it.

Chaos theory and the story of its founding provides to leadership with these mandates an encouraging perspective on the perception of multiple and hopelessly disjointed and incongruent viewpoints within an institution. The founders of the theory often transgressed organizational boundaries within their own academic structures and cultures, which initially emphasized disciplinary differences and could have kept their isolated research results inert. In ways we need to examine further for their implications for organizational reform, the chaos and complexity researchers overcame the obstacles to collaborating across academic departments, divisions, fields, institutions, research organizations, and corporations, in the nonprofit and for profit sectors. For educational leaders and all academics, James Gleick's book on chaos theory's "making"—and making it—is a heartening guide and rationale of academic organizational reform of structures and policies (1987). The stories of the founders of what Briggs and Peat (1989) and Gleick (1987) and Wilson (1998) call a theory of the "whole" provide a sensational rationale for helping institutions understand the value of the diversity that exists by definition within the organization, and the mandate for new ways to negotiate it for increased learning. In other words, what is seen initially as a liability, the diversity that exists and seems to threaten coherence, is necessary both to acknowledge and to leverage for greater learning and organizational health.

Chaos theory itself provides an alternative to the logical sense of crisis and deteriorating morale of an institution depleted by its constant wars within itself and the self-absorption that limits the institution's responsiveness to external forces and fluctuations in society. In dynamic organizations, these self-perceptions of fragmentation and disunity are bound by time and space, and are unnecessary sources of distraction and detraction from the dignity and excitement of the work people do at an institution in all its manifestations. Turning around this perception is vital for a leader. This is why chaos theory is so useful in enabling a leader to identify the nature of what Parker Palmer refers to as "our common work"[14] and the role that each element plays in contributing to the "whole."

A further example of how the understanding of chaos theory can produce a positive attitude toward sources of conflict and even despair, when we think that our institutions are hopelessly divided by conflict, is seen in our paradigm of the "turbulent universe." If chaotic incompatibilities resolve into coherence from looking at ourselves as from space in chaos theory's long-term lens, we learn about our coherence by looking at space for clues about ourselves. Thus a leader can regard the various chaotic stages of forming and reforming stars and galaxies, each moving in a perfect order in relationship to other solar and universal systems, on its own path, sometimes merging, colliding, contacting, expanding. Star growth shows how elements of stars become the "matter" of new life (including the chemicals that make up our bodies) as stars develop greater chemical complexity and expire into the universe as sources of new planets, earth, and life forms.

If we have internal conflict, we can "look up" and regard the planet Jupiter as a model of constructive chaotic behavior. While the planet's surface seems to be only random turbulent swirling, its climate is really moving in one direction, clockwise. However, within this orderly turbulence is a state of constant disorder, a permanent storm system vaster than the size of the U.S. Moreover, it appears that this storm system, called the "red spot," revolves in the opposite direction of the planet's currents. The storm, while turbulent within, keeps its intrinsic shape and boundaries intact from the climate of the planet as a whole. It moves back and forth across the surface in a certain predictable pattern and path. It is orderly in and of itself and in relation to the planet as a whole. It does not change the essential climate of the whole planet, nor does it interfere with the planet's ability to keep its moons or its stable path in the solar system.

In other words, the structure, rhythm, shape, and behavior of the turbulence shows an overall order and stability. Leaders can extract from this "hugely" successful model of natural systems behavior the knowledge that it is possible that elements "organized" to disrupt or challenge or "disturb" or "perturb" the institutional climate, and probably will never change their opposition to aspects of our organization—its mission, policies, leadership structure, and. so on—will not destabilize the institution or culture. It can continue to survive and thrive as an organized system. We can transcend fears for the institution's resilience to withstand turbulence. In fact, each unit on campus, organized around a certain purpose, can be understood in its own way as a persistent storm system, in harmony with the whole institution even as it moves according to its own rhythms and defines its own agenda. Who knows—perhaps research one day will reveal the stabilizing or perpetuating role of the storm system for Jupiter.

## Individual Evaluation of Learning

How the institution uses feedback to modify and continuously adapt should be a key factor in overall institutional assessment and evaluation of institutional success. Those institutions undergoing change can experience the satisfaction of documenting the processes in which they are responsive to structured feedback. The same principles of assessment would apply throughout the institution, organized around "self-similarity" of functions. A practical example of an assessment process that leadership can help an institution to develop is the practice of structured feedback from students about courses and programs. An institution is as viable, relevant, and "smart" as its ability to generate and use feedback.

As learning institutions, the feedback from our students is a key component to institutional development. The institution depends for its adaptive functions on the quality of the feedback. If students feel their feedback is going to be used in a meaningful way to affect or result in change, they will produce helpful feedback. If faculty feel that evaluations are designed to help them continuously to strengthen their skills, to encourage their best efforts, and to help them and our institutions be responsive to the learning environment and its continual new possibilities, they will take the feedback seriously enough to act on it in the form of adaptations and modifications, and the institution will be able to model the successful "complex adaptive behavior" of a dynamic learning system. Faculty must feel that administration will make the supportive changes that are called for in responding to student feedback, and that the institution overall, in its policies, structures, reward system, resource allocation, and ethos is organized around responsiveness to their feedback.

But in order to develop a feedback structure that works productively to keep continuous input in the system, we need to base evaluation processes on what we actually know about learning. Learning, I would submit, is itself a chaotic process. If we consider that our knowledge of the world at any point in time is a well-ordered and balanced system, and we apply dynamic systems behavior to our understanding of the learning process, we see that this mental order is initially perturbed and destabilized by the new energy of any input (in this case, information, ideas, questions, assignments, access, and exposure to different ways of thinking and knowing). The student entering a school or program or class may have felt in "control" of his or her ways of knowing. Now the student can feel demoralized, confused, and upset. This initial stage of turbulence, "not knowing" or "unlearning" or "relearning," can be experienced as a failure. In fact the ferment is critical for the following stages of learning, in which the disorder will "self-organize." "Suddenly," it seems, the student "sees" or "gets it" (the "click"). Then further questions will destabilize that "order," which will fragment into new lines of inquiry. In other words, mental processes absorb the energy, and the mind follows laws for complex adaptive dynamic systems: gets "smarter."

While we may structure our learning environments in linear and periodic fashion, we know that learning is aperiodic, occurring in fits and starts, jolts and disruptions; and the process remains turbulent as new information (feedback from the environment) is constantly absorbed. It may take a student most of a ten-week course to master a principle that then can be used by the student, but by then, the course is practically over. How do we measure a student's (or faculty member's) success then? How do we measure the fact that a student may realize what was learned six months or two years after the course was ended? What kinds of questions now can let us know that the catalytic process was begun? To answer these questions, we need to know how dynamic systems work, how chaotic processes occur over time. We need to see evidence of "chaos" to know that the system is working.

Just as important, how can we let the student be conscious of the nature of this dynamic process? For the student, not knowing how the learning process operates can result in the student initially concluding that he or she

a)  does not have the capacity (intelligence, background, interest) to take the course,
b)  does not belong in the program,
c)  should not be at the institution,
d)  the faculty is not appropriate. The student prematurely can give up on herself or himself, the program, or the institution.

This is traumatic not only for the student but for the faculty and the institution as a whole. The institution is destabilized by the loss of the student: the student's lack of confidence in the program, the loss of revenue, the unrealized investment in the original costs of bringing the student to the organization, and the loss of morale on the part of staff, faculty, and students as a whole. My point is that in many cases the student gives up in the first stages of a program or course unnecessarily, misreading the indicators through not knowing that learning naturally follows this chaotic path.

In fact, the challenge of a learning organization is a literacy, which enables our members to assess how each of us is succeeding in the environment. If students and faculty are aware of the natural chaotic processes, including fluctuation, flow, and turbulence of a learning system, they can prepare for those periods in which learning is experienced as "chaotic." In fact, students can be taught to recognize those moments of traumatic disorder as positive "strategic indicators" of the learning process. When resistance, confusion, "thinking I knew it and now I realize I had it all wrong," and other responses occur, students and faculty can "read" these as encouraging signs that the process is working and that "self-organizing" and new forms of order and mental organization are right around the corner. Systems theory would also emphasize the role that the learner plays in his or her own learning: the necessity for interactions and interventions (for example, going to see an advisor or the faculty member, consulting someone, and so forth).

From this point of view, the entire learning and teaching dynamic is a series of planned and emergent "interventions" as well as "actions" and interactions bringing "energy" into a system. Students, faculty, and the institution as a whole are served more fairly when people view themselves and each other in the context of the natural behavior of chaotic processes in dynamic systems. Thus, evaluation can strengthen the morale of an institution. I see exciting opportunity for institutions in the work to ensure that evaluations across the institution reflect the natural timetable for learning. Questions, observations, self-reflection, and other indicators should recognize the catalytic role of lectures, assignments, tests, exercises, meetings, requirements, advising, and other learning events, in terms of how they actually destabilize the existing "order" and mental models. We should look for evidence of change (i.e., turbulence), from students, faculty, and administration, evidence of a system "working" chaotically, as it should, structured around intervention and feedback.

## Encouraging Diversity as a Principle of Wholeness

Diversity of the learning environment is held out as a primary value of institutional leadership. Promoting diversity is like promoting life itself. In a learning organization access and exposure to a variety of different ways of thinking, experiencing, being—are a condition of learning; as an ecological, aesthetic, and physical principle, diversity is fundamental to organizational viability and renewal; as a principle of reality in the universe, it is necessary for intellectual accuracy in calculations and conclusions based on representations of the environment. For organizational integrity, curriculum, research, and learning, diversity is essential. Leadership's challenge is that diversity is often considered an obstacle to institutional coherence—that it represents chaos, fragmentation, seeds for adversity and alienation. In this view, institutional stability and order would be served by diminishing diversity, walling up and out what is "different." How we think about diversity, therefore, determines organizational success.

If we use chaos theory's "step back" approach and compare the astronaut's holistic perspective of earth with an earthly, fearful self-diagnosis of chaos, we can see new ways that chaos theory can be used to leverage the vision of the whole for the understanding of the role of diversity in the coherence of the institution.

From the celestial and realistic vantage of the whole, relationships among diverse cultural, organizational, and disciplinary elements within the institution appear. The ways that they exhibit "self-similarity" in their functioning is evident. One can see that however varying in size, function, and states of equilibrium, each belongs to, and does not threaten, the coherence of the organization.

The advantage of this viewpoint is that it provides the leader with an inclusive paradigm that can be communicated to the learning community in a way that will enable its members to see how it all fits together, including their role in making the system work. In this holistic view of the organization's deep structure, to apply an anthropological linguistic term, various organizational elements convinced of their essential differences can see what they have in common and how and why to work together and to learn with and from each other. The institution can develop ways to integrate and allow "flow" among the various elements, whether departments, divisions, disciplines, organizations, clubs, offices, roles. The technology of such a vision can include a view of the institution from "the outside," such as its mandates in terms of market forces, as a historic construct (for example, its economic and social role in its community and region), or its mission (for example, the role that alumni have played, its commitment to community access and service, its dedication to excellent teaching, its research function).

Understanding that attitudes toward diversity in an institution are expressed "across scales and function," I can point to an academic experience that framed for me the role of chaos theory as an intellectual construct, which could inspire organizational and curricular reform. Recognizing that service to an institution to win support for liberal arts and graduate learning required firsthand experience working with state and national agencies, I held a federal appointment as U.S. Scholar in Residence for the United States Information Agency in Washington, D.C. As an American Studies scholar, and cultural historian specializing in literature, I was responsible for articulating to foreign and U.S. official and academic audiences the essential characteristics of American culture. This required both an interdisciplinary and international—that is, "outside" and holistic— perspective, which meant intellectually going "outside" of my department, discipline, school, college, and country. The challenge of the job was in the fact that both foreign and U.S. colleagues wondered whether such a diverse culture as ours could be seen to have "a" culture. How could it, given the diversity of cultures within the national ethos? Could our culture, given its change, complexity, and diversity, be understood as a meaningful and coherent construct? From the foreign countries in which I was working, U.S. culture had obvious signifiers but "culture" was understood to be based on those things that do not change. U.S. colleagues asked if the diversity of our country makes impossible any categorical statements about it as an entity. Yet in the global context I had experienced as a Fulbright scholar teaching American studies, I had seen what Jefferson saw in the Constitution as an "expression of the American mind"—that emanating from the experience on this continent were stories, buildings, bridges, ideas, inventions, laws, institutions, occurrences, and habits which seemed to be interconnected with patterns of themes and imagery. Seen from "away," the disciplinary differences in which "texts" are defined and read, these expressions taken together over time revealed patterns of thought about time, community, success, nature, authority, aging, and identity. While the expressions are diverse among themselves, they are distinguishable from artifacts of other diverse cultures.

In the early 1980s, chaos theory, then just emerging in formats for non-scientists to begin to use, came to my aid as scientific evidence of what someone in the humanities could observe about a complex culture. Chaos seemed a paradigm for how a cultural dynamic system could be characterized by diversity, change, and complexity. My effort to describe the U.S. from a global viewpoint was the same as looking at earth: from space (a foreign country) and time (a historical overview), it was possible to see patterns in icons, images, and institutions which appeared unrelated. Whether in the "story" of Martin Luther King, the Brooklyn Bridge, McDonald's, the Constitution, baseball, the expression "have a nice day," or notions about progress or time, one could see in the deep structure a people's history, psychology, and experience. The historical overview permitted us to see ways that each group and set of ideas and actions influenced other groups and the culture as a whole over time, how they led to perturbations in national life, fragmented into various branches, self-organized, and created new forms—for example, the influence of jazz on American life, culture, and politics, as well as music, or the influence of eastern thought on Emerson and the transcendentalists, in turn influencing Thoreau, in turn influencing Gandhi in South Africa, in turn influencing national Indian and then global politics, in turn influencing Martin Luther King, in turn influencing the American civil rights movement, in turn influencing . . . .

Further, the insights from chaos theory supported the necessity to include all the histories of our people, instead of seeing any one group as the "right" or "model" group and the others as not belonging or "irrelevant." This thinking challenged scientists in every field. Founders of chaos theory, who by definition were looking at "the whole" and thus at the way multiple disciplines converge, had to overcome each discipline's preconception about what data belonged, what questions should be asked to yield the "correct" answer, what belonged in the field and the study, and what the "right" answers were. When the question revolved specifically about the change in a complex system, new understanding could be achieved about the nature of the whole, which revealed how entities which had been considered "marginal" were central and essential to a system's behavior.

Chaos theory causes a re-valuation of all those elements in a system previously understood to be disturbing, insignificant, "noise," irrelevant, or "wrong." A leader's view of an organization which is inclusive of all the elements within it, with clarity on how and why all the elements belong and relate, and a commitment to ensuring that diversity exists, can help a system to achieve an intellectual, cultural, and organizational equilibrium.

It may seem difficult if not impossible to experience from within and up close the coherence of the institution as a whole, when it speaks with so many voices and messages. Thus the job of the leader in any organization, who has responsibility for "the whole" and speaks on its behalf, can be supported by the scientific knowledge that the existence of simultaneously coexisting, competing, conflicting, various points of view does not mean that the institution is not functional or whole and cannot sustain a coherent self-image of its common work.

## Problem Solving

In the natural world, the cosmos is defined by multiple entities in multiple ontological states, going from order to disorder to new states of order, one element influencing the other. Organizations are structured in the same way. When problems occur, the existence of diverse elements can seem the cause of the problem. But the problem is often a result of lack of coordination and integration and flow among the various elements. The solution, therefore, is to reconstruct "the whole."

For example, in my college we recently had an issue whereby just as we were ready to submit a balanced budget to the trustees (order), we fine-tuned our data processing (energy intervention) and discovered a potential loss of half a million dollars revenue (disorder). In such cases, we can remember dynamic systems theory: news is information energy we can learn from; a small intervention can modify the system and put it back into equilibrium. We discovered that accruing tuition losses in our residential undergraduate program would put us into operating budget deficit. It turned out that an unprecedented number of students simultaneously in the past number of weeks had decided to take off-campus "field semesters." These provide students full academic credit (and thus faculty receive full pay and are at full workload) but for which students only pay half tuition. Up to this point, there was no way to predict how many students would take advantage of this program, and there was no policy controlling it. In the institutional scheme of things, this was a tiny aspect of one program, which had gone relatively unnoticed by the budget office and college planning; it did not enter into long-term projections, and would not have been noticed now if it had not "gone wrong" and led to potential turbulence in the system.

To balance the budget and restore order, loss of half a million dollars in expected revenue from the academic program had to be compensated for. The various constituencies gathered around the table to represent "the whole" offered competing and contradictory solutions. From the finance side, it was obvious that students had to pay more tuition for field studies and that the numbers of students accepted into the program had to be regulated so that the institution could more accurately project enrollment revenue and adjust expenses and resources in budget planning. But student affairs thought revenue would be not as severely influenced if students were allowed to have the field semesters when they wanted them. They would continue in their programs, which would build retention. If students withdrew because of disappointment in their opportunities for research leaves, far more revenue would be lost over the long-term. Student services was concerned about contractual responsibilities in how the institution may have represented such opportunities. Academics was concerned with questions of the quality of the academic experience which gained the students full credit, and wanted to institute a system whereby fewer students were accepted into the program and could be monitored carefully in terms of their learning outcomes for "quality control." Academics and student services were wary of implementing a system that limited students for any one term, because of a lack of agreement over the criteria to be used to select students for the opportunity. Meanwhile, faculty were advising students to take advantage of this opportunity, not aware that the decreases in revenue would put the budget into crisis and threaten the financial stability on which their own jobs rest. Student services objected vigorously to the notion of raising tuition or fees in the program, feeling it was counterproductive to do so if students then withdrew.

From the president's point of view, everyone was right. Every viewpoint held by institutional officers was logical and correct within in its context. How to develop a policy, a set of policies, that address the truth of each perspective and would serve the college as a whole? After the various viewpoints were discussed, data shared, and feedback from students, faculty, and staff was generated and analyzed, a policy was put into effect that was collaboratively arrived at: faculty understood their advising function as to limit the number of students accepted to any one term of research leaves; tuition would not be raised; the academic nature of the experience would be further documented, analyzed and monitored; retention of students participating in this program would be monitored for further policy decision. The effort to make a decision based on the needs of "the whole," combining academics and operations, required the overlap, collision, affiliation, coalition, alliance, and conflict within multiple divisions of the college. It required, when conflict arose between various entities, asking, what other points of view need to be at the table? Whose viewpoint is being left out? What kinds of collaboration and integration of data would identify the need for policy or a policy change before it becomes a potential crisis? What systems need to be in place for this to occur?

The leadership goal was to ensure that the resolution did not destabilize the college in the effort of trying to "fix" a problem. While the solution to the budget deficit seemed logical and simple at first, a more draconian approach (such as eliminating the option of such field semesters on a tight budget, or raising the tuition to cover full costs of faculty involvement) would have caused problems for every unit successively—in terms of budget, financial aid, retention, faculty relations, student affairs, accreditation, and campus morale. The solution involved a systemic adaptation, increasing coordinated feedback mechanisms structured in earlier ways into the system, and other policy changes. The solution was multiple, smaller rather than larger in scope, requiring slight changes in various units, and was both long term and short term. Even so, as we could predict, the decisions were "energy" and "interventions," and caused turbulence throughout the system. Directors, faculty, and other staff anticipated such turbulence, and feeling that solutions reflected "the whole" and were fair and reasonable, had a less threatened and calmer approach to supporting concerns on the part of individuals and groups. The result was that there was a little short-term turbulence but not a "crisis."

## Crisis Management as Confidence Building

What is a crisis? Chaos theory challenges our assumptions of what constitutes crisis and what we can do about it. From the lens of chaos theory, we can stand back and carefully assess the situation. What seems like a crisis may be initial turbulence that will self-organize. On the other hand, recognizing early on the indicators of a problem is critical for providing an intervention, which can keep a situation from getting "out of hand." The role of leadership has new opportunity with this knowledge to convey a sense that the organization is functional and resilient.

An example of how this leadership role can be served by chaos theory is how airline pilots can assure passengers during turbulence. As the plane suddenly jerks and bounces wildly around, and passengers worry about the stability and resilience of the aircraft, the crew's competence, and their own vulnerability, the pilot's voice is heard over the loudspeaker. "Folks, we've moving up through 23,000 feet through some clouds. There's going to be some bumps but we have reports that we'll get through this turbulence in about fifty miles. Then we'll turn off the seat-belt sign. But although they tell us up ahead we can expect a fairly smooth ride, as always we encourage you to keep your seat-belts fastened in case of unexpected turbulence." Now that the experience of chaos has a name, "Cloud," and a recognized behavior, "turbulence," people relax. The plane is bouncing violently, but one has been given a way to "read" the chaotic experience and know its meaning, shape, cause, and duration.

In such ways, the visionary gift of leadership can enable the members of an institution, who are bound up together, comprising each other's fates, and whose careers and lives are dependent upon its ability to withstand turbulence, to know what to expect as the organization goes through transitions in the turbulent world of today's higher education. A projection of the kinds of behaviors that can be anticipated in any institutional work is important to communicate to the community. Leadership can play an instrumental role in conveying a sense of where the bumps are up ahead, what can be expected from a new initiative, probable outcomes of market forces, and so on—all natural in the course of being a dynamic and thriving organization. Leadership can define and prepare members for the kind of system behavior that chaos has revealed to us—the flow of order, in which order fragments into disorder, disorder resolves into order, in both predictable and predictably unpredictable ways.

But the analogy between passengers on an airplane and members of an institution breaks down in the most wonderful ways. In dynamic learning organizations, every person has the ability to influence the system and not have to wait, gratefully but helplessly, for the institutional leadership to take the organization through the waves and constant flow of chaos. In an environment in which there is "sensitive dependence on initial conditions," the butterfly—an image of a light, delicate, freely moving creature—is powerful. In chaos theory, we learn that system stability is served with interventions, early and often. Continual adjustment and assessment provide an equilibrium that fosters an atmosphere of confidence in the work of the institution and the meaning and purpose of everyone's work together as an interdependent system. The lesson of "the butterfly effect" from chaos and dynamic systems theory is that everyone has a role. No leader can act alone; no member of the institution can act alone; no institution can act alone, out of context of society and other related social, economic, political, and educational forces. Effectiveness in an organization, the ability to play a constructive role and to contribute best from one's "whole" being: this is a function of one's ability to collaborate, to respect one's impact on the interdependent system, and one's dependence on every other unit. The challenge and joy of leadership of learning organizations is encouraging the dependence and integration of each member and entity of the institution, so that each member functions as a butterfly, causing not storm systems, perhaps, but actions which "perturb" and infinitely revitalize and stabilize the system. In this way, leadership models its most important role: conveying a confidence in the institution itself, its coherence, its capacity to trust and be trusted, its resilience, and even its potential for the wildness that characterizes learning and growth.

## Conclusion and Further Reflections

Academe is supposed to be different from "the real world" in meaningful ways that serve society. It can provide a liberation or waiver from real-world parameters so that people can step back and take the necessary time and risks to think new thoughts, try out new ideas and practices, assess, reflect on, develop what has been learned, and advance knowledge in long-term and practical ways for society. Higher education's purpose is fundamentally a means of "chaotic order," the stable storm system of society's Jupiter, an ongoing stage of phase-transitions, of continuous experiment, challenge, being provocative, providing ferment, and rigorously testing the "state-of-the-art." Through teaching and research, it is a means by which society's intellectual assumptions are constantly disordered and re-ordered in continuous discoveries, which become new learning formations and applications. These formations and reformations splinter, spiral off, and acquire their own self-organization in new and emergent disciplines and fields and schools and centers and ways of knowing . . . before reforming again.

Paradoxically, the "comfort level" of higher education in this chaotic function seems to decrease the more that higher education reforms itself in response to new needs and possibilities. There is a perception that much of the organizational and intellectual leadership of innovation and challenge is happening outside of academe today. But two ideas challenge this perception. First, just as in chaotic systems there is an interplay of order and disorder, as one merges into the other, higher education has a role that is both flexible and inflexible. It is simultaneously and continuously opening up new fields and meeting emergent needs with advances in knowledge about learning and the world, yet proceeding cautiously, often reluctantly. It conserves and preserves essential features of learning and research, and leadership of the most innovative programs respects the tension, which keeps academe grounded. Second, the concept of "outside academe" is being expanded in stellar ways. Our own institutions develop more complex elements, and replenish and renew and seed other institutions. Today there are far more intersections between traditional academe and other institutions. In truth, higher education spawns learning organizations, which form new learning units and contribute back to higher education, new fields, research, and learning.

In this volatile and creative atmosphere, which is redefining the look and experience of higher education, academic leadership has both a new and a revitalized traditional role to play. We need a vision of how all these different entities can function as an interdependent network of organizations, each with their own cultures, rhythms, and missions. Academic leadership can identify the strength and resilience of institutions in their chaotic nature, providing encouragement for institutions to be *more* chaotic based on a fearless new value and reading of the chaotic elements in every thriving complex dynamic system. In so doing, academic leadership can restore the traditional leadership role, and provide new impetus and mandate, for higher education's catalytic, perturbing, essential "disorderly" role in society's continuous learning that the world needs now.[15]

What does the world need now, and how can higher education meet this need? As we persistently endeavor to build the capacity of every person for a more resilient, loving, wiser society, we call for citizen leadership and responsibility, and a more meaningful and useful education for still greater numbers of citizens. Is what is useful and necessary changing? I would argue that we still have the learning needs identified by the Sphinx: how and why do we belong to each other and the earth?—the holistic, integrated, relational knowledge that drives global strategic thinking and problem solving, and technological, symbolic, and computational literacies. The leader's vision of the whole is everyone's need: to view the dynamic, complex, diverse environment as coherent, meaningful, and valuable. Seeing the environment holistically and with empathy comes from the cognitive ability to integrate diverse kinds of information, to make connections and discern patterns among different entities, to relate *this* to *that, you* to *me, now* to *then.* A new kind of integrated thinking is required for a world that is round, alive, new, and renewing. A new kind of optimism is required. A new kind of trust and faith in both the environment and our ability to negotiate it, learn from it, and continue on. We still have five billion years to figure out what to do before the sun up and becomes a red giant, swallowing earth in nature's evolving chaotic plan. So we can't give up now.

## Notes

1.  Order theories have different names depending on the scholars who advance them and the discipline(s) in which they are presented. In addition to "chaos theory" and "nonlinear dynamical systems theories," there is "complexity" theory: a good introduction is M. Mitchell Waldrup, *Complexity: The Emerging Science at the Edge of Order and Chaos* (Touchstone 1992).
2.  See Edward O. Wilson, *Consilience: The Unity of Knowledge* (Vintage Books 1998). E.O. Wilson uses the term "consilience" consistently with the findings of chaos theory, to mean the way that different elements appearing totally distinct are discovered to be infinitely related, defining an overall cosmic unity based on interdependence of systems that transcends disciplines.
3.  In 1993, The American Council on Education published *An American Imperative*, which describes the response of leaders throughout society—political, union, workforce, educational—to evaluate how higher education is serving America's most urgent needs. The individual essays yield a consensus that, in editor Robert A. Atwell's conclusion, students graduating from our institutions need skills, attitudes, competencies, and abilities necessary for the cultural, political, and economic success of the nation. The essays pointed to the needs to negotiate complex and changing environments, to work productively and collaboratively with diverse people, to integrate diverse kinds of information, to identify resources, to do strategic and global problem solving, and to exercise a service ethic toward society.
4.  Nobel Prize Acceptance Speech, Stockholm, Sweden, 1951.
5.  For example, Stilgoe writes of "the necessity to get out and look around, to see accurately, to notice, to make connections" for "an education in visual acuity" (pp. 13–14).
6.  For example, "The ecologically literate person has the knowledge necessary to comprehend interrelatedness . . . , a broad understanding of how people and societies relate to each other and to natural systems, and how they might do so sustainably . . . , a comprehension of the dynamics of the modern world" (pp. 92–93).
7.  The scientists who write about chaos are extraordinary writers. Some who have contributed to my understanding and appreciation as a nonscientist of the specific concepts of the theory include Gleick (1992), Waldrup (1998), Prigogine (1984, 1998), Kauffman, (1992, 1995), Peat (1991), Bok (1996), Gribbin (1984), Gell-Mann (1994), Cambel (1993), Briggs & Peat (1989), Wheatley (1999), Lederman & Scharmm (1989), Bohm (1987), and Abraham (1994).
8.  Wilson prefers this term to coherence for its specific original meaning as used by William Whewell in 1840 as "'a jumping together' of knowledge by the linking of facts and fact-based theory across disciplines to create a common groundwork of explanation" (1998, p. 8).

9. James Gleick, *Chaos: Making a New Science* (1987), provides poignant examples of scientists whose research recovered completely new ways to interpret data that was considered useless—and which, therefore, jeopardized their own professional progress.

10. Scott Sanders, *Hunting for Hope* (1998), brings a new respect for understanding the physical and psychological necessity for hope, from the point of view of a scientist and humanist concerned with earth's survival, and ours.

11. Wilson attributes these laws to physics: "The central idea of the consilience world view is that all tangible phenomena, from the birth of stars to the workings of the social institutions, are based on material processes that are ultimately reducible, however long and torturous the sequences, to the laws of physics" (Wilson, 1998, p. 291).

12. This fundamental challenge is brilliantly addressed in various disciplines, whose authors portray the struggle to create a coherent self amid chaos in terms of dynamic systems. In *The Protean Self: Human Resilience in an Age of Fragmentation*, Robert Jay Lifton (1993) uses the language of chaos. In his psychological analysis, Lifton sets the challenge to construct a coherent self in "the restlessness and flux of our time," the confusion as people feel "buffeted about by unmanageable historical forces and social uncertainties," a time when "leaders appear suddenly, recede equally rapidly, and are difficult for us to believe in when they are around . . . [and] we come to view ourselves as unsteady, neurotic, or worse" (p. 1). In Antonio Damasio's *The Feeling of What Happens: Body and Emotion in the Making of Consciousness*, from a neuroscientist's point of view: "If you are looking for a haven of stability in the universe or change that is the world of our brains" one should consider the body and mind as "rock-solid stabilities," which, although "ephemeral and continuously reconstructed at the level of cells and molecules" are a positive image of coherence "while the world around us changes dramatically, profoundly, and often unpredictably" (Damasio, 1999, p. 142).

13. In *Leadership and the New Science*, Wheatley argues that chaos theory helps us to envision an organization as an organic whole, following dynamic systems laws of nature (Wheatley, 1999, 2nd ed).

14. Cited by Donna Shavlik. Parker Palmer uses this term in programs at the Fetzer Institute. See Palmer (1981).

15. This role of "agents of change" and challenge were urged on higher educational leadership in Atwell's introduction to *An American Imperative*, developed as a Report of the Wingspread Group in Higher Education (1993).

# References

Abraham, R. (1994). *Chaos, Gaia, Eros: A chaos pioneer uncovers the three great streams of history*. San Francisco: Harper.

Atwell, R. A. (Ed.). (1993). *An American imperative: Higher expectations for higher education: An open letter to those concerned about the American future*. Report of the Wingspread Group on Higher Education. Racine, WI: The Johnson Foundation.

Barry, D. (1991). *Dave Barry's only travel guide you'll ever need*. New York: Fawcett Columbine.

Berry, T. (1988). *The dream of the earth*. San Francisco: Sierra Club Books.

Bohm, D., & Peat, F. D. (1987). *Science, order, and creativity*. New York: Bantam.

Bok, P. (1996). *How nature works: The science of self-organized criticality*. New York: Springer-Verlag.

Briggs, J., & Peat, F. D. (1989). *Turbulent mirror: An illustrated guide to chaos theory and the science of wholeness*. New York: Harper & Row.

Cambel, A. B. (1993). *Applied chaos theory: A paradigm for complexity*. Boston: Academic Press.

Damasio, A. (1999). *The feeling of what happens: Body and emotion in the making of consciousness*. New York: Harcourt.

Dewey, J. (1981). The school and social progress, in J. McDermontt (Ed.), *The philosophy of John Dewey*. Chicago: University of Chicago Press.

Eisley, L. (1964). *The unexpected universe*. New York: Harcourt, Brace, & World.

Gardner, H. (1993). *Frames of mind: Multiple intelligences*. New York: Basic Books.

Gell-Mann, M. (1994). *The quark and the jaguar: Adventures in the simple and the complex*. New York: W. H. Freeman.

Gilligan, C. (1982). *In a different voice*. Cambridge: Harvard University Press.

Gleick, J. (1987). *Chaos: Making a new science*. New York: Viking Penguin.

Goodstein, D. L., & Goodstein, J. R. (Eds.). (1996). *Feynman's lost lecture: The motion of planets around the sun*. New York: Norton.

Gribbin, J. (1984). *In search of Schroedinger's cat: Quantum physics and reality*. New York: Bantam.

Jackson, J. B. (1984). *Discovering the vernacular landscape*. New Haven: Yale.

Kauffman, S. A. (1992). *Origins of order: Self-organization and selection in evolution*. Oxford: Oxford University Press.

Kauffman, S. A. (1995). *At home in the universe: The search for laws of self-organization and complexity*. Oxford: Oxford University Press.

Lederman, L. M., & Scharmm, D. N. (1989). *From quarks to the cosmos: Tools of discovery*. New York: Scientific American.

Lifton, R. J. (1993). *The protean self: Human resilience in an age of fragmentation*. New York: Basic Books.

Marty, M. E. (1968). *The search for a usable future*. New York: Harper & Row.

Marty, M. E. (1981). *The public church*. New York: Crossroad.

Marty, M. E. (1992). *The glory and the power*. Boston: Beacon.

Mossberg, B. (1982). *Emily Dickinson: When a writer is a daughter*. Bloomington, IN: University Press.

Nicolis, G., & Prigogine, I. (1989). *Exploring complexity*. New York: W. H. Freeman.

Orr, D. W. (1992). *Ecological literacy: Education and the transition to a postmodern world*. Albany: State University of New York Press.

Palmer, P. (1981). *The company of strangers*. New York: Crossroad.

Peat, D. F. (1987). *Synchronicity: The bridge between matter and mind*. New York: Bantam.

Peat, D. F. (1991). *The philosopher's stone: Chaos, synchronicity and the hidden order of the world*. New York: Bantam Books.

Prigogine, I. (1998). *From being to becoming*. San Francisco: W. H. Freeman.

Prigogine, I., & Stengers, I. (1984). *Order out of chaos*. New York: Bantam.

Sanders, S. R. (1998). *Hunting for hope*. Boston: Beacon.

Stengers, I., & Prigogene, I. (1997). *The end of certainty: Time, chaos, and the new laws of nature*. New York: Free Press.

Stilgoe, J. R. (1998). *Outside lies magic: Regaining history and awareness in everyday places*. New York: Walker and Co.

Thomas, L. (1971). *The lives of a cell*. New York: Viking Press.

Waldrup, M. M. (1992). *Complexity: The emerging science at the edge of order and chaos*. New York: Touchstone.

Wheatley, M. (1999). *Leadership and the new science: Discovering order in a chaotic world* (2nd ed.). San Francisco: Berrett-Koehler.

Whitehead, A. N. (1967). *The aims of education*. New York: Free Press. (Original work published 1929).

Wilson, E. O. (1998). *Consilience: The unity of knowledge*. New York: Vintage.

# CONTRIBUTORS

**Jeffery P. Aper** (*Ph.D., Educational Research, Evaluation, and Policy Studies, Virginia Polytechnic Institute and State University*) is associate professor of educational administration and policy studies at the University of Tennessee, Knoxville. He is the coauthor of the recent book *Exploring the Heritage of American Higher Education* and the author or coauthor of some 20 articles on a variety of higher-education topics.

**Bob Barnetson** (*Ph.D., Higher Education, University of Calgary*) is the research and communications officer for the Alberta Colleges & Institutes Faculties Association. His research interests include higher education policy, performance indicators, and labor relations.

**Ronald Barnett** (*D.Lit. (Ed.), Higher Education, University of London*) is professor of higher education and dean of professional development at the Institute of Education, University of London. He has acted as a consultant to national bodies on higher education in the United Kingdom. He is the author of several books on higher education, most recently *Realizing the University in an Age of Supercomplexity.*

**Marc Cutright** (*Ed.D., Higher Education Leadership, University of Tennessee, Knoxville*) is communications director for the Center for Social Organization of Schools, Johns Hopkins University, Baltimore. He has been an institutional advancement professional for twenty years, and was a Fulbright Scholar at the University of Calgary.

**John T. Dever** (*Ph.D., English, University of Virginia*) is dean of academic and student affairs at Tidewater Community College, a 30,000-student, four-campus institution in Virginia. Previously, he was dean of instruction and student services at Blue Ridge Community College, Virginia. A former American Council on Education Fellow, he has studied, presented, and written on strategic planning and leadership in higher education.

**John A. Downey** (*M.A., Counseling Education, Boston College*) is interim dean of instruction and student services at Blue Ridge Community College, Weyers Cave, Virginia. He has served as coordinator of counseling services at BRCC, and in similar capacities at Bunker Hill Community College, Boston.

**Bryant Griffith** (*Ph.D., Educational Theory, University of Toronto*) is professor in the School of Education, Acadia University, Wolfville, Nova Scotia, and has taught kindergarten through graduate levels. He is a past president of the Canadian Society for the Study of Higher Education, and his research and writing focus on the philosophy of education.

**Adrian Kershaw** (*M.A., Sociology of Education, University of Calgary*) is vice president for community and distributed learning services at the University College of the Cariboo, Kamloops, British Columbia. He has been an instructor and administrator in higher education in British Columbia and Alberta for more than twenty years, has published on technology-mediated teaching and learning, and has provided technology-planning support to institutions in British Columbia.

**Jeffrey B. Lanigan** (*M.A., History, University of Tennessee, Knoxville*) is professor of history at Blue Ridge Community College, Weyers Cave, Virginia. Appointed in 1990, he has served four years as chair of the BRCC Planning Committee, and is currently chair of the Faculty Senate.

**Lynn Speer Lemisko** (*Ph.D., History and Philosophy of Education, University of Calgary*) is an assistant professor in the Faculty of Education, Nipissing University, North Bay, Ontario. Her work, which is grounded in the philosophy and historical approach of R. G. Collingwood, investigates the ways in which past educational thought interpenetrates present educational thinking.

**Bernard H. Levin** (*Ed.D., Virginia Polytechnic Institute and State University*) has been a professor of psychology at Blue Ridge Community College, Weyers Cave, Virginia, since 1973, and is presently the head of the college's administration of justice program. He is the author of numerous articles on planning, the past president of the Southeastern (U.S.) Association for Community College Research, and chairman of the BRCC Planning Committee.

**Barbara Mossberg** (*Ph.D., Literature, Indiana University*) is the president of Goddard College in Plainfield, Vermont. She has been a Senior Fulbright Distinguished Lecturer, a U.S. Scholar in Residence for the United States Information Agency, and has held a Mellon Foundation Fellowship, among many honors. She is a published poet and the author of an award-winning book on Emily Dickinson. Dr. Mossberg lectures widely on the application of dynamical systems theories to leadership and learning, and has a book in progress on the topic.

**James R. Perkins** (*Ph.D., Educational Leadership, Florida State University*) is president of Blue Ridge Community College, Weyers Cave, Virginia. He began his career in community college education in 1968 as an instructor of mathematics, and has since served in various leadership capacities including division chair, dean of instruction, and president.

**Susan Safford** (*M.S., Organizational Development, Central Washington University*) is dean of student development at the University College of the Cariboo, Kamloops, British Columbia. She has been involved in adult education for more than twenty-five years as a teacher and administrator, with particular emphasis on the provision of educational access and support to students on campus and in widely distributed small communities. Her research interests include organizational change.

**Jean (Prinvale) Swenk** (*Ph.D., Education, Stanford University*) is director of institutional effectiveness and planning at National University in San Diego, California. She has been in higher education for a decade, including positions as assistant to the vice president for academic affairs, and a faculty member in education. Her research interests include organizational culture and strategic planning, the integration of technology into the classroom, and accreditation.

**Higher Ed**

Questions about the
Purpose(s) of Colleges
and Universities

Norm Denzin,
Josef Progler,
Joe L. Kincheloe,
Shirley R. Steinberg
*General Editors*

What are the purposes of higher education? When undergraduates "declare their majors," they agree to enter into a world defined by the parameters of a particular academic discourse—a discipline. But who decides those parameters? How do they come about? What are the discussions and proposed outcomes of disciplined inquiry? What should an undergraduate know to be considered educated in a discipline? How does the disciplinary knowledge base inform its pedagogy? Why are there different disciplines? When has a discipline "run its course"? Where do new disciplines come from? Where do old ones go? How does a discipline produce its knowledge? What are the meanings and purposes of disciplinary research and teaching? What are the key questions of disciplined inquiry? What questions are taboo within a discipline? What can the disciplines learn from one another? What might they not want to learn and why?

Once we begin asking these kinds of questions, positionality becomes a key issue. One reason why there aren't many books on the meaning and purpose of higher education is that once such questions are opened for discussion, one's subjectivity becomes an issue with respect to the presumed objective stances of Western higher education. Academics don't have positions because positions are "biased," "subjective," "slanted," and therefore somehow invalid. So the first thing to do is to provide a sense—however broad and general—of what kinds of positionalities will inform the books and chapters on the above questions. Certainly the questions themselves, and any others we might ask, are already suggesting a particular "bent," but as the series takes shape, the authors we engage will no doubt have positions on these questions.

From the stance of interdisciplinary, multidisciplinary, or transdisciplinary practitioners, will the chapters and books we solicit solidify disciplinary discourses, or liquefy them? Depending on who is asked, interdisciplinary inquiry is either a polite collaboration among scholars firmly situated in their own particular discourses, or it is a blurring of the restrictive parameters that define the very notion of disciplinary discourse. So will the series have a stance on the meaning and purpose of interdisciplinary inquiry and teaching? This can possibly be finessed by attracting thinkers from disciplines that are already multidisciplinary, for example, the various kinds of "studies" programs (women's, Islamic, American, cultural, etc.), or the hybrid disciplines like ethnomusicology (musicology, folklore, anthropology). But by including people from these fields (areas? disciplines?) in our series, we are already taking a stand on disciplined inquiry. A question on the comprehensive exam for the Columbia University Ethnomusicology Program was to defend ethnomusicology as a "field" or a "discipline." One's answer determined one's future, at least to the extent that the gatekeepers had a say in such matters. So, in the end, what we are proposing will no doubt involve political struggles.

For additional information about this series or for the submission of manuscripts, please contact Joe L. Kincheloe, 128 Chestnut Street, Lakewood, NJ 08701-5804. To order other books in this series, please contact our Customer Service Department at: (800) 770-LANG (within the U.S.), (212) 647-7706 (outside the U.S.), (212) 647-7707 FAX, or browse online by series at: www.peterlangusa.com.